HUMANE MIGRATION

HUMANE MIGRATION
ESTABLISHING LEGITIMACY AND RIGHTS FOR DISPLACED PEOPLE

CHRISTINE G. T. HO AND JAMES LOUCKY

Kumarian Press
An Imprint of Stylus Publishing

Published by Stylus Publishing, LLC
22883 Quicksilver Drive
Sterling, Virginia 20166-2102

Design by Pro Production Graphic Services
Copyedit by Bob Land
Proofread by Beth Richards
Index by Robert Swanson
The text of this book is set in 11/13 Adobe Garamond

Printed in the United States of America

∞ All first editions printed on acid free paper that meets the American National Standards Institute Z39-48 Standard.

Library of Congress Cataloging-in-Publication Data
Ho, Christine G. T., 1943–
    Humane migration : establishing legitimacy and rights for displaced people /
Christine Ho and James Loucky. — 1st ed.
        p. cm.
    Includes bibliographical references and index.
    ISBN 978-1-56549-320-9 (cloth : alk. paper) — ISBN 978-1-56549-319-3
(pbk. : alk. paper) — ISBN 978-1-56549-380-3 (library networkable e-edition) —
ISBN 978-1-56549-381-0 (consumer e-edition)
    1. Emigration and immigration. 2. Human rights. I. Loucky, James. II. Title.
JV6035.H6 2012
325—dc23
                                                                    2011040329

Bulk Purchases

Quantity discounts are available for use in workshops and for staff development.

Call 1-800-232-0223

First Edition, 2012

10 9 8 7 6 5 4 3 2 1

Contents

Preface

MIGRATION—OR MORE COMMONLY, *IMMIGRATION*—is distinctive from the plethora of issues facing humanity in that it raises fundamental questions about rights to move, which often become synonymous with the right to be. Today it also provokes, as it often has in the past, a litany of negative associations and fears. Cast as a source of social discontent and a threat to safety, jobs, and even purity, immigrants today attract little welcome either in the United States or elsewhere. Even compassion for refugees is on the wane. But even as anti-immigration rhetoric and policies expand, they are tempered by reality. Economic growth has demanded cheap labor, and aging populations in industrialized powers require new and young workers simply to sustain a viable future.

Whether considered a threat, or the essence of potential well-being, immigration requires a thorough and objective examination, particularly because of its complex connections to the many transformations now enveloping the world. Migrants are not just propelled by forces unprecedented in their global, economic, and political reach, they also challenge concepts and assumptions that are rapidly becoming outdated.

Decades of research have led to tremendous advances in our understanding of the determinants, scope, and implications of contemporary mass migration. Significant new terms reflect current dimensions and complexities when added to conceptual staples like push-pull theories and sending-receiving communities. Mobility, circulation, pluralism, syncretism, and transnational identities are among the themes that reflect contemporary movements of people, along with ideas, commodities, and practices. This book seeks to contribute to a critical anthropological understanding of the continuing significance of migration, and the positive role it can and will play in the future. Through consideration of the close association of migration with dominant global forces, and with subsequent retrenchment and antipathies, we also perceive how alternative framing of migration as normative and justifiable enables us to recognize more sensible policy options, some of which are being pursued in various countries.

There is another compelling reason that motivates us. Whether humanity can sustain a collective social ethic when crises loom on a global scale is becoming the question at hand—or perhaps more accurately, the question is whether humanity can risk not fulfilling that ethic. As evidence of planetary environmental stress becomes ever more incontrovertible, inclusive as well as holistic thinking is imperative. References to tipping points, environmental refugees, and climate responsibility were nearly nonexistent a few years ago; they are now becoming the defining issues of our time. Related notions of borders, national sovereignty, citizenship, and loyalties are also very much in contention. All are associated with movement. All also compel us to try to reach agreement on what rights people should have, whether movement is among them, and whether it matters if it is involuntary or a matter of choice.

Terminology matters. Words have tremendous power—from provoking wars to promoting solidarity. They often convey errors and misrepresentations, especially when their definitions are overwhelmingly negative. Degrading descriptors (like "alien," "illegal," or cruder versions) and metaphors (such as "invasion," "hordes," or "rising tide") imply criminality, disease, or danger. Use of negative language also implies undesirability and a rationale of exclusion from destination countries, thereby denying people decent living conditions and access to jobs commensurate with their skills, while also hindering them from participating or fully integrating into new societies. Rather than using labels like "illegal" or "undocumented," which put emphasis on the person rather than a condition that is often temporary or involuntary, we use designations like "immigrants" and "migrants," "people on the move," and "new Americans." Ultimately such terms encourage accuracy and promote respect and understanding. In addition, we use the term "American" throughout the book, being fully aware that it might be the source of enormous contention and debate.

With much already written about migration, what was it that inspired us to write our own?

Christine: I am an immigrant myself. I grew up in the twin-island, Caribbean nation of Trinidad and Tobago, where more than half the population are of African descent, where more than one-third have ancestors from India, where only about 2% claim "whiteness," and only 1% claim Chinese ancestry. Moreover, the society I come from practices "racial mixing" expressed as a "color gradient." So, the idea of "people of color" is not a meaningful one, not only because very few are colorless, but because those with power are a numerical "minority," the mirror image of the situation in the United States. This forced me to learn a new meaning of the word "minority," which had to do at least as much with power as with numbers.

Not surprisingly, arriving in the United States was quite a culture shock for me. I spent the first year crying and being homesick. Apart from grappling with strange and exotic American customs, which I have since adopted, much of the shock had to do with the American obsession with race, expressed in geographical segregation and other forms of social exclusion and racial isolation and, its corollary, the denial of class cleavages. Although my personal story is not one of suffering but one of those shining immigrant tales of success and I am very grateful for the bounty and opportunities afforded me, I could not help but notice the contradiction between American ideals and reality: I found the treatment of "people of color" in America quite unfair.

However, it was not until I studied anthropology at UCLA that my intuitions about what was happening all around me took a more cerebral shape, inspiring my quest for self-understanding and igniting my concern with inequality and social injustice. Although I did not encounter it until much later in my intellectual development, the concept of structural violence has been very important to me. Armed with newly acquired knowledge of how culture and society worked, I joined the professoriate of the United States hoping it would allow me to give public voice to the plight of people, including immigrants, who suffer indignities of all sorts. In other words, I feel a responsibility to speak out and to document the truth. Such are my motives for this book, which I hope will make a difference.

James: I am an anthropologist, in stance and profession, in addition to having an immigrant heritage. My father was a refugee from Czechoslovakia who fled across the Iron Curtain, one of the most pernicious borders humans have ever erected, after learning of his imminent arrest for Christian church activities. After the classic transatlantic passage past the Statue of Liberty, he arrived in upstate New York in 1950. There he worked in factories and on furnaces to support a growing family with my mother, whose parents were immigrants themselves. In addition to immigrant roots, I grew up in a remarkable multicultural household, since we moved (when I was five years old) into the ground floor of a large rooming house for foreign graduate students. Sharing supper, stories, and stamps with people from countries the world over instilled in me an intense curiosity and deep appreciation for cultural differences.

Fieldwork in highland Guatemala during the 1970s was both transformative and serendipitous, as it was followed by the exodus of hundreds of thousands fleeing massacres and repression in Central America during the 1980s. Many headed to Los Angeles, and my study of anthropology at UCLA soon became entirely applied in nature, through work with ecumenical and solidarity groups, attorneys, and especially refugee families and communities themselves in their efforts to build awareness and justice amid grave degradation of human rights. I began working closely with the first Maya organization in Los Angeles, IXIM (Integration of Indigenous Mayas), and in turn with Maya communities across a growing continental diaspora. I participated as well in health and educational programs for children from Mexican and Central American families, including along the US-Mexico border. Many of my colleagues and mentors are people who have experienced considerable disruptions in their locations and lives, yet also levels of resilience and cooperation that I have come to understand and to try to emulate.

Our collaborative effort has attempted to shed light on some of the particularly complex and contentious issues that immigration raises. We share the effort and responsibility for the whole, and especially for Chapters 1, 6, and 8; Christine took the lead on Chapters 2, 3, and 5, while James was primary author for Chapters 4, 7, and 9. We also wish to thank Jim Lance for his enthusiasm, patience, and above all, his sharp editorial eye.

The challenges associated with immigration, and especially the divisive and damaging measures that often meet it, call for greater humanitarian understanding than has prevailed to date. In a world where unacceptable deprivation coexists with unimaginable opulence, more informed dialog and ethical response are essential. We offer this book in that spirit, to help affirm greater inclusiveness and, in turn, the transformation in social relations that will be required in the years ahead.

—*Christine G. T. Ho*
Miami, Florida
—*James Loucky*
Bellingham, Washington

1

Seeing the Humanity of Migration in the Migration of Humanity

The dog barks but the caravan moves on.
—Arab proverb

Migration is one of the predominant and persistent characteristics of humanity, occupying a central place in the sweep of human history just as in current affairs. Often short in distance and duration, sometimes long and prolonged, movement lies at the core of our being, powerfully determining who we are as individuals and groups, and as species. It is clearly implicit in the global spread and collective impacts of Homo sapiens. Commonly conflated with immigration, migration is also arguably the most explosive social issue of our time. Few other dimensions of social interaction entail as many human rights and wrongs.

Anthropology reveals not only the ubiquity of migration across time and space but also its vital role in many of the critical challenges we face. The emergence of bipedalism among early humans provided enormous benefits, enabling mobility to range far and wide. From origins in Africa, our hominid ancestors spread across the planet. Food and water were tied to specific places, often varied by season, requiring foraging peoples to move according to available resources. With the shift to food production, a mere eight or 10 millennia following a lengthy foraging past, societies became more sedentary. But rarely did migration halt, as growing populations required food from beyond urban concentrations.

Today, nearly every place on Earth has been affected by, and often fundamentally transformed through, movement of people, because migration solves a host of problems. Shortages, destitution, war and conflict, and natural disasters regularly compel people to move. At the same time, migration represents new life, liberty, and pursuit of happiness. Simply put, if opportunities do not come to people, people move toward opportunities.

To move or not to move: has that become the question? Or are there a set of complex questions along with assertions and trajectories that must be addressed if we are to foresee a benevolent future? Population growth, ethnic and social change, and the transformations we have come to call "globalization" are all migration-related. So, too, is the looming displacement inherent in the seemingly inexorable advance of global climate change.

Movement is critical as well to how we live our daily lives. Human growth and development, along with the creation of new households with marriage, often entails movement. For all our technological sophistication, even people in industrialized societies continue to find worth and to be valued through belonging, to family groups and communities as much as to countries. We interact through social relationships as well as work, and moving is integral to both, as is evident in how we respond to shifting opportunities of education or employment.

Multiple forms of movement meet human needs, having significant social and cultural facets as well as political and economic dimensions. Thinking of migration in terms of "mobilities" rather than a singular or bounded move is useful. Facilitated by new modes of transportation and mobile communications, relations between people and places continue to be formed and reconstituted through meeting and networks, as well as through separation and dispersed trajectories. Migration, basically, is both a contemporary reality and, as we shall see, an inevitability.

The sobering implications of human capacity to affect our surroundings are everywhere being realized, provoking challenges to long-held assumptions about limitless economic growth, the inevitability of widening inequities, and the inviolability of nation-state borders. All of these are intertwined with movement in convoluted ways. As a result of intense overuse of Earth's natural resources, humans may have spawned what some are calling the "Anthropocene"—a stage of human history marked by such profound human impact on Earth's ecosystems and climate as to be considered a new geologic age. Migration is one of the foundations of this age. It will also be part of emerging realities that require living within nature and reaffirming commonalities and inclusion.

From this evolutionary and geographical perspective, flows of people, along with their goods and knowledge, represent diverse and powerful means for mutually beneficial interconnectedness. But if migration is such a profound feature of evolutionary history and contemporary reality, why is it understood so poorly and negatively? One reason is that people operate not only as members of groups but also as individuals within immediate surroundings and experiences, with new ones reasonably perceived as threatening. Movement also entails disruptions, which accompany those who move and which discomfort those in areas where they settle. The proliferation and intensification of related global processes can further mask the positive role that migration plays. History and the cross-cultural record reveal how strongly and repeatedly economic and political forces drive migration, even as it may seem today to be unprecedented in origins and scope.

Movements of individuals and groups are intrinsic to contemporary global economic and political reality, rather than surprise or aberration. Far from being incomprehensible, the contemporary world is grounded in a set of converging factors that have identifiable roots and trajectories that operate through imbalances of power as well as impetus of synergies. Flows of people as well as of goods and knowledge have never been greater or more diverse. Yet they continue to be powerful ways that people change destinies along with destinations. If we are to design reasonable responses to what otherwise threatens to be an increasingly confrontational future, historical and comparative inquiry appear essential.

The Emergence of Nation-States and Borders

For millennia, humans roamed the planet relatively freely. With the emergence of nation-states, however, freedom of movement became highly restricted as borders placed barriers to population movement. Few people are aware that borders emerged in human history only three and a half centuries ago with the rise of the nation-state in 1648. In that year the Peace of Westphalia was signed at the end of the Thirty Years War in Europe. This treaty brought into existence a new type of political entity based on the idea of sovereignty—radically different from previous forms of political organization. The notion of state sovereignty implied not only autonomy inside the political unit, but the replacement of "frontiers" by "borders" and the recognition of borders by other nation-states (Giddens 1990).

Before the birth of the nation-state, human beings lived in political arrangements such as empires, made up of many economic systems ruled by a single political authority, the emperor. They also lived in monarchies, ruled by a king, a single individual who possessed absolute power and divine rights (Castles and Miller 2009). Empires and kingdoms both had cultural and power gaps separating aristocratic rulers from the peasants in the village, who were not citizens, but subjects of the king (Guibernau 2007). Also absent was the idea of a national culture transcending the gulf between the ruling class and villagers. The rise of the nation-state, then, was a milestone not only because it established rigid borders but because it demanded greater equality between the rulers and the ruled (Held and McGrew 2007).

The process of nation-building is made up of two parts: state formation, which is a political process, and nationalism, which is a cultural force that produces the feeling of belonging. State formation requires an economic system that provides not only access to material resources but allows greater communication and movement between social classes (Held and McGrew 2007). State formation is also necessary to legitimize the power of the ruling class and to promote loyalty to the state by providing security, order, and democratic processes for the people to achieve their goals.

Nationalism, as a cultural process, hinges on the idea of citizenship, the most important link between state and nation because it defines responsibilities as well as a set of civil, political, and social rights (Castles and Miller 2009; Guibernau 2007). However, the notion of citizenship is contradictory because, at least in principle, all citizens within a political community should be entitled to equality of rights, along with institutions guaranteeing these rights. The idea of citizenship is also problematic because it forms a mental partition between the insider (independent, responsible, trustworthy, moral) and the outsider (dependent, irresponsible, immoral, undeserving transgressor), drawing lines of inclusion and exclusion between citizen and noncitizen and creating a categorical divide between those entitled to rights and those deprived of them (Guibernau 2007; Inda 2006; Ngai 2004).

Understanding nationalism also makes it easier to understand hostility to immigrants. According to Benedict Anderson (1983), who defined a "nation" as a sovereign, "imagined community," a nation actually exists only in our imagination and is completely dependent on the feeling of belonging. As sovereign entity, a nation is a "community" in the sense that there is brotherhood, and it is "imagined" in the sense that every member of a nation imagines fellow members to be similar, even though the vast majority do not know each other and most will never meet. In short, all communities larger than face-to-face villages are imagined.

Simply put, the emotional bonds tying members of a nation together are so deep that it feels like an extended family (Guibernau 2007). Nationalism's sibling, patriotism, then becomes a form of political love, inspiring people to regard fighting and killing in wars as heroic deeds. Nationalism is a love so profound that dying for one's country is seen as an act of moral purity, and the powers of nationalism and patriotism are perhaps the mightiest and most enduring ideologies that humankind ever invented (Falk 1999). Thus, hostility toward the "foreigner" and depicting immigrants as threats to society are essential for maintaining this homogeneous imagined community.

As a result, countries with immigrants have had to formulate policies and practices about the meaning of citizenship: who is a citizen and how newcomers can become citizens, given increasing diversity in many nation-states. Not surprisingly, members of the majority ethnic group enjoy the greatest citizenship rights. In contrast, members of ethnic minorities are usually assimilated, often marginalized and excluded, and sometimes exterminated (Castles and Miller 2009; Bodley 2008). Thus, rights differ not only according to the dominant power but also according to culture, race, class, gender, and other social attributes.

For the most part, the borders of nation-states have been beneficial over the centuries. More recently, however, borders have become dysfunctional: they promote self-interest and ethnocentrism, and they undermine any sense of community and civic engagement. Even worse, border crossing has become confused with danger, resulting in a nationalism expressed as xenophobia, policies of exclusion, the criminalization and imprisonment of immigrants, and the militarization of borders. This outcome is most unfortunate because the principle of democracy espoused by many nation-states should guarantee to all members of civil society equality of rights, whether citizen or noncitizen.

With the emergence of states and, in turn, colonial empires, people and places became even more connected through movement. The Industrial Revolution provoked mass shifts from farms to cities, while colonial expansion and wars produced mass movements in the form of scattering and resettlement, sometimes over long distances and long periods of time. Movement is also implicit in trade, which is a defining feature of human societies and omnipresent today. Both migration and immigration—movement across national borders—have accelerated to unprecedented levels with the emergence of the contemporary era of globalization. People are forced and drawn to move as never before. Revolutionary changes and accelerations in transportation and communication have so "shrunk" the world that people are now able to reach nearly every possible location, with unprecedented speed. They bring with them perspectives and potential, but also problems.

Mass Movements, Global Unease

That much of the world is on the move is self-evident, in light of the proliferation of intercontinental travel, social media, and consumer goods from every corner of the world, as well as the increasingly transboundary nature of many communities, careers, and even identities (Sheller and Urry 2006; Kaye 2010). People everywhere enjoy the bounty and product diversity of what we now call, somewhat redundantly, our "global world." There is much less content or consent, however, about the seemingly unstoppable flows of people in this new world. Backlash in more industrialized countries, and growth of fundamentalisms elsewhere, are hardly surprising amid the increase of new unknowns and mounting unease associated with challenges to established worldviews. Researchers are confronted by global developments at least as much as the public. Assumptions and vocabularies are under scrutiny as never before. New categories and models can seem outdated almost as soon as they are proposed. Certainly this is the case for migration. Debates about benefits versus costs continue unabated, while binaries such as forced and voluntary, refugee and immigrant, and legal and illegal are increasingly open to question. The pervasiveness of fluidity and mobilities (Cresswell 2006) cast growing doubt on the viability of nation-states and justifications for separating people from places where they can sustain life.

While the scale of contemporary migration and prevalence of mobilities may be unprecedented, mass movements are nothing new. Emergence of larger population centers, sustained by agriculture, encouraged movement to cities for their perceived or real opportunities compared to the hard and often denigrated rural life. Rural-to-urban movement continues to unfold, along with flows from the global South to the global North, in the face of persistent and growing regional and global inequalities.

Today's global political economy is grounded on axioms that encourage, and even require, migration. An assumption of growth as preferred and perpetual undergirds much modern production. Profits are realized with expansion and concentration of resources. Business practices like outsourcing, an undermining of food security (sometimes of entire countries, as well as small farmers themselves), and top-down control of labor and other forms of dispossession impose poverty—virtual slavery even—on much of the developing world (Bacon 2008). Social and psychological dislocations accompany the physical disruptions this global order generates.

Not only is migration fundamental to the elite-driven system that has evolved, so too is instability. Tremendous insecurity is inherent in a situation, as exists today, in which a person in the top one-fifth of humanity earns on average 150 times more than that of a person in the bottom quintile. The conflicts and suffering arising from such gaping and growing chasms are hardly surprising.

The mounting dissension that accompanies growing divisions, in turn, provokes efforts to dampen unrest by containing people within predictable and prescribed orbits. A veritable global immigration panic has emerged in recent years. People on the move tend to be blamed for moving in the first place, and for a host of ills that may or may not result. Far less common is acknowledgment of history or underlying factors. Such understanding is admittedly more difficult than simply parroting accepted models and mantras. Connections and implications are also conveniently masked by dominant political interests and media manipulation. Fear itself is a powerful motivator. When times are tough, xenophobia is easy to incite, and policing can become normal. Far easier to shoot first—metaphorically or militarily—and ask (or not ask) questions later.

Add to this "the big one," the looming geo-ecological crisis for which climate change seems far too mild a term. Catastrophic or irreversible destabilization of climate portends more massive disruption ahead, unless (and perhaps even if) mitigated. The poor, as usual, are most affected. But this time, even the wealthy will not be spared, in part because of the numbers of people who are likely to have no option but to move. Past crises in the United States alone—the Dust Bowl, the Rust Belt, and Katrina—suggest what may lie ahead with major changes in weather patterns, melting glaciers, rising oceans, and severe degradation of ecosystems on which life depends. Forced displacement, on a scale previously unimagined, seems unavoidable. Some predict a 90% chance that 3 billion people will either move or go hungry in the next century as a result of climate change (Brahic 2009; International Organization for Migration 2008). Less foreseeable are the divisions and methods of exclusion that may accompany these prognoses.

Today, humanity faces a turning point, provoked by planetary tipping points. Transformation must be immediate and comprehensive in how we "do business"—from wise resource utilization and equitable distribution, to granting legitimacy and rights whatever people's background and circumstances. Instead, we ominously see countries turning away immigrants and even refugees, sometimes despite long histories of migration and commendable prior policies. Border crossings are coming to be viewed as fears, rather than facts. These fears are multifaceted, ranging from perceived threat to national sovereignty to unpredictable futures. Borders liberalized not long ago are now portrayed as being out of control. From Western Europe to North America and elsewhere across the globe, apprehension and alarmism shift easily to nativism and repudiation, as they have throughout history (Chavez 2001).

But little is inexorable. Disturbing scenarios are not inevitabilities, given the power of human dignity and the synergies of strategizing and acting together. Rising popular movements are challenging the morality and continuation of the system that has become dominant, just as the massive world economic meltdown in 2008 confirmed its inherent instabilities.

The Beneficence of Migration

Migration is so intertwined with the expansion of global capitalism, and so ubiquitous today as it has been historically, that it can only be understood as normative rather than as aberration or threat. Migration is both a logical outcome of macroeconomics and geopolitics and a key factor in future developments on a planetary scale. Viewing it as a common interest and solution is far more reasonable than treating it chiefly as a problem, which is the prevailing sentiment underlying recent debate. Migration falls much more in the realm of human rights than it does under criminal justice.

The pervasive characteristic of global labor is strong evidence that the nature of migration is primarily beneficial. But asserting, as we do, that freedom of movement also remains an inherent right is quite another matter.

One way to approach these controversies is to consider what motivates people to move, often over long distances and durations, at considerable financial and psychological costs. A common theme throughout human history is that most people do not move unless necessary, which explains why an element of coercion is frequently part of the reason for migration. The dynamics provoking movement may be as persuasive as they are powerful, but they are also imbued with promise as they provide avenues for creativity in the unfolding of new lives and livelihoods. People and places change through migration, often dramatically. So, too, do families and communities left behind, as do new destinations and social configurations. A multitude of life histories as well as fictionalized accounts illustrate how, although migration is frequently grounded in suffering, it can also bring out the very best in people.

We know a great deal about migration through comprehensive and long-term studies (Castles and Miller 2009; Portes and Rumbaut 2006), but much is easily missed or misperceived. Rapidly changing circumstances generate a range of reactions, from anxiety in the face of unpredictability to confusion and mistrust amid crises. Through comparative and historical inquiry, as well as reflection, we can come to see ourselves on the same path as others. We can empathize since most people have experiences of migration, and migration narratives are common to most cultural traditions. Commonalities also serve to encourage deeper recognition that whatever the contentiousness, common good is best served by working together to address the challenges at hand.

Recognizing the elements that give migration its power and pervasiveness is essential. Engaged inquiry means examining not only who moves but also who benefits from those moves. We can look for patterns that arise in new situations or emergencies requiring refuge. We can probe the critical role of social networks in successful adaptation. We can also examine social forces that enhance the formation as well as transformation of ethnic communities. In turn, the global character of migration today requires us to address dilemmas that tend to be more recent in origin: the emergence of transnational communities and identities, the importance of children and issues of youth associated with the unknowns facing new generations, and scenarios of mass displacement associated with global economic and environmental crises.

Never before have such issues been so crucial. They require frank dialogue and cooperative interchange across borders of many kinds if we are to overcome misconceptions and policy errors. Sharing what is already known about how, why, and how often people move, as well as what feelings are evoked, increases the likelihood of asking the right questions. In turn we can also make more effective responses. At the very least, grounded knowledge and opportunities for meaningful participation help prevent policies that are unilateral or myopic, and potentially counterproductive as well.

Given that migration is intrinsic to being human, it requires a time perspective that is long term rather than immediate, and an approach that encompasses the moral as well as the practical. Human and humanitarian concerns are ultimately at least as critical as any issues of national sovereignty. The world cannot be safe unless it is safe for everyone. Migration is far more than an unlikely result of global interdependence and rapid communications and transportation, although these are important drivers. Migration is both fundamental to being human and a matter of common interest. It is vital that we address whether there is—still—a right to move. Freedom of movement is implicit in human history and codified in international law. What are the consequences of jettisoning something so essential, as seems to be occurring in the assertion of a "new normal" today, and particularly following the stunning events of September 11, 2001?

What could result from considering migration within a human rights discourse? The politics of language reveals numerous accounts of misuse of power, but also possibilities for ethical reframing and civic reaffirmation.

As migration is the logical outcome of macroeconomics and geopolitics, examining movement as an entitlement is reasonable. What might be gained by speaking of people instead of units of labor, markets, and supply chains? Treating people as members of families and communities, rather than as numbers and problems, is far more likely to produce sensible responses to vexing yet unavoidable dilemmas, such as those relating to social well-being, family reunification, and the best interests of emerging generations. Compared to advancing narrow interests and unilateral national agendas, prospects are considerably brighter through prioritizing common sense and common interests.

From Politics of Exclusion to Communities of Inclusion

What we focus on largely determines what we leave out. As Nobel Prize–winning Turkish novelist Orhan Pamuk observes, "If you focus on clashes, you will get clashes, but if you focus on harmony, you will get harmony." Anxiety and innuendo about how immigration either causes or deepens divisions, economic declines, or cultural deterioration disregards substantial evidence that people who move from one place to another are, in general, at least as likely to have high aspirations and valuable human and labor potential as longer-term residents. Amid the fierce and bitter debate, then, we must highlight evidence and logic that may run counter to the prevailing claims of pundits and politicians.

The United States has experienced deep challenges that come with dramatic long-term demographic and social changes associated with a long history of immigration. Europe is following suit, relatively later than the United States with respect to magnitude and consequence, but with similar public alarm over uncertainty about appropriate immigration policy (Hill 2010a; Castles and Miller 2009; Lucassen 2005). Other regions of the world are experiencing similar growing pains. Ultimately, policies and practices that make inclusion, and thereby hope, possible are far more valuable to everyone than policies and practices that exclude. Whether from the weight of evidence, or pragmatic recognition that the ominous financial implications of aging populations place tremendous value on the far younger immigrant, change toward a more favorable outlook with respect to immigration is inevitable (D. Myers 2007).

One of the main problems in visualizing, much less implementing, immigration reform is the huge divide between the worlds occupied by people living in new communities and countries and those of many native-born or longer-term residents. The disconnect between migrants' lived experiences and public policy is larger still. Legal, language, and economic differences exacerbate the human tendency to avoid or not engage with those who are different. Authorities—whether employers, law enforcement, or those working in social or educational institutions—have considerable power to influence lives and livelihoods, all the more so for people who work in an underground economy. As a result, undocumented people tend to live "shadowed lives" (Chavez 1998), shying away from census workers, police officers, and institutions representing authority.

The long interest of anthropology and other social sciences in the dynamics and human implications of transnational migration provide considerable potential for contributing to migration reform. No longer stuck in a tradition of seeing cultures as distinct entities, researchers for decades have been emphasizing the interconnectedness of a global world as well as how differences are constructed rather than simply emerging through separation of discrete groupings. Immigration represents a significant arena for production of difference, particularly through anti-immigrant discourse and policies that perpetuate hegemonic ideals of nationhood and identity while continuing to disempower others. Attention to lived experiences, a hallmark of anthropology, seems invaluable for helping to develop fair and humane migration policy.

Opportunities for meaningful interaction, through which people get to know and trust one another, are fundamental to a healthy, democratic society. So, while uncertainties are part and parcel of migration, success in dealing with it requires comprehensive efforts that are rooted in understanding its vast and comparative history. Cross-national understanding certainly helps. Acknowledging communities and countries that pursue effective and humane paths for including newer citizens is as important as taking note of more ineffective or violent cases. Comparative and historical inquiry that considers all the elements that make up migration allows us to see how migrants experience disruption and dispersion, and how they—and those among whom they settle—then deal with transition and uncertainty. More often than not, the result is mutually beneficial syntheses in which people come together to rethink relationships and what they mean.

As people grapple with new modes and mores, their discomforts also create wider opportunities for circumspection, and even change, for wider society as well as themselves. The materialism and the erosion of primary ties and values associated with greater affluence, for example, provide lessons for all. In one case, a letter sent home to Iraq by a young man studying at Yale is as relevant today as when it was penned in the mid-1960s:

The more a society advances in a technical and material way, the more its people grow complicated and distant from one another. Everyone here . . . is an individual. The innocent, simple man who accepts things at face value, the nice guy who worries about people and not just himself, that person disappears.

—Sabar (2008, 202)

The collective experiences, stories, and codes and modeling of ethics within immigrant and refugee communities hold tremendous value far beyond those communities in themselves. Human resources and funds of knowledge are sometimes recorded, more often transmitted in intergenerational and face-to-face interactions. Anthropologists have long heralded the way in which cultural diversity reflects and builds the creative capacity that enables humanity not only to survive but also to thrive. Differences, in other words, need not be feared but can instead be seen as strengths, potentially and tangibly.

The hardships, treacherous journeys, and resilience embodied in refugee and immigrant experience are as durable as they are dramatic. The shared memories and morals to the stories are central to whom people have been and who they are becoming. They shape emerging identities and the ethnogenesis of new communities. By acknowledging these accounts, we not only affirm the basic rights of those recounting but also commonalities with those experiences. *E pluribus unum* is more than a historical motto. It continues to be the strength of a country that has been and remains fundamentally multicultural, and so also quixotically American.

Ultimately, whether perceived as "management" or as inevitability, collective responses to immigration that acknowledge the humanity and worldviews of those on the move are most likely to result in more engaged civic participation. However currently ignored or maligned, migrants themselves are a critical voice for helping to determine what is fair and wise with respect to services and settlement policies. Worldwide, in fact, the dreams as much as the demands of immigrants are provoking a rethinking of society, and indeed of the future.

Goals and Outline of This Book

This book considers a number of pressing questions about the causes, circumstances, and consequences of global migration. As much as we believe that questions must not go unanswered, we also affirm that answers must not go unquestioned.

We address moral as well as practical aspects of migration, adopting a broadly comparative, interdisciplinary, and engaged approach. Contemporary patterns are examined in light of what has gone on before, and experiences of other countries provide a basis for evaluating our own.

Movement and settlement involve many actors and agencies, not just people on the move. Some seek shelter from violence, engendered at home or through geopolitical forces. Others embark on perilous and costly routes in response to consumer demand for products they help produce cheaply. By acknowledging the shared responsibilities for creating, perpetuating, and potentially modifying migration, we open the way for more humane alternatives to what often prevails.

We hope to challenge readers to rethink prevailing misconceptions about immigrants and to visualize them as new neighbors, working and living in cities, towns, and rural places throughout various countries. Their many contributions are evidence of the deep resilience and promise that newcomers represent, particularly for adopted communities but also for those from where they have come.

In Chapter 2 we place migration in a wider context by probing the root causes of international migration, particularly global processes that are unprecedented in their power to encourage the crossing of borders. We also scrutinize transnational systems that transport people across national borders, such as guest worker programs and human smuggling, as well as colonial ties and military interventions that create refugees and asylum-seekers. We then turn our attention to personal motivations—such as hunger, starvation, the inability to find work, the desire to be reunited with family—that inspire migrants to make family sacrifices and risk their lives to relocate, as well as to create remarkable strategies for survival.

We shift our gaze in Chapter 3 to the climate of fear that has gripped virtually every immigrant-receiving country. We analyze groundless myths and fallacies buttressing these fears, such as job theft, welfare dependency, and the threat to American culture and identity. We also scrutinize past and present US immigration laws aimed at excluding "undesirables," highlighting the immigration law of 1924 that set many legal precedents and Arizona's SB1070 for racial profiling. Also examined are contemporary hate crimes and institutional racism directed at the Chinese in the nineteenth century and the Japanese in concentration camps during World War II. Most important of all, we look at how immigration has become fused with crime and terrorism in the American imagination.

Immigration overlaps closely with borders, the subject of Chapter 4. For the United States, "the border" is synonymous with our 2,000-mile marriage to Mexico. Bordering, however, is something humans do everywhere, and in countless ways. Tremendously valuable and vibrant exchanges occur, along with problems. Growing reliance on security as solution is revealed to be rather myopic, and often draconian as well. In time, the nature and functions of borders, as well as their particular histories and advantages, have to be acknowledged if there is to be a long-lasting resolution of the dilemmas of migration, in North America and worldwide. Borders also produce suffering for migrants, requiring family sacrifices, fracturing families, and forcing many to lead "shadowed lives."

In Chapter 5 we scrutinize the institutional processes that have resulted in immigrants, particularly the undocumented, being treated like criminals. First we examine the US immigrant detention system, whose practices violate international human rights laws, as well as the connection between skyrocketing rates of immigrant incarceration and the growth of the US prison industry. Next, we look at "technologies of governance," the bureaucratic machinery designed to keep immigrants out, founded on a philosophy of punishment. We also compare the differences in treatment of Cubans and Haitians by the US immigration system. Last we look at how a border fixation has resulted in the needless death and suffering of immigrants at the US-Mexico border.

Nearly every human culture has a migratory narrative as part of its history or mythology, and many countries today do so as well. As perception mixes with reality, new understandings and interpretations arise, including of people and worlds that are different. Multiple challenges associated with immigration can be seen through the experiences of other countries. A comparative perspective enables us to discern what has been problematic but also what has worked and what, in turn, might work in our country. Income generation, intellectual talent, and legal arrangements that support loyalty and belonging are central to the transborder arrangements we consider in Chapter 6.

In the United States, perhaps the only aspect of immigration on which there is broad agreement is that policies in place are not working—or, as more usually stated, the current system is "broken." Chapter 7 explores some of the basic tenets of US immigration policy, along with different explanations of what might occur. Few deny that the system in place entails enormous wasted resources, in the form of costs of enforcement as well as lower productivity, depressed wages, and uncollected tax revenues. The system is equally costly in terms of human lives and dignity. Instead of remaining hostage to laws and accepted practices that foster exclusion and exploitation, we propose instead that benefiting from the human capital represented by people who are among our most productive and youthful is both preferable and possible.

The vibrancy of immigrants in the United States and around the world, and the numerous contributions they make both to adopted communities and to those left behind, lead us to consider how we might better ensure the mutual benefits that their diversity and deep resilience represent. Chapter 8 focuses on rights, including rights of people to move and of communities to strive for some control over people and processes that emanate from afar. Movement may be inherently human, but the complexities of responsibility, legitimacy, and citizenship turn out to be anything but straightforward.

In the final chapter, as throughout the book, we look to what can emerge through recognizing immigrants as new members of society. As communities are more inclusive, they also become safer and healthier. Openness and welcome, places to meet and socialize, along with an area's aesthetics have been identified as the three main qualities that attach people to their community and to each other (Knight Foundation 2010). Our society, as others elsewhere, promises to become more vibrant and sustainable if it can continue to successfully uphold a long-standing commitment to both diversity and democracy.

2

Globalization and Why Migration Happens

You might as well sit in your beach chair and tell the tide not to come in.
—Michael Bloomberg, mayor, New York City,
testimony before US Senate Committee to restrict immigration

What is globalization? Globalization is a worldwide process that changes what happens at the local level on many different fronts (Ho and Nurse 2005). Its global reach took many centuries to accomplish, particularly on the economic front, which is its most powerful. More recently, it has accelerated, intensified, and become more contradictory and paradoxical. Globalization is contradictory because it incorporates greater numbers of countries into a global economic system while creating divisions between and within countries. Globalization is also paradoxical because it stimulates migration and simultaneously provokes an anti-immigrant backlash.

In this chapter we examine economic globalization as one of the most powerful drivers of international migration today. In addition, we look at bridges connecting nations that enhance the crossing of borders—such as trade agreements, international finance and trade organizations, guest worker programs, labor recruitment, human smuggling, trafficking and the "migration industry," military interventions, and colonization. Furthermore, we consider personal motivations and local conditions that propel people out of their homelands: hunger, starvation, the inability to find work, and the desire to be reunited with family are a few of the many situations that inspire migrants to leave their families and risk their lives to relocate.

A report to President George H.W. Bush in 1990 on the causes of immigration to the United States, which also offered policy suggestions for how to contain it, stated that the main motive for migrating north was economic (Harris 2010). If the chief driver of migration to the United States is economic, then effective immigration policies must balance corporate hunger for cheap labor with the rights of migrant workers (Kaye 2010). This principle contrasts sharply with immigration policies today, which merely give birth to new institutions such as *coyotes,* born of fortified borders (Lopez 2007). Restrictive policies, in turn, impact the sending countries and the people left behind, and also elicit challenges by human rights organizations in defense of immigrant rights. In this way, the paradoxes spiral in feedback loops throughout the global migration system.

Economic Globalization and Migration

How does economic globalization promote international migration? Economic globalization works by producing profound changes at the local level, in its quest for new markets. Market expansion is accomplished by introducing capital-intensive methods of production into economic sectors of developing nations that are nonmarket or premarket (Massey 2009). Historically this has resulted in peasants being expelled from their land and is very common in land tenure systems, such as those in Latin America, that tolerate large holdings of wasted land by the wealthy while limiting peasants to tiny plots (Galeano 1997). Peasant dislocation has also resulted from the conversion of communal property rights into exclusive private property rights and the denial of rights to "the commons" (Harvey 2003). "The commons" is a concept used to describe a shared natural resource, such as water or air, to which everyone should have free access. The term "tragedy of the commons" comes from a famous article by Garrett Hardin (1968) that explained what happens when many individuals, acting in their own self-interest, deplete a resource, knowing full well that abusing it will lead, in the long run, to its disappearance.

The absorption of developing countries into global networks of trade and production, as well as the expansion of markets, have not only displaced subsistence farmers from their land, the key to national food security, but they have destroyed their livelihoods. In contemporary Mexico, peasant displacement has followed on the heels of government agricultural policies that have reduced access to electricity, fertilizer, and water, as well as slashing credit subsidies, price supports, and agricultural extension services for small farmers (Andreas 2000), while providing highly technical training for commercial growers to produce export crops (Stanford 2008). The sale of communal farm lands and denial of water rights have displaced small farmers, transforming them into landless wage workers (Andreas 2000; Galeano 1997; Harvey 2003).

As a result, many small farmers and farmworkers have abandoned agriculture, migrating from the countryside to find work in cities, where they have joined an avalanche of "human surplus" in shantytowns, because cities have more people than work. In Mexico, 20 million people work as day laborers, street vendors, unofficial taxi drivers, and so on (Nagengast 2009). In Caracas, Venezuela, these people are called *toderos* because they do a little of everything (*todo*) in order to survive (Galeano 1997, 249). Unemployment and underemployment in the cities rob them of the right to work, making them doubly poor because urban life confronts them with images of wealth, such as fancy cars and mansions, to which they have no access.

When peasant expulsion occurs on a grand scale, local labor markets become saturated, unable to absorb the rivers of workers pouring into the cities. Migrants are then driven into the international labor market at a disadvantage, which sets in motion migration across the planet (Harvey 2003; Massey, Durand, and Malone 2002; Sassen 2007). In other words, when people are displaced from their traditional livelihoods, they become a mobile population of wage workers, actively selling their labor in whichever market will accept them. Under these conditions, migration serves as a type of self-insurance policy against unemployment or underemployment for families who send members to labor markets in different locations—rural, urban, or overseas—to diversify their income portfolio (Massey 2009).

Even for farmers who switch to commercial export agriculture, migration is important as self-insurance for protection against crop failure or sudden drops in commodity prices, when dealing with unfamiliar crops and technologies. In countries with weak capital and credit markets, migration can also serve as a self-financed bank account when a family member works abroad to accumulate savings that can be used either for investment or to purchase consumer goods (Massey 2009). In effect, economic globalization, also known as "free trade" or as the neoliberal "Washington Consensus," is one of the most powerful instigators of worldwide migration today and is a major root cause of a world on the move (Castles and Miller 2009; Guskin and Wilson 2007; Massey 2009).

Migration is also a reaction to trade policies, "the globally connected business engines that promote and support it," including forces such as "global supply chains, money flows, nomadic businesses, inequality and

trade policies" (Kaye 2010). Trade agreements such as NAFTA produce social and economic changes in sending countries that not only encourage migration across borders but also create transportation, communication, and
social links that make it easier (Massey 2009). The connections between the
United States and Mexico forged by NAFTA also serve as bridges for migration across the border (Navarro 2009). As a result, more Mexicans have
moved to the United States since the passage of NAFTA than in any other
period of American history (Bacon 2008; Nagengast 2009).

A classic example of economic globalization promoting migration is the
North American Free Trade Agreement (NAFTA), the 1994 treaty signed
by the United States, Canada, and Mexico (Bacon 2008; Lopez 2007; Nagengast 2009). The architects of NAFTA (agribusiness, banks, manufacturers, and multinational corporations) promised to reduce migration out
of Mexico by revitalizing the Mexican economy, creating jobs, narrowing
the wage gap, improving health care, saving the environment, lowering tariffs, eliminating trade barriers, and encouraging privatization (Lopez 2007;
Navarro 2009). Not surprisingly, they rejected the free movement of labor
across borders (Bacon 2008; Navarro 2009), so as to keep labor cheap.

After the passage of NAFTA, the Mexican government converted the
ejido system of small farming communities into condominiums, co-ops,
partnerships, joint-stock companies, and private businesses (Harvey 2003).
One year later, 1 million Mexican farmers left their land, while the Ministry
of Agriculture predicted that 1 million more farmers would leave their land
each year for the next 15 years. Between 1993 and 2000, from 1.3 to 1.7
million jobs were lost in rural Mexico (Bacon 2008). Thirty percent of farm
jobs in Mexico, affecting 2.8 million farmers plus millions of family members, were lost in the wake of NAFTA (Nagengast 2009). At the same time,
1 million Mexicans reached the age of fifteen, while the Mexican job market contracted by 200,000 jobs (Lopez 2007). Overall, 15 million peasant
farmers in Mexico were displaced from subsistence agriculture and forced to
turn to other crops, abandon their land, or seek wage work (Lopez 2007).

The result in Mexico has been the collapse of family farming, which
has been replaced by commercial export agriculture, a trend strongly encouraged by the International Monetary Fund (IMF) and the World Bank
in many developing countries (Escobar 1995; Harvey 2003), which undermines Mexico's food security. Export agriculture also profoundly restructures
food production systems worldwide and contributes to global food instability by exerting pressure on countries to dismantle domestic agriculture
and open local food markets to cheap imported food. The case of Mexico
is particularly ironic because it has been transformed from the birthplace of

corn into an importer of corn. The Mexican government was pressured to abolish subsidies and price supports for corn production in order to comply with NAFTA requirements and IMF demands (Bacon 2008; Stanford 2008). Corn is the single most highly subsidized crop in the United States, making it possible for American farmers to produce corn at 40% of the cost in Mexico (Lopez 2007). Surplus corn stocks in the United States were sold to Mexico, a practice known as "grain dumping" (Bacon 2008). With cheap US corn flooding the Mexican market, the price of corn dropped 70%, putting Mexican corn farmers out of business. At the same time, the cost of corn tortillas rose 50% and the cost of food, housing, and essential services rose 247% (Lopez 2007).

The impact of NAFTA on Mexico can be compared to the impact of the 2010 BP oil spill in the Gulf of Mexico on the lives of those whose livelihoods depend on the sea, except that in Mexico the primary resource is land. In contrast to its promises, NAFTA has brought hardship, not prosperity, to ordinary Mexicans. Also contrary to public perception, those who have benefited most from NAFTA have been agribusiness, banks, manufacturers, major corporations, and the Mexican elite who have made huge profits either from export agriculture or export manufacturing (Navarro 2009). Ironically, corporate investment and the cross-border operations of NAFTA have created new migration streams, rather than eliminating them (Sassen 2007). Even worse, NAFTA has undermined the labor rights of working people in all three countries and polluted the environment (Bacon 2008).

The Unholy Trinity and Migration

The destruction caused by the IMF, the World Bank, and the World Trade Organization (WTO) across the globe has earned them the title of the "unholy trinity" (Cavanagh and Mander 2004). The IMF and the World Bank were created together in an agreement signed at Bretton Woods, New Hampshire, in 1944, to reconstruct the global economy after the end of World War II. The WTO was created in 1994. All three powerful, global institutions not only create the rules for economic globalization but design its operating systems, using a single formula, aimed at forcing developing nations to cultivate identical visions, policies, and standards.

Adopting a shared vision of the developing world, they work hand in hand for common goals, which include deregulating corporations, privatizing all things public, preventing developing nations from protecting their natural resources and their labor forces, and nullifying safety standards and laws. Together, they try to ensure that in developing nations all assets should be owned by foreign corporations; all production should be aimed at export, and its corollary, all goods consumed locally should be imported; all currency used for transactions should be borrowed from foreign banks; and health care and education should be owned and operated by foreign corporations for profit, charging fees for services (Cavanagh and Mander 2004).

Armed with this ideology, the IMF formulated "structural adjustment" policies to help developing countries qualify for loans, with the goal of "monetary stabilization." Accordingly, IMF policies require developing countries to impose "austerity measures" by slashing government spending on health care, education, and the environment, as well as eliminating government subsidies not only for basic necessities such as food grains and cooking oils but also for local agriculture (Cavanagh and Mander 2004; Guskin and Wilson 2007). Such measures place enormous hardship on the population and ignite social protest, such as the riots in Greece in May 2010, when the Greek people were getting a taste of IMF austerity for the first time, unlike their cousins in the developing world who have experienced it for decades.

In addition, the IMF "encourages" national exportation by nurturing export industries such as commercial agriculture, export-oriented manufacturing, and export processing zones (EPZs). It also supports national importation through the elimination of tariffs and duties on imported goods. In addition, IMF policies require developing countries to open up their financial markets to short-term financial speculation, which encourages financial bubbles and instability, such as the financial crisis in Asia in 1997–1998 (Cavanagh and Mander 2004). The IMF also pressures developing nations to devalue their currencies, which increases operating costs for local companies forced to pay more for imported machinery and spare parts paid in dollars (Escobar 1995).

To add insult to injury, IMF policies also require developing nations to increase interest rates to attract foreign firms, which promotes the acquisition of local companies and a rise in domestic bankruptcies (Cavanagh and Mander 2004). In effect, IMF policies have destroyed local economies and increased local unemployment as foreign firms have taken over many economic sectors and government revenues have declined in order to pay back the national debt. Furthermore, the death of domestic agriculture has threatened local livelihoods and reduced survival options for small producers, forcing them to become wage laborers, first in domestic job markets but later in international economies (Sassen 2007).

Another IMF requirement is the privatization of government services (Escobar 1995). The aim of privatization is to shift responsibility for social services away from state machinery to a variety of market-based nongovernmental organizations (NGOs) as well as small groups and individuals (Inda 2006). What is achieved by the privatization of common natural resources such as water, land, and forests is the enclosure of the commons. Privatization converts the bounty of nature, which should be free, into private property owned by individuals, groups, and corporations, turning them into new instruments for generating profit (Harvey 2003). The most common result of privatization on ordinary people has been dispossession. Outspoken political activist Arundhati Roy (2001, 43) defines privatization in this way:

> Essentially it is the transfer of productive public assets from the state to private companies. Productive assets include natural resources. Earth, forest, water, air. These are assets that the state holds in trust for the people it represents. . . . Their lives depend directly on access to natural resources. To snatch these away and sell them as stock to private companies is a process of barbaric dispossession on a scale that has no parallel in history.

In 2000, bankers, economists, government ministers, and engineers gathered in the Hague at the World Water Forum to discuss privatizing the world's water by putting a market value on water when 1 billion people in the world have no access to safe drinking water even when it is free. In parts of the developing world, poor people were denied water because they were unable to pay for it. They were forced to turn to polluted water, with the result that many died from a cholera epidemic (Harvey 2003). Furthermore, the World Bank has played a central role in producing water scarcity by converting Earth's natural water supply into market opportunities for water corporations. Indeed, the water business is regarded as an extremely lucrative industry, its potential being estimated by the World Bank to be around $1 trillion (Shiva 2002). As Roy (2001, 42) put it,

> There is a difference between valuing water and putting a market value on water. No one values water more than a village woman who has to walk miles to fetch it. No one values it less than urban folk who pay for it to flow endlessly at the turn of a tap.
>   When all the rivers and valleys and forests and hills of the world have been priced, packaged, bar-coded and stacked in the supermarket, when all the hay and coal and earth and wood and water have been turned to gold, what then shall we do with all the gold?

The World Bank was created originally to finance the reconstruction of Europe after the end of World War II, but when Europe rejected the mortgaging of its economic future to foreign bankers, the World Bank declared its mission to be eliminating poverty in the third world and turned to marketing its loans to the newly independent nations of the developing world (Cavanagh and Mander 2004). Today it has an organizational structure in which the United States (21%), the United Kingdom, Germany, France, and Japan together control almost 45% of the vote—while 22 Latin American countries control less than 10% (Escobar 1995; Galeano 1997). This institutional structure allows the global financial elite and US foreign policy to dictate how the problem of poverty and its solutions should be framed.

Furthermore, the World Bank's unstated mission appears to be helping global corporations to establish control over natural resources and local markets (Cavanagh and Mander 2004), since most of its loans and contracts have been awarded to multinational corporations and "experts" from the industrialized world, although projects are subject to "competitive" international bidding (Escobar 1995). This mission is accomplished by funding contracts on large projects such as dams, roads, power plants, electrical grids, and communications links that provide the infrastructure for the export of raw materials as well as finished products (Cavanagh and Mander 2004; Escobar 1995; Galeano 1997). Such projects suggest that the welfare of the poor is not the World Bank's top priority; for example, it favors the building of huge hydroelectric dams instead of smaller projects supplying much-needed water to local populations. Even when publicly funded, giant water projects tend to dispossess the weak and benefit the powerful, such as construction companies, industries, and commercial farmers (Shiva 2002).

As the financial twin of the IMF, the World Bank shares its economic ideology, equating economic development with export-oriented production, as well as foreign borrowing and foreign investment. In the spirit of its stated mission to eliminate poverty in the third world, the World Bank distributes huge sums of money to the developing world. However, its greatest achievement has been to transform the habit of developing countries' borrowing into an addiction, as they borrow ever-larger sums to service the interest and principal on older loans, to the point where the cost of debt servicing has exceeded the ability to repay (Cavanagh and Mander 2004). In fact, the governments of several industrialized countries cancelled the debt of the 18 poorest countries in 2006 when it was obvious that it would be impossible for them to repay their national debts.

The IMF and the World Bank have strangled many governments of the developing world with the promotion of high levels of debt. In 1980 the total external debt of all developing countries was $609 billion; in 2001 it totaled $2.4 trillion, thanks to 20 years of structural adjustment (Cavanagh and Mander 2004). In the 1990s the majority of highly indebted countries paid $3 in debt service to industrialized countries for every $1 received in development aid (Sassen 2007). Debt service ratios to gross national product (GNP) stand at 123% in Africa, 42% in Latin America, and 28% in Asia (Sassen 2007, 153). Debt payment requires new loans to cover interest, dividends, amortization, and so on, which then require more and more new loans, in an endless spiral. In 2001 Sub-Saharan Africa paid $3.6 billion more in debt service than it received in new loans and credits, and spent four times more on debt service payments than on health care (Cavanagh and Mander 2004, 57). In short, the World Bank has been a major contributor to the global debt crisis.

Contrary to popular wisdom, foreign aid has failed to promote prosperity. Rather, foreign aid has created greater dependency by placing enormous burdens on governments when it is coupled with the national debt. It has also served as a subsidy for US exports. For example, foreign aid has been tied historically to buying US goods at prices ranging from 30% to 50% higher than goods purchased elsewhere (Galeano 1997). In addition, loans from the US Agency for International Development (USAID) and the Inter-American Development Bank (IDB) require that at least half the cargo must be transported on US ships at freight rates double those of other shipping lines. Furthermore, insurance for merchandise being shipped and banks expediting the shipment must be US-owned.

The third arm of the unholy trinity, the World Trade Organization, was founded in 1994, half a century after its older siblings. In essence, the WTO is a "closed tribunal of trade bureaucrats" (Cavanagh and Mander 2004, 65) whose operations are conducted in secret. It is dedicated to setting global limits on government regulation of environmental, food safety, and product standards, as well as to protecting intellectual property rights of corporations in rich countries. It exists mainly to serve the interests of global corporations and the US government over those of civil society and developing nations. For instance, agriculture was brought under the jurisdiction of the WTO in 1995 to undermine food security in developing nations by forcing them to import US agricultural products and sell them at prices lower than domestic crops (Cavanagh and Mander 2004).

As international trade mushroomed at the end of World War II, the United States exerted great international pressure to establish the WTO because its predecessor, the General Agreement on Tariffs and Trade (GATT), did not sufficiently promote corporate interests over labor rights, human rights, and environmental protection. A loose and flexible GATT no longer served the interests of leading US corporations, so it needed to be replaced by the WTO, which operates by formulating one-size-fits-all rules to control every level of government in every member country and applying permanent trade sanctions against noncompliant countries. Not surprisingly, the WTO system of dispute resolution and most of its rulings have favored the United States (Cavanagh and Mander 2004).

Developing countries have discovered, albeit a tad late, that membership in the WTO has hamstrung their prospects for economic development. For example, they agreed to ban limits on imports, cut tariffs on many industrial imports, and promised not to increase tariffs on all other imports. In so doing, they essentially signed away their right to use trade policy to enhance domestic development and to use import substitution for industrial development.

Simply put, the WTO sets strict limits on how much a government can protect a nation's health, security, and environments, while the WTO does nothing to limit the excesses of global corporations and financial speculators. Nor does the future look too rosy. WTO agenda items for the future include prohibiting public policies that favor local investors and suppliers over foreign ones, limiting the protection of local farmers from foreign competition, limiting the protection of forest and water resources from foreign exploitation, and privatizing public schools and health care under the control of global corporations (Cavanagh and Mander 2004, 69).

Not surprisingly, the combined impact of the unholy trinity on the people of the world has been categorically negative. Together the IMF, the World Bank, and WTO have devastated the working class of developing nations, especially the lives of women and children, creating desperate conditions that drive them toward the migration industry or human traffickers to carry them to jobs wherever they can be found.

Labor Recruitment and Migration, Part I: Guest Worker Programs

We used to own our slaves; now we just rent them.
—Edward R. Murrow, *Harvest of Shame* (1960)

By definition, guest worker programs are government-sponsored projects that import people from one country to another, exclusively for purposes of labor. In the United States, there are two types of guest worker programs: the H-2A program for agricultural work and the H-2B program for nonagricultural work. Guest worker programs everywhere are deeply flawed because they are founded on exploitation. The profits of business and industry are more highly valued than the welfare of guest workers who are bound to their employers by law—in effect, becoming a pool of workers unable to change jobs or to defend their rights when they are exploited or abused (Guskin and Wilson 2007). It is no wonder that guest worker programs have been described as "buying people in bulk" and "turning people into a commodity" (Bacon 2008, 234).

The inner workings of guest worker programs have been documented in a Southern Poverty Law Center (SPLC) report titled *Close to Slavery* (2007a). As the title implies, workers are treated more like slaves than guests, beginning with an unregulated and profitable recruitment process in the home country. Recruiters charge exorbitant fees to cover travel, visas, and recruiter profit, which forces migrants either to get loans at high interest rates or provide collateral, such as deeds to their homes.

Although US laws require employers to reimburse workers for travel and visa costs, these laws are seldom enforced. As a result, guest workers often arrive at their destinations with debts ranging from $500 to $10,000, not including interest, which is almost impossible to repay, given their paltry earnings (Guskin and Wilson 2007). In post-Katrina Louisiana, for instance, guest workers for hotel jobs paid up to US$5,000 in advance, which placed them not only deeply in debt but also at the mercy of unscrupulous employers.

In addition to usurious recruiter fees, guest workers are routinely abused in the following ways: they are cheated out of wages, held captive by employers who seize travel and identification documents to prevent them from leaving, forced to live in squalor, and denied medical care for injuries on the job (SPLC 2007b). When they complain about such abuse, they are either threatened with deportation or deported. For example, in November 1986, a group of 100 sugarcane cutters in Florida stopped work to protest their low pay and being cheated out of wages. The company responded by calling in riot police with attack dogs and then shipping the entire crew, not just the protestors, against their will, back to Jamaica (Guskin and Wilson 2007).

Let us consider one moment in American history when such misguided values almost changed. Back in the 1990s there was a short-lived attempt to craft a law that would provide acceptable wages, decent living and working conditions, protection from employer abuse and limited immigration amnesty for immigrant workers, in exchange for time spent as a guest worker (Bacon 2008). It was called the AgJobs bill, authored by Congressman Berman (California) in cooperation with the United Farm Workers, but it died when President George W. Bush was elected. The AgJobs bill died because of the efforts of the Essential Worker Immigration Coaliton (EWIC), formed in 1999, a corporate trade association with an insatiable appetite for seasonal, temporary workers.

The EWIC proposed expanding guest worker programs that would deprive workers of all rights but would allow annual visas conditioned on work for a specific employer. Such proposals are reminiscent of the Bracero program, which was notorious for abuse and dehumanization. After September 11, 2001, EWIC proposals became the bible of immigration reform in Washington, DC, because they were reframed as answers to national security dilemmas and marketed as instruments of tracking and border enforcement (Bacon 2008).

Since 2001 all immigration reform proposals in the United States have included guest worker programs by manipulating language and substituting the phrase "guest worker" for euphemisms like "essential workers" or "new workers" (Bacon 2008, 115). Some have even proposed to increase penalties for lack of documentation and others to eliminate the possibility of family reunification. In the final analysis, however, every proposal for "comprehensive" immigration reform since 2001 has contained guest worker provisions, a key EWIC principle.

Labor Recruitment and Migration, Part II: Direct Recruitment and Labor Exportation

Today, direct recruitment has fostered new migration streams, but it is not a pretty picture. In an exposé titled *The Dark Side of the Dubai Dream,* the BBC documented unbridled exploitation and squalid living conditions in the construction industry in Dubai to which migrant workers had been recruited (Allen 2009). The everyday life of migrant workers in Dubai contrasts sharply with popular stereotypes of Dubai as a glamorous retreat for the rich and famous. Frolicking is out of the question for the 1 million migrant workers who have been recruited from the poorest parts of the Indian subcontinent. Their destitution has made them extremely vulnerable to empty promises made by recruitment agents who charge recruitment fees amounting to 2,000 British pounds or more, forcing them either to borrow money or sell family land hoping to repay the sum in 18 months.

Once in Dubai, the migrant workers were not paid the wages promised, which was not enough to send remittances home. Although some migrants worked directly for the largest construction company in Dubai, most were employed by subcontractors who made them work 12 hour shifts, six days a week, and seldom paid them overtime, as law requires (Allen 2009).

Most workers also lived in hidden camps under appalling conditions. In one camp, 7,500 migrants shared 1,248 rooms, the latrines had no water supply and were overflowing with raw feces, raw sewage had leaked all over the camp so that stepping-stones were necessary to avoid walking in sewage to and from the barracks, and the roads were water-logged and full of garbage. Although Dubai authorities had inspected the camp and fined the company 2,000 British pounds, the company blamed the migrants for the situation, claiming that their standards of hygiene and cleanliness were primitive. Workers throughout the Gulf are not likely to complain for fear of losing their jobs and being deported (Gardner 2010).

The infrastructure of the global economy—including global markets and global money flows, communications technologies, and transnational networks—facilitates labor export (Harvey 2003; Sassen 2007). There is no doubt that the state plays a major role in promoting and supporting the organized export of workers, both for government revenue and for private profit. Organized labor export has increased recently, raising interesting questions about the relationship between rising unemployment, the closing of local small businesses, and growing government debt (Sassen 2007).

For example, China has begun to export its cheap labor to far-flung destinations such as Saudi Arabia, Sudan, Niger, and Nigeria, where they toil in the oil industry (T. Johnson 2009). Most have been recruited from rural villages with promises of double and even triple the wages they make at home. Many describe being tricked and deceived about wages and working conditions. Those who complained and refused to work were deported and sent back to China. Some were victims of human trafficking.

Human Smuggling, Trafficking, and the Migration Industry

People-smuggling is a business partnership, however unequal, in which the *movement* of people produces profit. In contrast, people-trafficking is based on trickery, deceit, and coercion, which generates profit from the *sale* of sexual services or the *sale* of labor. With a common goal of profit, both industries have grown exponentially, human trafficking having become the fastest-growing industry worldwide because of skyrocketing profits: US$5–$10 billion per year (Castles and Miller 2009, 203). In reaction, the US government launched antitrafficking legislation in 2001 and has been praised for its efforts. The effectiveness of such laws, however, is debatable because today the United States stands among nations in which modern-day slavery resides.

Ironically, some believe that stricter laws and enforcement have generated greater demand for traffickers by people with legitimate claims to refugee status but no legal access to it. For instance, studies of smuggled and trafficked Chinese workers have revealed complex global networks, almost impossible to dismantle through law enforcement, in which "foot soldiers" were caught and punished but high-level executives escaped easily. A 2006 US report estimated that 800,000 individuals are trafficked across borders every year, and the United Nations estimates that 200 million people are involved worldwide and that 50,000 women are trafficked to the United States each year (Castles and Miller 2009, 203). Even more alarming, the US State Department published a "Trafficking in Persons" (TIP) report in 2010 estimating that more than 12 million children and adults may be victims worldwide (Chen 2010).

Women and children are trafficked all over the world for the sex industry because they are the most vulnerable. Some agree to the trafficking because opportunities for legal migration are so limited; others are tricked by false promises. Consider, for instance, the teenage girls of Zimbabwe who wanted to escape destitution, starvation, and disease following the collapse of the Zimbabwean economy, the disintegration of its health-care system, and the spread of a cholera epidemic. The girls' only hope for survival appeared to be in crossing the border into South Africa on their own. Many traveled hundreds of miles from the Zimbabwean capital of Harare to Musina, a mining town on the border. There, the South African government opened an office to process their asylum claims. After being documented, they disappeared (Bryson 2009).

A study by the International Organization for Migration (IOM) found established routes used by human traffickers in South Africa to recruit and transport girls and young women to cities from the countryside to work as prostitutes or maids (Bryson 2009). They are extremely vulnerable because they are so desperate and because there is no shortage of young girls. Some do not admit to being victims because they are too ashamed; others do not see themselves as victims because they are grateful to have a job. Some force themselves into prostitution to get money; others force themselves into temporary marriage for security. Some were raped on both sides of the border when they crossed.

Because of its sensationalist value, media attention is often riveted on young girls inducted into sex slavery by prostitution rings, but government data suggests that labor trafficking is more common, especially in nonunderground industries such as hotel work and nursing homes (Chen 2010).

Awareness has grown, over time, about the seriousness of the human trafficking problem. A representative for Lawyers for Human Rights, whose job is to prevent illegal detention or deportation before applying for refugee status, stated that he does not try too hard to get young girls released from a government deportation center because he cannot be sure they will not be captured by traffickers (Bryson 2009). While it is not possible to know precisely how many people are being trafficked, there is general agreement that the worldwide inequalities produced by economic globalization fuel human trafficking.

The social networks and cross-border connections that enable human movement have also spawned a migration industry. The cast of characters is a motley crew, made up of labor recruiters, remittance agencies, banks, travel agents, interpreters, immigration lawyers, immigration and customs officials, transportation providers, NGOs that assist migrants and refugees, and human traffickers, among others (Castles and Miller 2009). In short, the migration industry is a complex system connecting large groups with small operators in countries of origin and destination as well as in transit, providing infrastructural needs not met by governments. Migration would most likely fail without agents and brokers, who have a vested interest in perpetuating migration because their livelihoods depend on it.

Another dimension of the migration industry is the notion of managed migration. In fact, the substance of a proposal at the WTO meetings in Hong Kong in 2005 was to manage the movement of people in the same way as the movement of capital and goods (Bacon 2008). Not surprisingly, human rights and immigrant rights organizations have presented strong opposition. Instead of allowing the WTO to regulate migration in the best interests of employers, these organizations have proposed that all countries ratify and implement the 1990 UN International Convention on the Protection of the Rights of All Migrant Workers and Members of Their Families.

The UN convention also supported basic human rights such as family reunification, equal treatment in matters of employment and education to that of citizens of the host country, and protection against collective deportation. From the UN perspective, the protection of these rights would be the responsibility of both sending and receiving countries. In other words, the United Nations, human rights organizations, and immigrant rights organizations believed that government, industry, and business should view immigrants not simply as units of labor to be bought and sold as commodities or to be imported and exported but as human beings who deserve dignity and rights.

Colonization, Military Intervention, and Migration

International migration is a system of exchange in which the movement of people is encouraged by previous connections of many types, including those of colonization, military conquest, and political domination. As emphasized previously, migration is the outcome of interaction between two or more countries at many levels, with the interactions generating ties that mobilize border crossings. Over the centuries, financial, technological, informational, transportation, social, and cultural bonds have been nurtured between the developed and the developing world, creating ties of interdependence and dependency that lock them in an enduring embrace across time and space.

Old colonial ties constitute one such type of interdependence that facilitates the movement of people from former colonies to the land of their former colonizers (Castles and Miller 2009; Harvey 2003; Sassen 2007). For example, after the end of World War II, 350,000 Irish citizens, as well as immigrants from former colonies in the Caribbean, South Asia, and Africa, flooded the United Kingdom to make up for labor shortages in post–World War II reconstruction, essentially serving as a reserve army of labor. Although the Irish were not exactly welcomed, the nonwhite immigrants were subjected to unparalleled discrimination in education, employment, and housing. The hostility was so strong that the British government was persuaded to pass the Commonwealth Immigrants Act in 1962 to limit their entry. However, this law was considered inadequate because it allowed family reunification, bringing more nonwhite immigrants into the country. So, colonial immigration was brought to a complete halt by the Immigration Act of 1971.

France was also flooded by large-scale immigration from former colonies in North Africa by 1970: Algeria (600,000), Morocco (140,000), Tunisia (90,000), Senegal, Mali, and Mauritania, as well as overseas departments such as Martinique and Guadeloupe (Castles and Miller 2003, 74). Although they were all French citizens, they provoked racial violence and the formation of extreme-right political parties. Between 1945 and the early 1960s, 300,000 people migrated from Indonesia, a former Dutch colony, to the Netherlands without much opposition. However, after 1965, black immigrants from Aruba, Curacao, and Surinam, former Dutch colonies in the Caribbean, provoked protest. In Europe, the countries with the largest number of immigrants from former colonies were Britain, France, and the Netherlands.

Far beyond the wildest dreams of the colonial era, military interventions, direct and indirect, also propel human migration by creating connections between countries through imperial relations of power. For instance, the US war in Vietnam in the 1960s generated a huge flow of refugees from Vietnam to the United States during the 1970s and 1980s, most settling along the West Coast, but many spreading to other parts of the country. These refugees were entitled to and given generous resettlement packages wherever they landed. Similarly, the US war in El Salvador motivated large numbers of refugees and migrants to flee their war-torn country in the 1980s and 1990s and to settle mainly in California (Guskin and Wilson 2007; Sassen 2007).

The presence of US corporations, coupled with American economic dominance, also serve as neocolonial bridges that encourage migration from the Philippines and Mexico to the United States. Furthermore, US military bases, scattered across the globe, and US ballistic missile sites in Europe (C. Johnson 2010) are not merely military operations; they create social bridges between the United States and the countries in which they are located, as well as links between US citizens and the people of those nations that encourage emigration. Simply put, the United States generates migration networks across the globe because it is the hub of a military system binding regions together, even if these networks are unintended (Sassen 2007).

Mexico-US Migration: Up Close and Personal

Let us now shift our gaze toward more personal perspectives on migration. When the Mexican government removed subsidies and price supports for corn, hunger and starvation followed. Hunger and starvation also followed agricultural changes that benefited commercial farmers, brokers, and large corporations but not small, subsistence corn farmers who barely broke even from the sale of corn, seldom made a profit, and lost money if crop yields were low. "There is a direct correlation between the price of corn and beans paid to subsistence and small producer farmers in Mexico and undocumented migration to the United States" (Lopez 2007, 50).

Since 1994 endless hunger and malnutrition have become permanent residents of the Mexican countryside. Campesinos and their families are hungry and desperate for work. If they do not migrate, they may not survive. Hunger is the topic of everyday conversation in villages. Almost half of the plants grown in home gardens are for relieving stomachaches and diarrhea, which result from poor nutrition and poor sanitation. More to the point, almost every family can tell the story of a member who has died of starvation, usually a child (Lopez 2007). On a personal level, there is strong social pressure for the men (and sometimes women) of poor families in Mexico to emigrate to earn money to feed children who might otherwise starve.

Hungry migrants are desperate enough to risk everything, including their lives, for the hope of finding a job on the other side of the border. They feel they have nothing to lose except death by starvation (Lopez 2007). Thus, for those immigrants who risk everything, including their lives, for the hope of a better life, crossing national borders is a matter of survival, not a matter of choice. And, contrary to econometric theories about solitary individuals engaging in self-serving calculations, the decision to migrate is always made in consultation with the entire family and is never made lightly.

Obviously, not all migrants are hungry and starving; some are motivated to migrate by other factors. The shortage of jobs paying a living wage in Mexico, as well as the lack of opportunities to save money, except by migrating to work, is one such factor encouraging migration. Joanna Dreby's (2010) study of Mexican migrants in New Jersey proves the point; everyone in her sample had entered the United States seeking jobs. Not surprisingly, most were undocumented. In particular, female migrants complained that there was no work to be found in Mexico. One woman stated, "There isn't any work for women. Sometimes the women work helping to pick fruit, mostly lemons, and sometimes they make candies from coconuts to sell in other towns. Mostly, they do not work at all" (Dreby 2010, 11).

The enormous wage gap between Mexico and the United States provides an equally strong incentive to cross the border. Once in the United States, farmers and former government officials from different social strata found themselves working together, cheek by jowl, in landscaping, construction, factories, and private restaurants. Their typical wages ranged from US$8–$12 per hour, which is ten times the typical wage for equivalent jobs in Mexico (Dreby 2010, 11). Female Mexican immigrants mostly work in fast-food restaurants and factories, earning US$6–$9 per hour. In contrast, wage workers on farms in west-central Mexico earn between 16 and 80 pesos (US$1.60–$8.00) a day (Lopez 2007, 51). Wage workers in California agribusiness can expect to earn more in a single hour than in a whole day's work in Mexico. The wage differential between the United States and Mexico is unlikely to change because of a huge labor surplus in Mexico, especially since NAFTA.

Unemployment in Mexico is increasing rapidly, inspiring many migrants to come north. Even those with jobs are motivated to cross the border to the United States where they believe they will be paid more for their work and where their sacrifice of migration and hard work will provide a better future for their children (Dreby 2010). Consider the case of a 41-year-old father from a very poor family in a tiny town on the outskirts of Oaxaca. Until the age of 24 he worked as a farmer growing corn, chiles, and beans. When his children were ages six, four, and two, he and his extended family moved to the city where he worked unloading trucks, earning about US$10 per day, barely enough to feed his family. Having lost his land, he decided, with his family's consent, to accompany a friend to "el norte" (Dreby 2010).

Another important motivator of migration is providing better schooling for children in Mexico, which requires money. Although tuition is free through the university level in Mexico, other costs for those at the secondary level include fees, supplies, books, and transportation to larger towns with schools. Migrants hope that the money they send back from the United States will open educational doors for their children so they will not have to struggle as adults (Dreby 2010). Apart from better schooling, money sent from abroad also enhances the health of children and their caretakers left behind. Studies show that children in families with US migrants enjoy better health than children in families without US migrants. Remittances from the United States also contribute to home improvements for the family in Mexico, such as additions, renovations, and furniture.

Over the years, a culture of migration has developed, fueling the flow of migrants from Mexico to the United States (Dreby 2010; Hagan 2008; Kandel and Massey 2002). Throughout Mexico, there is a sense of longing for "el norte" and "a culture of migration" that has captured the imaginations of children and adults alike (Dreby 2010, 18). For instance, school principals in Mexico report low attendance at schools because their students' highest ambitions are to migrate to the United States. In addition, a sense of largesse is associated with "el norte," reinforced by migrant remittances, which have not only enhanced local families but also contributed to the larger community by installing streetlights on main streets, funding renovations of central plazas, and embellishing local festivals and celebrations.

Family Sacrifices

Although migration carries many benefits, there is a human cost in terms of sacrifice. The effects on families divided by borders vary according to gender and marital status. Studies show that the majority of Mexican migrants (81%) are solitary males, although more women are migrating recently (Dreby 2010). Not surprisingly, women are criticized more than men for leaving their children behind. Although the gap in job opportunities and wages between the United States and Mexico draws them north, sometimes they are unprepared for the sacrifice required by those, for instance, who work very dangerous jobs that can result in serious injuries and even death.

Mexican immigrants have high hopes that the benefits will compensate for their sacrifices. Job opportunities, however, seldom compensate for the hardship of family separation. On the one hand, migrant parents discover how hard life is in the United States: they live in unsafe neighborhoods and work hard in low-skill jobs for low wages, no benefits, and no job security. They also work long hours with little time to spend with family or friends. As one father put it, "Here there is no family life" (Dreby 2010). They are also restricted in other ways: they cannot drive or get car insurance, and they cannot travel by air. On the other hand, the emotional costs of family separations are felt most keenly by their children who feel abandoned. Children want constant reassurance from migrant parents that they still care about them; what they get are phone calls and remittances.

In essence, migration transforms the relationship between migrant parents and their children left behind into an "immigrant bargain" or "intergenerational contract" (Dreby 2010). Migrant parents expect two things to result from migration: First, that they will be economically successful in the United States. Second, they expect their children to love and respect them despite their absence, to behave well with their caretakers, to take care of themselves, to study hard, and to become professionals. Many parents believed that paying for schooling compensated for their absence, and some even planned to retire to Mexico after their children became professionals and could support them in old age.

While all children left behind experience loss after their parents leave, teenagers are the ones who have the greatest difficulty meeting their parents' expectations. They become angry and frustrated, lashing out at their caregivers and teachers. Some pretend indifference; others refuse to use the terms "Mom" or "Dad," calling their parents by their first names (Dreby 2010). Yet others refuse to migrate to join their parents. Even worse, when children become teenagers they defy authority and become uncontrollable, because most caregivers are grandparents whose authority is further undermined by absent parents who refuse to discipline their children—instead, exercising remote control or becoming friends.

The loss of control over teenagers has many negative outcomes, such as drinking, drug abuse, gang activity, and most importantly, low academic achievement. The latter is both heartbreaking and ironic because migrant parents have pinned all their hopes and dreams on their children's education. When children perform poorly in school, migrant parents send more money, which has little effect.

Studies have shown that Mexican children of migrant parents tend to drop out of school more so than children of nonmigrant parents. For example, 41% of children over age 14 dropped out of school, and 27% of those over age seven were held back a grade at least once, some many times (Dreby 2010). Most of all, children of migrant parents get no academic support, such as help with homework, from their grandparents, who tend to be poorly educated and some even illiterate. Furthermore, grandparents are not capable of the involvement expected from schools, such as joining PTAs or going to school meetings.

Fractured Families

Few Americans are aware of the power of immigration laws and border enforcement to fracture migrant families, generating hardship and suffering for them. When migrants leave their homelands to find work, often unauthorized, they are forced to leave their children behind because crossing the border with children is not only expensive but dangerous. Family separation can result in a whole generation of children growing up without their fathers (Lopez 2007). In some cases, fathers completely abandon their families in the homeland or start a new family in the host country with another woman. Abandoned women and their children are often left homeless in the country of origin with no means of support.

Even for immigrant families who have managed to reunite in the United States, despite the legal and institutional obstacles, they are still divided in terms of immigration status. Consider, for example, the Esparza family which, in many ways, is typical of many immigrant households in having members with wide variation in documentation—various permutations of citizen versus noncitizen, legal versus undocumented, naturalized versus US-born (Chavez 2008). Señor Esparza is alone in having become a legal immigrant, after many years of being undocumented. His new immigration status has enabled him to land a year-round job in the mushroom industry. His wife, however, remains undocumented, working for a company growing organic bush berries. Their two oldest sons remain undocumented because they were born in Mexico. However, their two daughters and youngest son were born in the United States and are therefore US citizens (Lopez 2007).

The existence of mixed-immigration-status families is a serious issue because the boundary between "legal" and "illegal" is not fixed. Being "illegal" is not a permanent condition. Many "illegals" become "legal" residents and even citizens over time (Guskin and Wilson 2007). More importantly, one family member being "illegal" does not mean all family members are the same, as the Esparza family illustrates. Moreover, by virtue of being born in the United States, two-thirds of the children of undocumented parents are US citizens, while three-quarters of the children of immigrants are US citizens (Fix 2007). Thus, a majority of the children of immigrants of all nationalities in the United States belong to families of mixed immigration status (Dreby 2010). Also, the denial of social services to undocumented parents is passed on to their citizen children, turning them into second-class citizens (Chavez 2008; Fix 2007; Zimmerman and Fix 2002).

Families have been shattered by detention and deportation, which separates parents and grandparents from children and grandchildren, and divides households composed equally of citizens, legal residents, and the undocumented (Guskin and Wilson 2007; Zimmerman and Fix 2002). Those who advocate deportation of "illegals" fail to understand that the undocumented are family members, partners, friends, neighbors, coworkers, and classmates. Apart from fragmenting families, heart-wrenching in its own right, policies preventing adjustment of immigrant status would also freeze individuals in certain statuses and keep families divided. Current immigration policies have ripped the fabric of society by tearing families apart. What we need now are family-friendly immigration policies.

Creative Survival:
Undocumented Migration and Smuggling

> How far away I am from the land where I was born
> Nostalgia sets my mind a-reeling
> And to see me so alone and sad,
>   like a leaf in the wind forlorn
> I would like to weep and die of feeling
> Oh, land of sun, how I long to see you . . .
>   —"Canción Mixteca," traditional Oaxacan folk song
>   (López Alavez 1915)

Despite the sacrifices and fragmentation entailed, undocumented migration from Mexico to the United States is the largest "illegal" migratory flow in the world. Indeed, statistics show that 80% to 85% of Mexicans arriving in the United States between 1995 and 2005 were undocumented, and that 55% of all Mexican immigrants in the United States in 2008 were undocumented (Dreby 2010, 10). Mexico also has the highest emigration rate in the world and 57% of all undocumented immigrants in the United States are from Mexico (Lopez 2007, 4).

Creativity and the bending of rules are indispensable for migration, especially for those lacking "papers," giving birth to the institutions of "illegal immigration" and migrant smuggling. It is estimated that the US economy requires 500,000 low-skill workers each year while US immigration policy has allowed the legal entry of only 5,000 low-skill workers per year (Oppenheimer 2010). Simple arithmetic tells us that the vast majority must enter the United States through the back door because the number of would-be migrants far exceeds the quota of entries allowed by law. In addition, undocumented migration would not be possible without the existence of a migrant smuggling industry.

However, undocumented migration can be viewed from different perspectives. Undocumented migration is often perceived as a criminal act, as "illegal immigration." A contrasting perspective is offered by Michel de Certeau, the French philosopher, in *The Practice of Everyday Life* (1984). He suggests that instead of becoming passive victims of repressive institutions and the excessive power of the state, as argued by French philosopher Michel Foucault, ordinary people adopt "tactics of resistance" that obey their own logic. In de Certeau's view, these "tactics of resistance" and "ways of operating" are not loud acts of rebellion. Rather, they are silent everyday practices that make tiny alterations to the system and, in so doing, adapt it to their own interests and their own rules (de Certeau 1984, xiv).

Seen through de Certeau's eyes, illegal immigration can be interpreted as an act of civil disobedience. It would be merely one of the many quotidian technologies that subvert US immigration laws, which Mexican migrants refuse to accept at face value in order to survive and thrive. Illegal immigration as civil disobedience requires tremendous creativity and ingenuity. Instead of going quietly into the night to die slowly of starvation, farmers in Mexico have become masters of improvisation. They have taken matters into their own hands, declared emigration to be their only survival option, and become farmworkers in Salinas and Watsonville, California (Lopez 2007), among other strategies.

Surrendering to both personal and structural pressures placed on them to leave their homeland, Mexican migrants have used creative "tactics" to overcome institutional obstacles standing in the way of their survival. Stated differently, undocumented immigrants do not consider "illegal immigration" to be a crime but a means of survival (Lopez 2007), a perspective that harmonizes with de Certeau's notion of how people, in their practice of everyday life, constantly manipulate events to turn them into opportunities. It is also an example of "clandestine tactics" that bend the rules creatively to suit their own interests and "short-circuit the institutional stage directions" of immigration laws (de Certeau 1984, xiv).

Undocumented migration is a prime example of the ingenious methods adopted by the weak to outwit the strong. The presence of approximately 11 million undocumented immigrants in the United States is evidence of their success, the key to which is the emergence of powerful immigrant smuggling rings (*coyotes*) that are corrupt, highly sophisticated criminal organizations operating underground with vast networks that span both sides of every border and with tentacles stretching in all directions (Payan 2006). People-smuggling is one of the fastest-growing forms of organized crime in the world today. The activity is enabled by the existence of huge numbers of would-be migrants who are desperate enough to risk beatings, robbery, rape, shootings, and even death in their efforts to cross borders.

Equally important to the success of migration is that *coyotes* are not perceived as villains or criminals but as heroes who perform an essential service promoting family reunification and general well-being (Lopez 2007). Indeed, they might be considered "specialty travel agents" (Kaye 2010, 99). Nor do *coyotes* themselves view migrant-smuggling as a criminal act, and boast jokingly that it is not very difficult to outwit the border patrol. There is a story of three migrants, traveling for days on foot and running out of supplies, who hide in a remote storage shed within yards of a crossing point on the Arizona-Mexico border. At exactly 9:02 p.m. they leap to their feet, running frantically to cross the border at 9:12 p.m. just before the next border patrol shift begins at 9:15 p.m. (Lopez 2007, 64). Some migrants even have relatives who are *coyotes* who provide the service for free and give discounts to their friends.

Migration happens because people are forced to leave all that is dear to them, to risk their lives, and to work in an alien destination to meet their basic needs. This simple fact has eluded many in destination countries, who prefer to remain in willful ignorance, succumbing instead to myths. In the next chapter, we look at the climate of fear nurtured by myths and fallacies as well as some rigorous studies that refute popular misperceptions about migration.

3

The Global Immigration Panic

F = FALSE
E = EXPECTATIONS
A = APPEARING
R = REAL

Although fear of strangers has existed since time immemorial, during lean times, it is common to blame outsiders for problems built into society as a whole; the reason is that much of the world is on the move, given all the forces that propel migrants to leave their homelands. Indeed, in 2005, approximately 190 million people (3% of the world's population) lived outside of the country of their birth (Hossain and Carter 2007). Not unsurprisingly, the demographic changes set in motion by planetary migration have provoked a powerful anti-immigrant backlash in every immigrant-receiving country.

Immigration: An Emotional Issue

Fear is a natural emotion with which all animals are endowed, including humans. It is nature's gift to protect them from harm. However, fear can become dysfunctional, especially for humans, when it rejects logic, inhabits our emotions, blocks out facts, and cuts ties with reality. While fear is natural, it puts humans into a hypnotic state during times of stress, such as the current economic crisis, paralyzing them, like a deer caught in the headlights. In the case of fear of foreigners, the level of fear in all immigrant-receiving countries has reached a pinnacle of dysfunction in which people succumb to authoritarian suggestions because their emotions have been manipulated in the direction of panic, resulting in the denial of immigrant rights.

The expansion of world capitalism has spread economic crisis and social inequality everywhere, but how these developments are connected to international migration is often hidden from plain view. For the past four decades, globalization has produced prosperity only for a tiny fraction of the world's population. It has not only privileged the rich over the poor, it has benefited rich nations at the expense of poor ones. As a result, the quality of life for nonrich humanity has worsened dramatically, which has generated internal displacement and economic destabilization in developing nations and provoked mass migration to advanced industrialized countries. Fear of immigrants has followed in the wake of this mass migration.

In the United States, all workers have seen their real wages plummet. They also work longer hours for less pay while health-care costs skyrocket. They watch their bridges collapse and their local communities crumble and rail at the failure of their public schools. In the same breath, the global economy was pushed to the brink of collapse by the pirates of Wall Street who continue to rake in record profits and embellish their bonus packages, in spite of the financial meltdown. The gap between the rich and the poor is gaping. For instance, between 1985 and today, the inflation-adjusted average annual salary for CEOs increased by $1.8 million while the inflation-adjusted median annual household income declined by $1,699 (Kurzban 2008). No wonder fear grips the hearts and minds of many US citizens.

Quite naturally, this fall from grace has generated widespread fear. Thanks to business practices such as deregulation, deindustrialization, and outsourcing, operating procedures that became the norm in the 1970s, US workers have been sliding down a slippery slope toward poverty while their standard of living has taken a nose dive. Thanks also to trade and immigration policies, US workers have been pitted against those in the global labor market, while leaving high-wage US workers protected and untouched (Nagengast 2009). Working-class people in the United States are not imagining their downfall, which is very real. Their mistake, however, has been to attribute its root source to immigrants, the undocumented in particular.

Job Theft, Depressed Wages, and Unemployment: Fact or Fiction?

There are many Americans whose only experience with trade and globalization has been a shuttered factory or a job that was shipped overseas.

—US President Barack Obama,
speech delivered in India, November 2010

Fear of job theft, depressed wages, unemployment, economic decline,
overburdened social services, cultural loss, crime, and terrorism are classic ways in which fear of immigrants has been expressed (Chavez 2008;
Guibernau 2007; Inda 2006; Navarro 2009; Riley 2008). Let us consider
the extent to which these fears are real or imagined, bearing in mind that
myth-making, as a strategy, thrives on telling only partial truths. First, are
the fears of job theft well-founded? No. A more accurate way to describe the
job situation in the United States today is job flight rather than job theft.
While it is true that 2.8 million manufacturing jobs left the United States
between 2001 and 2004, it is not true is that these jobs were stolen by undocumented immigrants (Kurzban 2008).

In short, the notion of job theft is only half true. The whole truth is that
immigrants do not compete against US workers for the same jobs, nor do
immigrants lower domestic wages. In fact, a longitudinal study of the mac-
roeconomic impact of immigration by the Organisation for Economic Cooperation and Development (OECD) has documented that immigrants do
not steal jobs and do not lower domestic wages (Castles and Miller 2009).
In fact, immigrants were responsible for half of the growth in the US labor
market in the past decade (Congressional Budget Office 2005). In other
words, the numbers of jobs in the United States are not static, and the labor
market is not a zero-sum game. Instead, it is fluid, with one-third of the US
workforce turning over in any given year. For instance, in 2006, 55 million
US workers left their jobs, voluntarily or by force; in the same period, 57
million were hired (Riley 2008).

Simply put, immigrants do not displace US workers. Instead, immigrants complement them because of the skill distribution in the US workforce. Immigrants are found at the extremes of the US labor market, working
either as low-skill laborers or as highly educated professionals, while most
workers in the US fall in between these two extremes. One-third of immigrants did not graduate from high school, while one-quarter hold a college

or advanced degree (Riley 2008). Immigrants do not depress wages because they are not interchangeable with US workers. Furthermore, immigrants are not job thieves; they create at least as many jobs as they fill by spending more money on goods and services than older people and are paid less than the total value of new goods and services they produce (Guskin and Wilson 2007; Nagengast 2009). Although they increase the labor supply, they also generate economic activity as consumers. More importantly, the mass employment of the undocumented makes it possible for US workers to be upwardly mobile (Castles and Miller 2003; Riley 2008).

Immigrants are not to blame for the economic crisis or the growing gap between the rich and the poor, despite this popular myth. The unpleasant truth is that the wages and working conditions for ordinary US citizens have declined, so the average salary no longer supports a middle-class lifestyle. Formerly middle-class jobs, accepted by immigrants today, pay so little that US workers reject them. In turn, the downgrading of jobs pushes the distribution of income upward, so that wealth is concentrated in the hands of a few at the top (Nagengast 2009). Furthermore, economic growth in the industrialized world now depends almost exclusively on financial engineering and investment speculation instead of manufacturing widgets, which has shifted income from low-wage earners to high-wage earners, resulting in greater and greater inequality.

Although this inequality hurts US workers, it hurts immigrants even more. Many of them are concentrated almost permanently in an underground economy, where they are forced to accept menial, low-wage jobs and scandalous working conditions in a "race to the bottom" (Guskin and Wilson 2007). This situation is especially true for the undocumented who are locked into "3-D jobs" (dirty, demanding, and dangerous). Their undocumented status, their lack of education, their limited English, their fear of deportation, their difficulty finding another job, and their ineligibility for unemployment insurance, food stamps, or other benefits equip them to do little else.

Employers also prefer undocumented workers because their lack of rights and benefits makes them cheaper and more profitable (Bacon 2008). They are also reluctant to challenge their exploitation for reasons stated previously, and as a result they have far higher rates of fatal injuries on the job than other workers. In fact, a 2004 study shows that thousands of undocumented workers are injured on the job and at least one dies every day because of unsafe working conditions (Nagengast 2009).

Are declining wages fact or fiction? In 1997 a US National Academy of Sciences study found that the rising tide of low-wage immigrant workers since the 1980s has lowered wages by 1% to 2% in jobs not requiring high levels of education or fluency in English (Guskin and Wilson 2007). Those impacted most by this trend include 10% of high school dropouts, whose wages were lowered by about 4% between 1980 and 1994. However, the population of US high school dropouts is rapidly shrinking, which is why the demand for undocumented workers persists even during economic downturns and periods of high unemployment.

For example, Mexicans in New York have acquired a reputation for extremely high rates of employment, even in the face of large-scale unemployment. They work in construction, as line cooks, delivery men, deli workers, housecleaners, and gardeners; some work two jobs. One Mexican reported working 12 hours a day, seven days a week, for $3 below minimum wage and sending what he can back to Mexico. He remarked that he had a family, and if he did not work, they would not eat (Semple 2010b). The enforcement of employer sanctions has been useless and ineffective because of the practice of subcontracting, which shifts responsibility from employers to contractors (Castles and Miller 2003).

Are undocumented immigrants responsible for rising unemployment? A popular belief blames undocumented immigrants for contributing to unemployment. However, economic research has demonstrated that high school dropouts are the only people in the United States in direct competition with low-skill immigrants (Borjas 2006), who experience a wage loss of 4% (Riley 2008). Actually, rather than contributing to unemployment, immigrants enlarge the economic pie by performing different jobs from US workers. There is also a popular misconception that immigrant jobs would exist at higher wages, if only immigrants could be deported; in fact, those jobs would not exist at all.

Besides, jobs performed by the undocumented continue to be rejected by US citizens. For instance, the United Farmworkers challenged US citizens to take up farm work (Editorial, *New York Times,* 2010b). Stephen Colbert, the television host/comedian, was among the very few who accepted. Clearly, US citizens are not leaping at the chance to bend and stoop for eight to 12 hours a day planting zucchini or to carry around 50-pound loads. Besides, does it make economic sense to pay a US worker a salary of $50,000 or more to pick strawberries, simply because she or he is from the United States, especially if the price of strawberries would skyrocket for everyone?

So, the blame for "job theft," depressed wages, unemployment, and economic decline should be placed squarely on the shoulders of the businesses that engage in the practice of outsourcing US jobs overseas, not on immigrants. Similarly, the growth in undocumented labor should be blamed on businesses' insatiable appetite for cheap labor, not on foreign workers. Employers everywhere exploit undocumented workers, and governments everywhere serve as their accomplices by placing the interests of business above the rights of workers (Chomsky 2007). However, the solution to the "immigration problem" is not to restrict immigration or to eliminate labor rights but to honor the rights of all workers, both domestic and foreign (Bacon 2008; Guskin and Wilson 2007).

Tax Evaders and Welfare Magnets: Fact or Fiction?

Everyone is entitled to his [her] opinion, but not to his [her] own facts.
—the late US Senator Daniel Patrick Moynihan

Are immigrants tax evaders who are totally dependent on welfare and social services, and a general burden on the public purse? In reality, the un-documented pay the very same taxes as citizens: income tax, sales tax, and property tax, either directly or indirectly through rent (Guskin and Wilson 2007). In fact, they pay more in taxes than they receive in services, such as unemployment insurance or retirement benefits, because they are at the peak of their working years but are not eligible for most public services (Behdad 2005; Nagengast 2009; Riley 2008). For example, a report refutes the pop-ular myth populist demagogues circulate that undocumented migrants do not pay taxes. Several researchers cite a *New York Times* report dated April 5, 2005, that the Social Security Administration receives almost $7 billion a year in taxes withheld on fake Social Security cards (Bacon 2008; Chomsky 2007; Payan 2006). Ironically, fake documents benefit not only the govern-ment but taxpayers also.

If the worth of a human being is to be measured by the sum of taxes paid, then about 60% of US citizens should be considered worthless be-cause they receive more in government services than they pay in taxes (Riley 2008). Simply put, 60% of US citizens do not pay their way. In contrast, 3.8 million households headed by undocumented immigrants generated $6.4 billion in Social Security taxes, in 2002 alone, for benefits they will never collect (Lopez 2007). In other words, undocumented immigrants contrib-ute to Medicare and Social Security without receiving a check for decades because they are not eligible for benefits. Even if they were eligible, they would be unlikely to apply because they live in fear of discovery and depor-tation (Guskin and Wilson 2007).

Furthermore, the US middle and upper classes are beneficiaries of immigrant taxes due to their legal access to entitlements as citizens, according to tax reports. For instance, the Heritage Foundation, a conservative think tank, reported that the typical Latino couple paid $350,000 (in 1997 dollars) more in Social Security benefits than they will receive in lifetime benefits (Riley 2008). Others have estimated that immigrants and their children will each pay $80,000 more in payroll tax than they will ever receive over their lifetimes in local, state, and federal benefits combined (Lopez 2007). This is especially true of Social Security benefits, because 70% of immigrants are between the ages of 20 and 54, while 12% of US citizens are age 65 or older.

Is the welfare magnet theory fact or fiction? Is it true that immigrants, especially the undocumented, are irresistibly drawn to the United States to abuse welfare? The answer is no, because undocumented immigrants (one-third of all immigrants) are not eligible for federal welfare benefits. Even if they were eligible, they would not be willing to run the risk of arrest and deportation by revealing their existence through welfare applications to the government. However, welfare use among legal immigrants has increased since the 1960s. According to one report, between 1995 and 2004 when undocumented migration doubled, the national welfare caseload fell dramatically by 60%, in some states down by 90% (Riley 2008). In addition, analysis by the Urban Institute of welfare use found that less than 1% of unauthorized immigrant households receive Temporary Assistance for Needy Families (TANF) benefits, compared with 5% of US citizen households. Even George Borjas, the Harvard economist—a Cuban immigrant but a strong opponent of immigration—admits that the welfare magnet theory is flawed, with no empirical evidence to support it.

Is it true or false that the children of immigrants overburden the US school systems? Many studies of educating the children of immigrants distort reality and inflate the costs by including in their sample US-born children (two-thirds of children of the undocumented and 80% of legal residents) who are, by definition, US citizens and not "aliens" (Riley 2008). Although there is a movement to abolish the Fourteenth Amendment to prevent the children of undocumented immigrants from becoming US citizens at birth, this has not yet become legal (Rodriguez 2010). Furthermore, research shows that 47% of migrant children drop out of school before completing middle school and join the labor force between the ages of 14 and 16 because their parents need the money (Nagengast 2009). In fact, very few finish high school or continue to college.

What about the popular misperception that immigrants abuse health-care services? Despite the fact that dire poverty forces undocumented families to seek medical care in hospital emergency rooms, a 2005 UCLA study found that less than 10% of Mexican immigrants, legal and undocumented, who had been in the United States less than a decade reported using an emergency room, compared with 20% use of emergency rooms by US citizens (Riley 2008). Similarly, the RAND Corporation in California found in their study that immigrants, authorized and unauthorized, reported fewer health problems and made fewer visits to the hospital than US citizens. Furthermore, states like Arkansas, North Carolina, South Carolina, Georgia, Tennessee, Alabama, Mississippi, Arizona, Indiana, Iowa, Kansas, Utah, and Nebraska are extremely miserly in welfare spending despite the enormous growth in their immigrant populations.

However, the cost of schooling for immigrant children and health care for adult immigrants often falls disproportionately on the shoulders of state and local governments. Also the lion's share of immigrant taxes (60%) ends up in the hands of the federal government, which sometimes results in deficits in city, county and state treasuries (Chavez 2001; Guskin and Wilson 2007; Wolfert 2008). Nevertheless, this situation is not uniformly true of all states. For instance, the Texas comptroller reported in December 2006 that 1.4 million undocumented migrants contributed $17.7 billion to the gross state product of Texas in FY 2005 and produced $1.56 billion in state revenues, which exceeded the $1.16 billion they received in state services by almost half a billion dollars (Nagengast 2009). Similarly, in the state of Arkansas, with one of the fastest-growing immigrant populations in the United States, immigrants made direct and indirect tax contributions of $257 million in 2004, while they cost the state $237 million for education and health care (Riley 2008). More importantly, they generated $3 billion in business revenues.

Clearly, the welfare magnet theory is fiction because factual evidence supports the opposite. For example, Hispanic males have the highest labor force participation rate of any group in the United States. And, generally speaking, low-skill immigrants have a higher rate of labor force participation and lower rates of unemployment than US citizens (Semple 2010). The undocumented, in particular, have a labor force participation rate of 94%, with an unemployment rate of 5.8% (Riley 2008). These numbers are mainly due to the high demand for low-skill labor in the United States, which the undocumented can take advantage of by being more in tune with the business cycle, and migrating during economic booms. They are also more mobile, using their extensive information networks to help them move to locations with high rates of job growth. This lifestyle contrasts with that of US citizens, many of whom are tethered to specific places by home ownership and social ties. Latino immigrants migrate with a strong work ethic and commitment to hard work. In other words, the United States is a magnet for workers, not welfare cheats.

The welfare magnet theory is also refuted by the fact that California farmworker families almost never utilize public assistance programs such as welfare, despite earning less than $15,000 per year—almost one-quarter of them having incomes below the federal poverty level. Between 1994–1995 and 1997–1998, periods of declining wages, only 20% of farmworkers reported receiving unemployment insurance and only 10% reported receiving benefits from the Women, Infants, and Children Program (Lopez 2007). In addition, the Farm Worker Housing and Health Needs Assessment study of the Salinas and Pajaro valleys in California, conducted in 2001, showed that less than half of the poorest participants accessed unemployment insurance, food stamps, or Temporary Aid for Needy Families (TANF) for which they might have been eligible.

Besides, laws have been passed to reform the welfare system by placing strict limits on welfare benefits, even for *legal* immigrants who were once entitled to them. In 1996, President Clinton signed the Personal Responsibility and Work Opportunity Reconciliation Act, a law founded on welfare magnet theory, making legal permanent residents not eligible for benefits until they had resided in the US for five years or more. He also eliminated government programs such as Food Stamps, Supplemental Security Income for the elderly, blind, and disabled (SSI), Temporary Assistance for Needy Families (TANF), and Medicaid (Chavez 2008; Guskin and Wilson 2007; Riley 2008). Another proposal rooted in welfare magnet theory was Proposition 187, passed by an overwhelming majority in the November 1994 elections in California. Fortunately, it was declared unconstitutional by the courts, which ruled that immigration was a matter to be regulated by the federal, not state government (Chavez 2001; Massey, Durand, and Malone 2002).

In sum, as the evidence from Texas and Arkansas demonstrate, undocumented immigrants are not an economic drain but a net economic gain through secondary and tertiary effects, such as expanding the demand for consumer goods and services, expanding markets, and creating more jobs. In addition, foreign labor is a source of profit to the receiving country because the cost of raising and educating first-generation workers is borne by the sending society and the families of the workers, rather than by the host economy (Chavez 1998; Chomsky 2007). Paradoxically, despite facts to the contrary, fears of undocumented immigrants sponging off the American people persist.

American Identity and Cultural Loss: Fact or Fiction?

The Satanic Verses celebrates hybridity, impurity, intermingling, the transformation that comes of new and unexpected combinations of human
beings, cultures, ideas, politics, movies, songs. It rejoices in mongreliza-
tion and fears the absolutism of the Pure. *Melange,* hotchpotch, a bit of
this and a bit of that is *how newness enters the world.* It is the great possibility that mass migration gives the world, and I have tried to embrace it.
                                           —Salman Rushdie (1991, 394)

Are fears of American identity and cultural loss well-founded? More specifically, is the Latino threat real or imagined? In the Latino threat narrative,
all Latinos, including the undocumented, legal immigrants, and US citizens,
are now perceived as threats to the United States, for a variety of reasons
(Chavez 2008). First, Latinos are accused of destroying American values and
the American way of life by refusing to adopt Euro-American culture and
language. Second, Latinos are perceived as separatists, wanting to establish
independent nations within the United States by cordoning themselves in
insular, linguistic, cultural, and politically distinct enclaves, along the lines
of the Quebec model in French Canada (Chavez 2008; Riley 2008). Third,
Mexicans, in particular, are portrayed as "invaders," whose intention is to
reconquer parts of the US Southwest (Aztlan), once part of Mexico, and
making a mockery of the US-Mexico border (Chavez 2008). The fact that
the Latino population is now widely dispersed across the United States is
ignored. In the hearts and minds of the fearful, the solution is to stop the
immigration of all nonwhites.

For quite some time, right-leaning journalists and political commen-
tators such as Peter Brimelow, Victor Davis Hanson, Heather MacDonald,
Georgie Anne Geyer, and Patrick Buchanan, among others, have been pon-
tificating about the pollution of the Anglo-Saxon national character of the
United States and the erosion of English as a national language (Chavez
2008; Riley 2008). Unfortunately, their incendiary rhetoric has been granted
legitimacy by the late Samuel Huntington, formerly a Harvard political scientist, and scholars like Arthur M. Schlessinger Jr. They have argued that the
seeds of the United States' cultural extinction lie in the multicultural trajec-
tory of the nation, large-scale Latino immigration posing a serious cultural
threat that could divide the United States into two separate nations. This
argument, however, is transparently racist, a desperate attempt to preserve
the whiteness of the United States (Behdad 2005).

There is also a popular myth that Mexicans are criminals by nature,
responsible for an immigrant crime wave simply because they have defied

the law by crossing the border. In reality, there is no logical connection between immigration and crime. Data from a 2000 study show that the imprisonment rate of US citizens was five times that of the foreign-born. A 2007 study also reported that since 1994, violent crime in the United States fell by 34.2% and property crime fell by 26.4%, the same period of rising immigration (Riley 2008). Latinos are also perceived as threats because of high fertility rates that would change the demographic composition and, hence, the US political landscape (Chavez 2008). Another popular fallacy among anti-immigrant newscasters is that Latinos pose a health threat to the United States because they bring dirty, third-world diseases such as tuberculosis and leprosy.

Mastery of the host language is one of the hallmarks of immigrant assimilation. Historically, all immigrants to the United States have been accused of refusing to learn English, regarded as the official language by the dominant Anglo-Saxon majority. For instance, after the end of World War I, this accusation was directed specifically at Germans. Immigrants from Southern and Eastern Europe, the Irish and the Italian in particular, were also demonized when they first arrived (Chavez 2008; Ngai 2004). However, despite predictions of their unassimilable nature, they became assimilated, often in a single generation, and are venerated today as noble ancestors of the United States' white majority. Today, Latinos are the target of public accusations, accused either of failing to learn English or being unwilling to do so (Chavez 2008). However, the seamless assimilation of European immigrants of yesteryear exists only in the public imagination and depends on pure historical amnesia.

In reality, Latinos have assimilated, at least with regard to mastering the English language. A study of several generations of Latinos living in Orange County, California, documented their linguistic assimilation. The study found that in the first generation, one-fourth used English as much as Spanish at home; in the second generation, one-half used mostly English at home; by the third generation, the majority used mostly English at home (Chavez 2008). Similar patterns of English usage were found in the workplace. Furthermore, the 2000 US Census found that 91% of the children and 97% of the grandchildren of Mexican immigrants spoke English well (Riley 2008).

There is additional proof that Latinos do not reject English. Nationwide, almost 60% of providers of classes in English as a Second Language (ESL) reported long waiting lists, some up to three years, and in New York City there were only 40,000 slots for more than 1 million applicants (Chomsky 2007). The Pew Hispanic Center also reported in 2002 that 89% of Latinos believed that mastery of English was the key to success in the United

States. A recent nationwide survey of young US citizens found that 89% of foreign-born and 59% of US-born Latinos speak English and Spanish (Oppenheimer 2010). In addition, one-third of immigrants resident in the United States for less than a decade speak English well; this statistic rises to three-quarters for those who have resided in the United States for 30 or more years, according to 2005 census data (Riley 2008).

Clearly, the notion that Latinos have failed to assimilate is more an illusion than a reality. The idea that Latinos refuse to learn English exists only in the Euro-American imagination, sustained by the fact that many Spanish speakers are choosing to become bilingual instead of abandoning Spanish completely. The continuous inflow of newcomers being added to the Spanish-speaking population in the United States at any given moment also fuels this public misperception. If Latinos in the United States abandoned Spanish to become monolingual, like most people in the United States, it would be a liability in today's globalized world in which speaking more than one language is an asset that confers competitive advantage in job seeking.

Fear-Based US Immigration Laws of Yesterday

Despite being contradicted by the facts, the fear-based myths described previously have produced laws designed to exclude and punish immigrants. Nativism has been the strongest expression of hostility directed at immigrants to the United States, the roots of which can be traced back to the early nineteenth century, with some historians claiming that it emerged out of the national conflict over slavery (Behdad 2005). During this period, nativism became a legitimate form of nationalism. Indeed, nativist ideas and practices have not only played a key role in creating a sense of belonging, building community, and sculpting national identity, they have been powerful in shaping immigration policy and defining past and present norms of citizenship (Navarro 2009; Ngai 2004). Hence, its importance in nation-building should not be underestimated.

A case in point is the emergence of the Know-Nothing movement, a form of organized xenophobia. As Behdad (2005, 117) observed, "The rise of anti-foreign parties in New York and other cities in the eastern United States during the late 1830s, which eventually grew into the powerful Know-Nothing movement of the 1850s, helped transform xenophobia into an acceptable and powerful form of patriotism, which has survived to this day." Historians of the mid-nineteenth century have shown that people in the United States were hungry for a patriotic movement to rescue them from alien invasions by Irish and German laborers, as well as Jews, Poles, Italians, and Chinese, who were perceived as threats to the economy, the government, and US society at large (Navarro 2009). They found what they were looking for in nativism and the Know-Nothing movement.

Nativists framed "the immigration problem" as "a crisis" and "a state of emergency," the solution to which was to restrict immigration (Ngai 2004). The "crisis" framework was a good political strategy because it conjured up images of a war in which the United States was under siege by "aliens." Such simulations have proved successful in winning public support for policies to keep immigrants out and producing an ideology of consent (Behdad 2005). This strategy is still successful today, which explains why, more than a century after the demise of the Know-Nothing movement, its political philosophy continues to attract a large following. However, contemporary nativists have changed their name to the Tea Party movement, although they have retained the tradition of willful ignorance and denial of basic truths (Egan 2010).

As practiced in many other countries, the US brand of xenophobia (fear of outsiders) blends the fear of immigrants with race. However, the link is so strong in the United States it has been suggested that US immigration policy is racial policy writ large (Ngai 2004). New immigrants to the United States have always been racialized, although the process of racialization and its methods have changed from one historical period to another. From the beginning, race has been a critical dimension of their American national identity. For example, European immigrants have been able, over time, to disentangle their ethnic and cultural identity from their racial identity. In contrast, the ethnic and racial identities have remained twinned, keeping non-Europeans "foreigners" forever.

Let us consider how the coupling of race with US immigration law has evolved over time. It began with the Chinese Exclusion Act of 1882, designed to keep out the "heathen Chinee." However, the goal of keeping out "undesirables" was not perfected until the Johnson-Reed Immigration Act of 1924. This law not only fused immigration with race, it gave birth to the idea and the reality of the "illegal alien" by making entry into the United States without authorization a deportable offense for the first time in US history (Inda 2006). Legal channels of immigration were closed while the nation maintained the demand for cheap labor. Quite logically and naturally, this situation led to the growth of "illegal immigration," an idea that has occupied the center stage of public discourse since 1924 and remained the central motif of US immigration policy (Ngai 2004). The 1924 law also expanded the categories of deportability, eliminated the statute of limitations on deportation, and created the border patrol, in 1925. In addition, the Immigration Act committed the United States to the idea of setting limits on numbers of immigrants, a notion that persists today (Ngai 2004).

The crowning achievement of the 1924 law, however, was establishing a quota system that ranked immigrants according to race and ethnicity and, in so doing, redrew the racial map of the nation by creating a "hierarchy of desirability." Nativists were especially pleased with this law because it discriminated against southern and eastern Europeans, located at the bottom of the hierarchy, while privileging northern and western Europeans (Navarro 2009).

This hierarchy of desirability was founded on the idea that the United States should be a white nation descended from Europe, using the criteria of race and ethnicity (Behdad 2005; Doty 2003). In this hierarchy, all groups of European immigrants were assigned quotas on the basis of national origins (ethnicity) at the same time that they were classified as "whites" on the basis of race. This system of double classification legalized "whiteness" as a new racial concept by separating whites from nonwhites and, for the first time, brought into existence a white race composed of Europeans who had nothing in common except whiteness (Ngai 2004).

The purpose of this obsession with whiteness was to deny rights to certain segments of the population, African Americans being a case in point. Although they were granted citizenship by the Fourteenth Amendment, they were citizens in name only, being denied full citizenship rights through practices such as Jim Crow segregation, lynching, and being prevented from voting (Ngai 2004). Similarly, Native Americans, the only indigenous people in the United States, ironically were not granted US citizenship until the 1924 Indian Citizenship Act and, even then, only by an act of Congress (Navarro 2009).

The 1924 law also impacted Asian immigrants. By the 1920s the Chinese were less of a menace because their entry had already been outlawed in 1882. However, the Japanese and other Asians were seen as the threat of the hour because their racial status was ambiguous, particularly with regard to citizenship rights (Navarro 2009). In this political climate, a plan was needed to discriminate against Asians while not appearing to do so. A solution emerged in the notion of denying them the right to naturalization, the criterion for denial being their inability to assimilate.

The Japanese were certainly not reluctant to assimilate. In fact, the Japanese had bent over backward to become citizens of the United States. They had not only adopted Western dress and learned English, they enthusiastically practiced the Calvinist principle of hard work: buying farmland in central and northern California, forming partnerships to buy land, and signing contracts with white landowners to lease land as farmers. Nativists, however, were unimpressed by the adoption of American values and the display of civic virtue, instead interpreting them as a plot to take over California from white people (Ngai 2004). At this time Japanese Americans could only own land secretly, and only those who were lucky enough to find trustworthy whites to hold the title.

Subterfuge was required for Japanese exclusion, accomplished by manipulating language so that "national origins" was substituted for ethnicity and "ineligibility for citizenship" for race. Through such sleight of hand, whiteness was made a requirement for citizenship (Ngai 2004). The outcome of this process was the creation of a brand-new racial category of "Asians." The idea of "racial ineligibility for citizenship" (denial of naturalization rights) was particularly appealing to nativists because President Theodore Roosevelt had frustrated their efforts to keep out the Japanese by law when he opposed Japanese exclusion on grounds that he wanted to maintain friendly diplomatic relations with the Japanese government. Nativists also triumphed when the Supreme Court ruled that Japanese and Indians were racially ineligible for citizenship in two out of 25 Asian petitions for naturalization.

The 1924 law also affected Mexicans in the United States, an impact both ironic and paradoxical. Ironically, Mexican nationals were granted automatic US citizenship by the Treaty of Guadalupe Hidalgo in 1848 at the end of the Mexican-American War. Those who were part of the *ranchero* elite had chosen to remain in territories once belonging to Mexico and had become US citizens as a result of colonial conquest and the US annexation of the northern half of Mexico. Paradoxically, the Immigration Act of 1924 racialized Mexicans as "white" for purposes of naturalization because the labor demands of southwestern agriculture and diplomatic relations with Mexico and Canada required Mexico and the Western Hemisphere to be exempt from numerical quotas (Ngai 2004).

Proposals in the US Congress to include the Western Hemisphere in the 1924 quota system had been defeated because the exclusion of Asians and less desirable Europeans had produced a labor shortage on California and Texas farms (Ngai 2004). Mexican immigration had grown in leaps and bounds to meet the labor shortage after the Southwest had been transformed from ranch country into commercial farming with the building of transcontinental railroads and irrigation of the region. Unable to include Mexicans in the 1924 quota system, nativists then tried to keep them out on grounds of racial "ineligibility for citizenship." These demands were also rejected by the US Department of Labor, citing treaties, conventions, and acts of Congress to justify the entry of Mexicans. The success of agribusiness in keeping out Asians while letting in Mexicans underscores the enormous power of corporate interests to transcend race when it suits their agenda. Nevertheless, during the Great Depression, when their labor was no longer needed, approximately 400,000 Mexican individuals were deported, half of whom were estimated to be US citizens (Inda 2006).

Fear-Based US Immigration Laws Today

Sadly, fear of immigrants is alive and well in the United States, thriving in Arizona, among other states. Fear has a way of distorting one's sense of what is fair and what is right, compromising the democratic ideal of social justice. In addition, fear is often powerful enough to induce policymakers to "shoot themselves in the foot," producing laws that are not only unjust but against their self-interest. One example is SB1070, the most recent link in a long chain of laws enacted throughout US history and aimed at preventing "undesirable" immigrants from entering and settling in the United States. On April 23, 2010, Governor Jan Brewer of Arizona signed SB1070, the immigration law designed to stop "illegal immigration."

SB1070 authorized local police to stop anyone, based solely on "reasonable suspicion" (such as brown skin) of being an "illegal immigrant," to demand proof of legal entry, and to arrest individuals unable to provide documents of legal residence (Archibold 2010a). Furthermore, the law would allow any individual to sue any state, county, city, or town official or agency that did not enforce the law (Editorial, *New York Times,* 2010a). Although the US federal government filed a lawsuit against Arizona and the law was stripped of its racial profiling element by Federal Judge Susan Bolton, SB1070 remains profoundly self-defeating.

Let us examine the self-defeating logic of laws such as SB1070. First, this law is unlikely to achieve its main purpose, which is to stop illegal immigration. Why? Because lawmakers have failed to understand the root causes of immigration, such as economic globalization and other global forces. Equally, many US businesses, large and small, depend on undocumented workers because they can pay them next to nothing and withhold benefits. Most of all, the US economy demands 500,000 low-skill workers per year, while current US immigration laws only permit 5,000 slots for low-skill legal migrants each year (Oppenheimer 2010).

Second, it is highly unlikely that any immigration laws, either state or federal, as they are currently framed, will stop illegal immigration. Simple arithmetic tells us that as long as there are desperate job-seekers who have been dispossessed of their livelihood in their homeland on one side of the border and businesses eager to exploit cheap labor on the other side, fences, whether high- or low-tech, will not keep them out. In short, undocumented workers have become indispensable everywhere, even if they are not welcome. Common sense also tells us that as long as the US government provides only 1% of the legal slots needed per year, low-skill migrants will continue to come through the back door. There is no moral justification, however, for keeping them in slavelike conditions, even if they are indispensable.

Besides, if they disappeared, who would do their jobs? (Ho 2010). Who would plant vegetables, pick fruit, slaughter cows and pigs, gut chickens, package meats, mow lawns, clean hotel rooms, build houses, bus tables, and take care of children and the elderly? The answer, one might think, is US workers. However, US workers have rejected wages that undocumented workers have no choice but to accept. In addition, businesses can and do export (outsource) many of these low-skill jobs.

Besides, SB1070 has alienated Latinos, inspiring them to leave Arizona. In fact, there are reports of Latinos moving to the states of Washington, New Mexico, and Utah, motivated also by the fact that these three states do not require proof of citizenship or legal residency to obtain a driver's license (Korte and Valdes 2010). If one-third of Arizona's population (Latinos) leaves the state, they will take with them their tax dollars and purchasing power. They will also close down more than 35,000 Hispanic-owned businesses, the sum total of which would bring the Arizona economy to its knees. SB1070 could very well backfire on Arizona in a variety of ways. To begin, SB1070 has already inspired boycotts of Arizona, adding to the state's economic woes. Indeed, the *New York Times* reported recently on drastic declines in the tourism and convention industries, pushing Arizona out of its position in the top four US destinations to 23rd and prompting Arizona lawmakers to bow to the business lobby complaining about boycotts, canceled contracts, and declining sales (Oppel 2011).

Shadowed Lives

From a human perspective, one brutal side effect of current immigration laws is that the undocumented are forced to live "shadowed lives." Many immigrants and the vast majority of the undocumented are still viewed with suspicion, and sometimes hatred, and are treated accordingly. Seldom understood is the fact that they do not come to the United States to live on the dole. Rather, they are desperately seeking work to feed and clothe their families and to educate their children. However, they are confronted daily with legal and institutional barriers, not only to migration itself but also to survival in the host country. The plight of undocumented immigrants who have been displaced from their land and their livelihood is both tragic and heart-wrenching.

As an example, let us consider the lives of the Esparza family described in Chapter 2 (Lopez 2007). The husband has been working in the strawberry and bush berry fields of Watsonville, California, every growing and harvest season since 1985, traveling back and forth from Michoacan, Mexico, and hiring a *coyote* to lead him and about twenty other undocumented migrants across the mountains near Tecate. He married in 1990 and had two sons shortly after. In their hometown, the family lived in a two-room adobe house belonging to the husband's parents, each family occupying one of the two rooms. Each room was too small to accommodate more than a single bed, on which both parents and children slept. They were sharecroppers on a single hectare of land, growing corn, beans, and squash, for food.

In 1994 the husband returned to Watsonville while the wife and two sons migrated to a major city in Mexico to earn 2,000 pesos selling cactus stems. These earnings were pooled together with the husband's income tax refund and some savings to pay a *coyote* to traffic the wife and two sons across the border where the husband was waiting to take them to Watsonville (Lopez 2007). At first they lived in the husband's brother's garage. Later, they found a two-bedroom apartment that they shared with the husband's brother's family. Later, they moved to a one-bedroom bungalow that they shared with two other families. They now also have two daughters and another son and the husband has become a legal resident. The wife misses her mother and other family members terribly but declares that it is too dangerous to cross the militarized border and also too expensive, as *coyote* fees increase in proportion to the danger.

As deprived as the Esparza family is, their lives seem luxurious compared with the plight of Mexican laborers working in strawberry fields in San Diego, California (Chavez 1998). Although housing and other codes have brought improvements in recent years, not long ago workers set up as many as 300 to 500 "spider holes"—sleeping shelters made of plastic, cardboard, tar paper, wood, and other discarded materials—in canyons and on hillsides, covered by dense brush to avoid detection by immigration officials. Some are merely holes in the ground while others are lean-tos.

These camps offer no shelter during rains or storms or protection from cold nights. Heated rocks used to warm shelters have been known to ignite plastic and start fires, and workers have been burned or killed. There are no telephones to summon fire brigades or ambulances. These camps have no storage for food, no running water, and no toilets, which poses health hazards to migrants as well as nearby residents. Water is brought in abandoned pesticide containers and through irrigation hoses containing fertilizer and zinc solutions; nature's woods serve as toilets. Snakes, rats, and fleas are constant companions. Living under these conditions is difficult at best, and few workers last more than 10 months before returning home, although starting in the mid-1980s, women and children also resided in these camps.

For fear of discovery by authorities, the workers seldom leave the farms or camps except to go to a convenience store (Chavez 1998). Migrant workers are often used for jobs that result in accidents and injuries that jeopardize their earning potential. However, they tend not to seek medical care for fear of losing their jobs and also because they do not know where to find a local doctor or a local clinic. In addition, some employers refuse to take responsibility for the health of their workers, driving them to the border and telling them to go back to Mexico.

In other words, undocumented workers live "shadowed lives" fraught with fear, anxiety, and an acute awareness that at any moment they can be arrested and deported. They describe their lives as being in jail or living in a chicken coop (Chavez 1998). Apart from being robbed of bus money twice and fearing arrest by immigration officials during bus rides to work, one woman recounted her fear that her husband or children might have been arrested whenever they were late coming home. This fear is not groundless as it is common for spouses to be apprehended on the job, or children to be apprehended at school or at a bus stop, or just walking the streets.

To make matters worse, undocumented workers are seldom knowledgeable about US immigration law or their legal rights. There are also obstacles strewn across the paths of the undocumented that make the daily life barely possible. The idea is to pressure the undocumented to leave the United States by making life here a living hell (Riley 2008). Consider how hard it is for illegals to accomplish everyday tasks taken for granted by citizens such as getting a driver's license, finding a place to live, opening a bank account, applying for jobs, registering for school, and getting medical treatment (Dreby 2010). These tasks are made even more difficult when employers and landlords take advantage of them, knowing they have few options (Guskin and Wilson 2007). Their vulnerability also makes them favored targets of robbers. These not-so-subtle efforts to make the undocumented disappear have failed because the rate of return migration has declined, thanks to border fortification making it more dangerous and expensive to return to the homeland.

Hate Crimes and Other Atrocities

Once upon a time in the United States, hatred of immigrants was directed alternately at Asians, Jews, the Irish, and southern Europeans. Today, xenophobia has evolved into Latinophobia, which includes all Latinos, legal and illegal. Not surprisingly, there has been a rise in hate crimes targeting Latinos. For instance, in 1984, off-duty Marines went on "beaner raids" at night, beating, robbing, and setting one worker on fire. In 1989, farmworkers were "terrorized" by white youths shooting at them with pellet guns, driving through camps in four-wheel-drive pickups, demolishing their shelters, and wielding baseball bats and knives. In the same year, two young farmworkers were shot and killed by local teenagers while walking on an isolated stretch of road near nurseries and camps (Chavez 1998).

In April 2010, nine Mexican immigrants were attacked by young black men in Port Richmond, a working-class neighborhood in Staten Island, New York. Back in 2006, a Mexican immigrant who worked as a cook at the local IHOP restaurant was killed by three attackers. Attacks on Mexicans had reached such epidemic proportions that the police commissioner sent reinforcements to Port Richmond, and the Mexican consul general established a consular office to help Mexican immigrants (Semple 2010a).

In a similar hate crime in Long Island, New York, a white teenager, Jeffrey Conroy, was convicted of a hate crime and first-degree manslaughter in the killing of an Ecuadoran immigrant, Marcelo Lucero, in a racially motivated attack (Fernandez 2010). On hearing the verdict, the victim's family declared that Latino lives are worth nothing in the United States. It appears that attacking Latinos for sport has become quite popular among US teenagers.

Consider another case: a 17-year-old Latino high school football player who was dragged from a suburban house party outside of Houston, Texas, and attacked by two white assailants. Police said the attackers were enraged because the victim tried to kiss a young girl they believed to be white. They forced him into the backyard where they burned his neck with cigarettes, stomped him with steel-toed boots, and slashed his chest with a knife, trying to carve slogans. They stripped him naked and sodomized him with a patio umbrella pole, shoving it so far as to cause major organ damage. They then stood him up against a fence and poured bleach all over his body, shouting "White power!"

Clearly, this was no ordinary beating. He was hospitalized in intensive care for more than three months and had to endure more than thirty surgeries to repair his internal organs. He returned to school in a wheel-chair but had to use a colostomy bag. Although he recovered somewhat from his physical injuries, he could not endure the psychological trauma and has since committed suicide. Both attackers were convicted of aggravated sexual assault in November 2006. The neo-Nazi skinhead was given a life sentence, and his racist accomplice was sentenced to 90 years in prison. The prosecutor in this case told the Associated Press that in his many years of prosecuting brutality he had seldom encountered such bestial savagery (Southern Poverty Law Center 2007b).

To eliminate any illusion that anti-immigrant hysteria is something new or aimed exclusively at Latinos, let us examine the treatment of Chinese immigrants in California and the Pacific Northwest in the second half of the nineteenth century. Between 1840 and 1900, more than 2 million laborers left China for distant lands to work in mines and plantations, 25,000 of them migrating to California in the mid-1800s, attracted initially by the gold rush there. Beginning in 1848, thousands of Chinese were systematically targeted, humiliated, segregated, and purged from town and countryside by the working class in the United States, supported by the elite, government officials, and trade unions. The campaign was regionwide and covered the entire Pacific Northwest.

Mob violence could not have succeeded without the cooperation of local elites, the police, the judicial system, and the government, in particular the Democratic Party (Pfaelzer 2007). The labor movement was not blameless, as the Order of the Caucasians and the Workingmen's Party actively promoted anti-Chinese hysteria. The media also played a major role in depicting the Chinese as "the yellow peril." By 1860 the Chinese had abandoned gold mining, becoming a vital part of the California economy in railroad construction, although they were discarded when their labor was no longer needed.

By the turn of the century, more than half were deported, exiled, or dead, and the rest were herded into urban ghettoes (Pfaelzer 2007). Chinese miners and merchants, lumberjacks and field workers, prostitutes and merchants' wives were gathered up at gunpoint and marched out of town. The Chinatown in Antioch, California, was torched after Chinese prostitutes were accused of giving seven young men syphilis. In 1871 a mob in Los Angeles lynched 16 Chinese men and one Chinese woman, provoked by a Chinese wedding (Pfaelzer 2007). In 1876 the Chinatown in Chico was destroyed by fire. Chinatowns across the West were burned to the ground. While these and other forms of ethnic cleansing are horrifying, they apparently were not enough to satisfy US hostility, so much so

that the Chinese Exclusion Act was passed in 1882, banning Chinese immigration for 60 years.

Fear of the yellow peril was not confined to the Chinese but was extended to the Japanese and other Asians. Initially the Japanese had migrated as contract farm laborers to Hawaii in the early 1900s. Later on,
many moved to California for higher wages; by 1919, half the population
had become small farmers in their own right, controlling 450,000 acres of
agricultural land (Daniels 1981). They also built small businesses such as
retail outlets for the fruits and vegetables grown by the farmers, as well as
groceries, restaurants, and curio shops. Not surprisingly, Japanese prosperity
was greatly resented, producing a widespread movement on several fronts
to limit their success.

First, there were efforts to stop further Japanese immigration by law,
followed by efforts to prevent them from becoming naturalized citizens, as
well as efforts to deny citizenship to their US-born children (Daniels 1981).
There were also efforts to bar their children from public schools. These anti-
Japanese proposals bear a striking resemblance to proposals aimed at Latinos
today. To prevent Japanese from owning land, California passed Alien Land
Laws in 1913 and 1920, and the states of Oregon and Washington acted
similarly. The California laws were not declared unconstitutional until 1952.

Anti-Japanese sentiment reached its peak after the bombing of Pearl
Harbor on December 7, 1941, when the US government adopted a policy
of mass imprisonment of Japanese immigrants and their children. As Roger
Daniels (1981, xv) put it, "In the early months of 1942 the United States
government assembled and shipped off to concentration camps 112,000
men, women, and children, the entire Japanese American population of the
three Pacific Coast states of California, Oregon, and Washington." Questions were raised about the constitutionality of such a move without declaring martial law. However, the California chief justice at the time declared
that the constitutional rights of citizens were nullified under conditions of
war (Daniels 1981).

Entire families were systematically rounded up and taken initially to
assembly centers, while waiting for internment camps to be constructed. In
California, these centers consisted of horse stables at racetracks. They were
only allowed to take belongings that could fit in one suitcase. Their property—land (owned by their US citizen children), businesses, houses, cars,
fishing boats and equipment, and all material possessions—were confiscated
by the US government and distributed to white US citizens.

After spending six months in the centers, they were moved in August
1942 to prison camps, surrounded by barbed wire and guarded by military

police, located in remote regions. For example, Manzanar in Central California; Tule Lake in Northern California; Minidoka in Idaho; Topaz in Utah; Heart Mountain in Wyoming; Granada in Colorado; Poston in Central Arizona and Gila River in Southern Arizona; and Rohwer and Jerome in Arkansas, all "godforsaken" places where no one had lived before or since (Daniels 1981). Life in the camps was not easy, as they lived in military-style barracks, in which families were separated from other families only by a cloth curtain. There was one incident of an unarmed elderly Japanese man being shot and killed by a guard because he had been taking a constitutional walk too close to the barbed-wire fence.

Beginning in 1943 there were proposals to return the Japanese to civilian life. However, there was loud protest on the Pacific Coast, where the proposals were labeled "a second Pearl Harbor." Therefore, they were scattered throughout the country, along the Eastern Seaboard and in the Chicago area. However, after the war ended, many returned in 1946 to the West Coast, where they were greeted with hostility and violence. They had to start over from scratch because their homes and all their possessions had been stolen. However, with the help of a small minority of white US citizens who wanted to see justice served, most were resilient enough to pick up the pieces of their shattered lives.

Border Games

Ever since 1924 US immigration policy and practice have focused on national security and keeping immigrants out by means of border enforcement. However, the danger of conflating immigration with national insecurity is not only that it has fueled an obsession with borders, but that it has also encouraged misguided immigration policies and practices. From a terrorism perspective, fortifying the US-Mexico border makes no sense because there are no known cases of terrorists entering the United States from Mexico or other parts of Latin America.

More importantly, the fixation on the Mexican border and immigration crackdowns of Mexicans and Central Americans are counterproductive because they compromise US national security by diverting precious resources away from serious intelligence-gathering that could identify the genuine terrorist article. There appears to be no better way to undermine US national security than to assign busy work to security forces chasing undocumented short-order cooks, busboys, and meat packers and turning them into decoys (Riley 2008).

Most of all, the US obsession with border enforcement has not been cheap. The cost of fortifying the US-Mexico border rose from $50 per undocumented entry in 1986 to $80 per entry in 1993, and then to $260 per entry in 1997. After the passage of the Immigration Reform and Control Act (IRCA) of 1986, the efficiency of the border patrol with respect to immigration declined precipitously as it turned its attention increasingly to drug trafficking (Massey, Durand, and Malone 2002, 118). Since 2000 the US federal government has increased spending for border fortification by 150% (Dreby 2010).

Clearly, border enforcement has been a dismal failure, considering that half a million undocumented migrants entered the United States in 2005 (Lopez 2007), and many more have crossed the border since then. Far worse than the squandering of taxes, however, is that militarization has not stopped the flow of immigrants but has caused unnecessary suffering and death. The US Criminal Justice System is currently groaning under the strain of dealing with only 2 million to 2.5 million prisoners (Riley 2008). The financial and bureaucratic cost of prosecuting and deporting 11 million people defies imagination. In the next chapter, we suggest ways to rethink the purpose of borders apart from manufacturing illusions of security.

4

This Land Is My Land,
This Land Is Not Your Land

The globe shrinks for those who own it; for the displaced or dispossessed,
the migrant or refugee, no distance is more awesome than the few feet
across borders or frontiers.

—Homi Bhabha (1992, 88)

In August 2009, after rescuing five men off the Sicilian island of Lampe-
dusa—sole survivors of up to 80 who had begun a three-week voyage by
dinghy from Libya—the Italian government came under intense criticism,
both for not doing enough to aid and extend asylum to Africans crossing
the Mediterranean and also from others for not dealing forcefully enough
to prevent such unauthorized journeys. A hemisphere away, US Border Patrol vehicles today routinely patrol even quiet cul-de-sacs of small communities. The growing assertion by federal immigration agents of a 100-mile
"border perimeter" in states bordering Canada angers many residents, while
others see it as an understandable new normal.

Borders are the most visible, and among the most vilified, targets in
today's heated arguments about immigration. The wide gap between realization that the current course is neither effective nor right, and ideas for
how to fix things, reflect the complex and even contradictory nature of
borders. The disconnect also reveals the emotionally charged and changing
understanding that people have about society itself, and especially who belongs and who does not. In the United States, the border with Mexico has
drawn enormous attention in the media and politics, and holds a prominent place in both literature and the formation of our national narrative.

65

Conundrums associated with borders do not vex policies and participants in North America alone, however. Worldwide, there is hardly a country unaffected by either immigrant or refugee flows, either as source countries or as recipients, and often as both. There is indeed an immigration and refugee crisis. However, the evidence shows that the crisis is largely one whose victims are immigrants and refugees themselves, as much as they are countries such as the United States.

Today more people are on the move than ever before. They remain disrupted for longer periods. Some move by choice, others by force, most by some combination of the two. Migrants everywhere are also increasingly subject to a variety of new and unimaginably intrusive and systematic policing. Everywhere we see erosion and even whole-scale abrogation of national laws and international accords designed to protect basic human rights—to move freely, not to be detained unjustly, to enjoy safety and citizenship. Just a half-century after the inception of the UN Convention Relating to the Status of Refugees (commonly known as the Refugee Convention of 1951, or simply the "Geneva Convention"), the countries that established a mandate to protect and assist the world's refugees are among those abandoning many of those principles. As a result, the lives of uprooted people around the world are under ever-greater threat, as is the viability of formal accords and existing practice to protect and provide for those who are displaced.

In recent decades, migration has increasingly come to be viewed as a security problem. A securitization of immigration is an outgrowth of insecurity, unemployment patterns, concern over crime, and the destabilizing effects of globalization, along with historically familiar xenophobia, far-right political activity, and new and more efficient rhetoric for shaping public opinion. But it also draws strength from policies of denial, which entail active forgetting about the positive and varied roles that migrants have played (Bigo 2002). Witness the discourse concerning human rights of asylum seekers. Differentiation between "genuine" and "fraudulent" migrants has contributed to something of a public panic, in which the very word "immigrant" conjures misgivings and, in turn, harsh narratives and practices of zero tolerance.

Anxieties appear to be more heightened today than ever before. To the modern lexicon of globalization, cyberspace, and digitalization have been added an assortment of terms that invoke fear: securitization, terrorism, and an array of "homeland" and border security measures. With the tragic events of September 11, 2001, the very notion of safety and security expanded to include a larger international dimension (Alden 2008; NACLA 2008). Racist, moralistic, or political grounds for exclusion that had been increasingly delegitimized in the development of a shared human rights doctrine over the second half of the twentieth century suddenly found new life in perceived dangerousness of the unpredictable and the criminal. Notions of a borderless world, well under way in the European Union, and even in discussion about what North American might mean, evaporated before a surge of demands for predictability and protection (Alper and Loucky 2009). Enforcement, exclusion, and even acceptance of preemptive actions and torture, became normative. Around the world, people on the move, whether immigrants or refugees, have assumed a sudden and substantial new burden—more dangerous and more undesirable than before. Such developments are even more sobering in light of prospects for greater disruptions in the world's ecosystems and economics in years ahead.

(B)ordering

Humans have a remarkable ability to define and to demarcate the world according to their needs and perceptions. Today we commonly conceive of borders as territorial delineations and spaces, drawn especially to denote countries. But other borders have existed for far longer than those of nation-states.

Human groups exercised territorial mobility and claims during the lengthy duration when subsistence was based on foraging. Our evolution in small groups was also grounded in social affiliation and shared identity, with allegiance to the group reinforced through cooperative work and affirmation of homeland. But cultures also evolve through intergroup exchange, as well as physical movement. So while there is a close fit between culture and place, neither is absolute. Cultural homelands share similarities with territories of many species in that they conform to natural barriers and perimeters of hills and mountains, valleys and watersheds, rivers and shores. Like those of other species, boundaries may be flexible, allowing seasonal movement or intergroup interactions. The emergence of states, which are generally grounded in intensive agriculture and anchored by the weight of larger populations, had significant bearing on assertions of borders. The assertion of sovereignty and borders has become even more unquestioned in the three centuries since nation-states became dominant.

Borders tend to be perceived, by people as well as by states, as essentially fixed and linear. But borders are better conceptualized as complex amalgams of flows and integration, as well as divisions and exclusion. Examining borders challenges prevailing models and practices not just with respect to nation-state borders but also with regard to intellectual, disciplinary, and institutional configurations. The comparative, holistic, and prospective aspects of an anthropological perspective encourage ways of thinking that can penetrate the bounded nature of nationalism and state security. Seeing how ethnicity, gender, and generation shape migration in turn helps us discern how policies may be enlightened or altogether unacceptable. Such framings can highlight the rise of borders within, such as those that emerge in patterns of segregation, while also indicating possibilities for borders beyond, as seen in new understanding of the international and intercultural roots of diversity within society.

Borders are central to assertions of legitimacy and either provision or denial of rights. They are also extremely complex in principle as well as practice. Borders share many characteristics, yet are hardly universal. They range from primarily symbolic to fiercely and forcibly demarcated. Some reflect binaries; others are far more fuzzy. A host of goals and instruments, policies and practices, abound—often on the same border, much less along the hundreds that are asserted worldwide. Most significantly, borders have countervailing dividing and merging functions. They can be guardians against, but also providers of opportunities for—often simultaneously.

In one, narrow sense, nation-state borders are facts on the ground, lines that mark who belongs and who does not. They have become an established feature in serving political and economic interests. But just as fundamentally, borders are products of the human imagination. As complex creations, borders have various origins, as well as multiple and fluctuating configurations. They serve several functions, including as arenas counterpoised against people on the move.

Yet, as creations and responses, borders are open to question and therefore also to change—even to "re-" or de-borderization (Agnew 2008). They can be disabling, established to prevent the unauthorized or harmful. But they can be disabling of possibility, of movement, and of synergies of intellect. Their equivocal character means they are inherently problematic.

Bordering, and the resulting fragmentation, may have long-term evolutionary implications as well. Smaller regions tend to have more simplified ecosystems, just as smaller organisms appear to be more suited to smaller islands. Divisions potentially promote the fraying of the fabric of nature and the associated social fabric. Borders are also the places where preoccupations about immigrants are most visible, and often expressed most violently, as both current and historical accounts reveal.

These inherent complexities are central to one of the most fundamental contradictions of a globalized world. Today at least 200 million people—

"real" human beings, with varying objectives, perceptions, and emotions—are in various states of geographic movement, which inevitably approach, challenge, transect, and frequently continue to transect borders in multiple ways and places. Countless others experience or exercise mobilities that are not geographic alone. Billions more may be susceptible to disruption if current environmental trends persist or worsen.

Probing what borders are all about—distinctions in eligibility, rights, access to resources, restrictions—is essentially an inquiry into a major way that humans have come to determine fortunes as well as fates. Borders represent some of the most inhumane species behavior—complicit in twentieth-century world wars, decimations of peoples in the centuries before (Wolf 1982), and fundamental challenges about who may have the best crack at the future. Fortunately, borders are also some of the most vibrant places imaginable for transmission and transformation, as well as transit. Acknowledging such functions and manifestations is vital if we are to successfully resolve the vexing problems inherent in a heavily armed, crowded, and bordered world.

"The American Border"

To be on the move is one of the quintessential characteristics of the United States, central to centuries of immigration from all corners of the globe as well as to a social imagination rooted in the frontier and westward expansion. With the rise to global prominence, another sensibility also emerged—intensified border control and rigorous scrutiny of others ("aliens") to accompany the power and wealth associated with global integration and economic liberalization. A strong sense of US exceptionalism colored the history and development of US border and immigration policies. It was not until the 1920s, however, that US immigration policy rearticulated the border as a racial and cultural boundary, with the US-Mexico border figuring centrally in the creation of "illegal" immigration (Ngai 2004). The prevailing climate closely reflected economic conditions, with immigrants welcomed when needed, and persecuted while still often exploited, in times of economic downturns.

The US-Mexico border is unique in many ways and also paradigmatic of characteristics and challenges that shape most borders of the world (Loucky and Alper 2008; Ganster and Lorey 2008). It has the distinction of being virtually the only place where a highly developed country meets, for nearly 2,000 miles, with a developing one. That contrast is central to the dynamic demographic, economic, political, and cultural interactions that link the United States and Mexico, for better and for worse (Ruiz 2000). Migration has been perhaps the most long-standing and contentious of issues between the two countries, even though immigration as a problem is a creation of the twenty-first century. Only in 1929, for example, did entering from Mexico without documentation become a crime. Increasing, and sometimes institutionalized, migration across a porous border was largely beneficial to US businesses, farmers, and consumers, as well as to migrants from Mexico. Concerns about cultural and linguistic change, poverty, and scarce jobs in times of economic downturn, however, increasingly came to dominate public discourse and policy by the end of the century.

With the end of the Cold War, new dangers also came into focus: terrorism, Islam, international crime—along with immigrants and refugees. Treating immigrant communities and would-be migrants as a threatening presence has come to characterize much recent politics as well as an insistent media, influencing, in turn, the views of many people in the United States. In the aftermath of 9/11, a brutal attack was manipulated further to ratchet up fears, provoking deep divisiveness in the name of patriotism while undermining fundamental constitutional rights. "Securitization" became the operative term, and one closely associated with migration (Tirman 2004).

The border—which in practice and perception meant the 1,969-mile (3.169-km) boundary with Mexico—was progressively militarized in an effort to "close" it. It has been transformed from long, unmanned stretches and rusting fences, or no fence at all, to a border now patrolled by 30,000 customs and border protection agents, and demarcated in places by multi-layered barricades. Along with dehumanization have come dangers, with border crossing increasingly entailing violence, along with greater powerlessness. At the same time, expenditures and surveillance have extended to the mainly isolated border with Canada (Alper and Loucky 2009). Accompanying these developments has been a shift within those borders, one increasingly transformed by a cultural war, one that pits myths of migrant criminality and dangers against calls for multicultural understanding and inclusion.

Besides assertion of new and heightened dangers, border and immigration policy is also intricately linked to how danger is perceived. Increasingly, the United States, followed by other countries as well, has been influenced by the growth of a kind of catastrophic thinking, visible in popular culture (ranging from *CSI* television shows to Tom Clancy novels), that is also cognizant of financial and governability concerns. Funding drives much policy these days, but so does the increasing recognition that ultimately the world includes at least some degree of ungovernability. Risk management strategies reflect this. If security and freedom are represented more as a continuum than opposites, the management of uncertainty becomes a matter of trying to avoid risk, with subsequent levels of transfer of responsibility, mitigation, and eventually even some acceptance (Muller 2008).

Sophisticated technology that enables an Orwellian surveillance society is increasingly essential to this new world. The comprehensive security-oriented policies embodied in the Homeland Security Act of 2002 project a reach of power through surveillance, exclusion, and retrenchment that is totalizing (Payan 2006). Heralded as an era of "smart borders," what appears (or is at least projected) is a panoptic system, grounded in sorting (using biometrics, profiling, and increasingly overt and even coercive searches), as well as enlistment of a broad array of agencies, community groups, media partners, and law enforcement to extend the more control-oriented border policies. Whether people on the move pose a threat—real or imagined—is certain to be a persistent theme of both foreign and domestic policy for years to come.

> I hear they're hiring workers to build this big new fence. . . .
> —Joke circulating among undocumented
> workers in the United States in 2007

Death Along the US-Mexico Border

It should come as no surprise that crossing the US-Mexico border has become more deadly, given the increasingly repressive strategies of controlling immigration and the urge to criminalize immigrants. A 14-mile corrugated steel fence was erected along the border between San Diego and Tijuana, Mexico, as part of Operation Gatekeeper launched by the US Department of Justice in San Diego in 1994 (Massey, Durand, and Malone 2002). The Gatekeeper package included two and a half miles of high-intensity lighting, night vision cameras, ground sensors, radio communication equipment, and growth in the number of border patrol agents by 45% (Payan 2006). It followed on the heels of a similar project, Operation Blockade, launched in El Paso, Texas, in 1993 (Andreas 2000). A third border package, Operation Rio Grande, was launched in 1997 in the area of Brownsville, Texas. The cost of the border campaign, known officially as "Prevention Through

Deterrence," has totaled more than $20 billion since the early 1990s, aver-
aging $2 billion a year in the 1990s, but growing to $6 billion per year by
2005 (Hagan 2008).

Despite the billions spent, the Blockade, Gatekeeper, and Rio Grande
projects have failed to accomplish their goal of keeping out migrants. Instead, the projects have succeeded in producing death by diverting migrants
away from urban settlements to remote and desolate parts of the border in
Arizona, New Mexico, and Texas (Massey, Durand, and Malone 2002; Oppenheimer 2006; Payan 2006). Ironically, border fortification has fueled
border crossing because the deported then remigrate to join family members left behind. Indeed, the evidence is quite alarming and underscores the
irony: since 1986, rather than decreasing, undocumented migration has increased by as much as 275,000 to 400,000 each year, estimates varying according to different sources (Andreas 2000; Payan 2006).

Fortifying the US-Mexico border has forced migrants to travel by foot
or in sealed and poorly vented vehicles over thousands of miles across deserts, mountains, rivers, and guarded checkpoints. Redirecting border crossing to empty desert, rugged mountains, and raging rivers has claimed many
lives, particularly deaths from heat exhaustion, hypothermia, suffocation,
and drowning because many migrants are ill-prepared for the arduous journey. The region has been nicknamed "America's killing ground" not only
because so many have perished but because it is littered with skulls, bones,
and bloated corpses of would-be immigrants (Lopez 2007). Conveniently,
the mounting death toll has been blamed on "coyotes" rather than on failed
government policies (Hagan 2008).

America's killing ground is fraught with danger and death not only for
adult migrants but for children as well. Between 1999 and 2004, 2,000
migrants lost their lives in the Southwest desert, many of them youngsters
crossing the desert trying to find their parents in the United States. Because
it is now so dangerous and expensive to cross the desert, many undocumented immigrants no longer return home to visit their children. Instead,
they send money home to pay for their children to cross the border to join
them, with the goal of family reunification and settlement on the US side.
In 2005 the border patrol caught 93,995 Mexican children under age 17;
between October 2005 and April 2006, they caught 53,397 Mexican children (Lopez 2007).

If the undocumented journey is fraught with danger for migrants from
Mexico, it is far worse for those from Central and South America because
they must cross not one but two guarded international borders as well as
the 1,000-mile length of Mexico. Not surprisingly, they experience twice as

many types of problems as their Mexican counterparts. For instance, some Hondurans reported traveling more than 3,000 miles and spending almost two months on the road before reaching the US-Mexico border, whereas 70% of Mexicans reported arriving in the United States within a week. Their first challenge is safe passage through the Mexico-Guatemala border towns of Tapachula, Tecun Uman, El Carmen, and La Mesilla, notorious for drugs, smuggling, and official corruption (Hagan 2008).

The Mexican government, supported by Central American governments, has launched its own interior and border program, *Plan Sur,* under pressure from the United States, to restrict transit migration and to control drug trafficking by increasing inspection, detention, and deportation along land and coastal borders (Hagan 2008). Thousands of Mexican troops have been posted in the southern states of Chiapas and Oaxaca to install checkpoints and border patrols, and they have caught, detained, and deported many Central Americans.

Thus, Central American migrants must find ways to elude Mexican police and army troops. Many do not triumph over either natural or social obstacles. In 2000, 120 migrants died close to the 600-mile Guatemala-Mexico border; by 2003 this figure had more than tripled, with Mexican authorities reporting 371 deaths at the border (Hagan 2008). More recently, 72 Central and South American migrants (Hondurans, Salvadorans, Guatemalans, and one Brazilian) were massacred in Tamaulipas in northeast Mexico near the Texas border by drug smugglers trying to extort them. There is also concern about human rights violations of migrants in Mexican territory (Archibold 2010b).

Along the US-Mexico border, the annual death rate has increased threefold since 2000, according to some estimates (Andreas 2000; Massey, Durand, and Malone 2002; Payan 2006). Some studies estimate an average death rate of 300 per year since 1995, peaking at 472 in 2005. In 1998 alone, 53 people died while crossing the Texas borderlands (Lopez 2007). Between 1999 and 2003, 600 unidentified bodies were found along the US-Mexico border. The death toll for the year 2001 was 1,233, with temperatures on the desert floor of 120–130 degrees Fahrenheit. One sociologist, traveling for research with a colleague through dangerous crossing points in desert areas southwest of Tucson, Arizona, in the summer of 2002, described heat so intense it melted the soles of her colleague's shoes (Hagan 2008). The US Border Patrol registered 400 crossing deaths in fiscal year 2007; the bodies of these unidentified migrants were buried in pauper cemeteries.

Alarmed at the spiraling death rate, efforts have been made on both sides of the border to prevent migrants from succumbing to dehydration and overexposure at remote crossings. The US Border Patrol has increased patrols by adding airplanes and helicopters. US church groups have also set up stations providing food and water. For its part, the Mexican government has established a humanitarian border unit called Grupo Beta to patrol the entire 2,000-mile border and to protect migrants. It has installed 55-gallon drums of water at strategic border points, posted warning signs, and arrested smugglers and gangs attacking migrants. In 2000 alone, Grupo Beta rescued 14,384 migrants (Lopez 2007).

Apart from the human cost of death, border enforcement has produced yet another irony: undocumented immigrants have become permanent settlers in the United States because it is now too dangerous and expensive to cross the border repeatedly (Andreas 2000; Durand and Massey 2004; Hagan 2008; Massey, Durand, and Malone 2002; Staudt and Coronado 2002). Furthermore, permanent settlement has resulted in the dispersal of immigrants away from a previous concentration on the border states (California, Arizona, New Mexico, and Texas), toward a wider distribution throughout the United States (Pacific Northwest, southern states, the Midwest, and the Eastern Seaboard). In short, permanent settlement has transformed migrants into immigrants. It has also increased the Latino population throughout the United States, a statistic that has provoked fears among white US citizens.

The Economics of Nativism

Border and immigration policies are complex, geographically varied, and susceptible to fluctuations in national and regional economies, related shifts in public opinion and political will, and even longer-term developments such as global climate change or environmental degradation. Today, the global age of migration (Castles and Miller 2009) is increasingly one of deepening tensions and restrictions depending on rather ominous new realities of the political economic order.

The history of the United States, like that of many countries, reveals how closely immigration policy follows changes in economic conditions. Immigrants and "foreigners," in general, are much more likely to be welcomed during periods of economic vitality, but targeted for hostility and exclusion when times turn tough. Graphing the ebbs and flows of US immigration policy, we can see a close fit with economic health. More open immigration policies and labor accords are associated with rising curves of economic productivity. Tighter regulations, restrictions, and policies of removal, on the other hand, appear soon after recessionary periods begin. Xenophobia, racial epithets, and incidents of physical violence tend to increase during economic declines. Anti-Irish campaigns in the mid-1800s were followed by a rise of anti-immigrant political parties, nativistic movements like the KKK, and anti-Asian exclusion laws at the turn of the century, ranging from opium scares to Hindu riots that drove Sikhs out of the Northwest (Zinn 1980). The twentieth century followed suit, with periodic roundups in times of rising unemployment, and cessation of permits and growing roundups in the mid-1960s that marked the end of the "bracero program" that had invited laborers from Mexico for two decades.

The historical patterns are beginning to be seen as well in the recession that nearly paralyzed the global economy in 2008. The first years of the millennium saw growing concern in many countries that immigration was not only on the rise but also increasingly out of control. Visions of a borderless world, seen as successful in the European Union and potentially viable even in North America, disappeared overnight with the events of September 11, 2001.

As more formidable barriers went up on the southern border of the United States, tighter border and visa restrictions began to emerge throughout the world. Even commitments to provide relief to refugees have waned. Humanitarian organizations, from the UN High Commissioner for Refugees on down, lament the growing "warehousing" of more and more refugees, particularly as world levels of food and other aid decline. Global economic developments, then, do not bode well for either refugees or immigrants overall. The pace of deportations and associated human rights abuses on every continent has yet to show any sign of slowing.

The ease with which economics can come to trump protection and rights is visible in a range of policy changes in immigrant-receiving countries experiencing rising unemployment in the current global recession (Migration Policy Institute 2009). In 2009 alone, cuts in numbers, duration, or even cessation of work permits, affecting millions, occurred throughout Asia (including Korea, Taiwan, Thailand, and Malaysia) and elsewhere (Australia, Russia, Kazakhstan, and Czech Republic, among others). Fast-track deportation of unauthorized immigrants has become standard. In the emirates of the Gulf, the threat of removal has become an integral part of the transmigrant experience. On top of physical and structural violence while laboring in the Gulf, deportation of thousands of workers back to India, Pakistan, the Philippines, and other Asian countries also means facing high unemployment rates and debts that they incurred to take jobs in construction, domestic work, and other manual labor (Gardner 2010).

Various plans to encourage repatriation have also been initiated, including the use of financial incentives in France and Spain. The economic slowdown in Japan includes rapidly rising rates of unemployment among Latin Americans of Japanese descent, *Nikkeijin*, who had been increasingly choosing to migrate to Japan in recent years. As a result, Japan has launched a substantial Voluntary Return Program that includes a lump sum paid for those who leave and agree not to return for at least three years.

Even more draconian measures mark policy in other countries. Refugee applicants are increasingly considered guilty, or at least excludable, until proven worthy. People may be denied opportunity to submit claims of persecution and, in turn, denied the possibility to qualify for political asylum. This is perhaps most evident in the emergence of China as a global economic powerhouse. Present and prospective trade ties with China are increasingly implicated in accounts of human rights abuses of refugees and immigrants in Burma (Myanmar), for example. With little warning, and scant media attention, stateless refugees, who include ethnic Karen and Rohingya, have since 2009 been rounded up, often beaten, and deported from both Bangladesh and Thailand, countries where some have been living for years after fleeing persecution at the hands of the Burmese military. Internally displaced communities in Sudan were similarly pressured into greater silence or submission. Not surprisingly, Burma and Sudan have become major suppliers of extractive resources to fuel Chinese economic growth.

The worldwide expansion of exclusion and exception is reminiscent of the creeping enclosure that dramatically reduced the commons in England and Europe a few centuries ago. Today's global economy has also been grounded in privatization as well as concretization of grand difference in wealth and power, not only between but also within regions. The familiar phrase—the rich get richer, the poor get poorer—has never been truer than today. The economy also rests on migrants, and migrations have similarly been the target of containment, which today is implicit in the dominance of policies that promote privatization and other forms of segregation. Refugee camps are the most visible of enclosures, but gated communities, expanded surveillance, and rising walls along borders are contemporary manifestations of efforts to either lock out or lock in. Warehousing people has also become a lucrative growth industry.

No Longer Distant Neighbors?

In the immediate shock of the attacks on the World Trade Center and the Pentagon in September 2001, Mexico was the first country that President

Bush heralded as an ally to the United States, much to the chagrin of Canada. Despite proclamations, however, it was quickly apparent that it would be politics as usual (and even more so) in the post-9/11 era. Whether in pursuit of terrorists or enforcement of borders, the United States has historically maintained a narrative of dominance in regard to Mexico, exercised through mandate of political and economic control.

In the United States, debates, and even research, about migration have been heavily one-sided in that the perspective of sending societies is rarely considered. Challenges and impacts are equally relevant for communities and countries of origin. Movement between Mexico and the United States is the largest sustained flow of workers in the world and is even more unusual in that over 98% of Mexico's 11 million migrants concentrate in one country: the United States. A view of and from the South is therefore critical, especially if we are to hope for mutual resolution of a relationship that has been misconstrued amid increasingly heated rhetoric. Alarm about a *reconquista,* a demographic and cultural reassertion over the sovereignty of the United States, could be dismissed as imprudent if not for how hyperbole and false claims are politically manipulated, while also influencing the direction of research.

Fitzgerald (2009) provides compelling evidence that emigration is fundamentally important to Mexico, but hardly an overt government strategy. Nation-states everywhere seek control amid the challenges of international migration and other forces of globalization. Like other sending countries, Mexico tries to benefit from the resources of the millions who have left. Efforts to embrace emigrants include encouraging investment of remittances, continued political involvement, and maintenance of national and cultural pride. Contemporary transnational and deterritorialized realities give rise to new forms of thinking about citizenship. Emigrant or extraterritorial citizenship may include provisions for dual nationalities and rights to vote from abroad, which, in the case of Mexico, first became possible in the 2006 national elections. The promises of emigration, on the one hand, and the limited capacity of states to retain control of citizens once they leave a country, on the other, ensure that moral, cultural, and financial ties will increasingly be the basis for new forms of a social contract that extend beyond and across nation-states.

The politics of absence are also probed in another book involving Mexico, the flavor of which we sense from its first paragraph:

Not only at the borders, but also in cities and towns throughout this North American country's heartland, immigrants are arriving in increasing numbers. Few speak the language of their adopted land, and most reside and socialize within an isolated cultural enclave. They continue to practice their own cultural traditions and celebrate their national holidays. The grocery stores are stocked with locally unfamiliar products that hail from the immigrants' homeland. These settlers maintain close political, economic, and social ties with their country of origin, and establish local organizations designed to promote its values. They vote in foreign elections, raise money for candidates running for office abroad, and meet with political party representatives from their country of origin while residing in the new land. Meanwhile, these immigrants also make political demands on the host country where they reside, although few choose to pursue formal citizenships there. Some live and work in the new country without proper documentation (read: "illegally"), and have even been involved in the unauthorized transport of drugs across state borders. Their presence is so pervasive that the local governments of the receiving state have been forced to adapt in many ways, providing additional services, linguistic and otherwise, to address the needs of the growing foreign population.

(Croucher 2009, 1)

Ironically, of course, the subjects in this case are the growing numbers of US citizens who relocate to warmer settings like San Miguel de Allende and beach communities along the periphery of Mexico. While dealing largely with migrants of privilege, by reversing the lens, this study helps confirm that the impacts of migration are inevitably mixed. Similar to feelings north of the border, US citizens in Mexico also tend to be uncomfortable with being considered either "immigrant" or "expatriate," especially as many seek to "belong" while also continuing associations with their homeland. Communications and financial technologies allow transcendence of territory in ways unimaginable scarcely a decade ago. The multiplicity of "belongings" is also political. State-given political rights still matter (Smith 2006), which helps explain why newcomers in Mexico, just as in the United States, do much to assert and expand new citizenship rights. Identity may be rooted in conditions and place of birth, but ultimately it is relational and contextual—made, not born.

The power differential between the United States and Mexico, including relative access to resources that can facilitate preservation of identity, influences the extensions and practice of transnationalism. We thus need to be careful with overly simplistic comparisons of north versus south migration flows in North America.

Contiguity, scale, illegality, regional concentration, persistence, and historical presence have been cited as six aspects of Mexican migration that make it particularly threatening to the United States (Huntington 2004).

Those elements, and their extensions through dual or complex allegiances, appear less threatening when we recognize the tremendous degree to which people worldwide are already exposed, and also predisposed, to Western culture (especially US values) through the media (Levitt 2001). Heightened global interconnectedness, then, influences the nature and practice of transnationalism. On many issues, we see similar views north and south of the US-Mexico border, particularly regarding both the wisdom and the efficacy of walls and more repressive enforcement. Greater connectedness is one of the great promises inherent in greater fluidity and transcendence in the contemporary world, even as there are counterassertions of states to control place and people. That seeming paradox is best engaged through more expansive and humane terminology, and opportunities for direct engagement across national, ideological, and generational borders.

The Immigration-Security Nexus

Fear of the unknown and the unforeseen is a human universal, and it is implicated in the roots of many conflicts throughout history. Anthropologists and psychologists suggest that ethnocentrism is a universal trait, something all cultures and countries have, though in varying degrees. It is rooted in part in a mistrust of what is different. Stranger-anxiety appears in most babies after seven to eight months, when finer capabilities for recognizing differences in appearance, voice, and smells develop along with greater awareness of the differentiation of self and other. Cultures depend on predictability and trust, especially nurturing these in small groups such as families. People who are more distinctive—strangers—warrant more scrutiny and suspicion.

History reveals that mistrust and denigration of those who are different is commonplace. Archaeology indicates how separate neighborhoods were set aside for visiting traders in the great Mesoamerican city of Teotihuacan, 13 centuries ago, suggesting that rulers worried about potential negative impacts on their subjects. Mobile populations, from pastoralists to gypsies, homeless to refugees, have been routinely subjected to suspicion and state controls.

Border and immigration policies and practices in the last decades of the twentieth century stand in sharp contrast to those at the turn of the century when, in the United States, the Statue of Liberty welcomed peoples from around the world, at least symbolically. Human history has been one of mobilities, which entail shifts in relationships and understandings, as well as in positions and places. Inherent in groups, from the household level to empires, are rules for membership. People are within, others outside. Much social theory has probed how groups function, how they maintain themselves as distinctive, and also how they interact with others. Ethnocentrism has been argued to be a cultural universal (LeVine and Campbell 1972), explained through a range of sociobiological, sociological, and even theological rationales. Discomforts associated with language, color, religion, and fertility seem to persist cross-culturally, though there is also considerable evidence of parallels in processes of integration and not just exclusion.

Strangers and immigrants, in particular, have long occupied an ambiguous space, both physically and psychologically. Philosophers and historians alike have reflected on how if an enemy or a crisis is not at hand, one is often invented to suit the political climate or divert attention from domestic woes. Biblically, Abel was the first scapegoat, with a series of woes resulting for his elder brother Cain and his offspring ever since. Immigrants worldwide conveniently fill a similar role. Tracking the history of US immigration policy, we can discern a close fit between economic vitality and relative restrictions regarding entry and enforcement. When times are good, and cheap labor needed, bring them in; when the economy sours, Operation Wetback and other exclusion acts quickly appear. Similarly, the political ecology of disasters and hard times are played out at the expense of immigrant workers and communities. Politicians run on anti-immigrant platforms, while wider civil liberties are also scuttled, especially as immigration is conflated with the Bolsheviks of today: terrorists.

Borders have become inexorably linked to the rise of the nation-state as the primary political unit, at least into the start of the twenty-first century. Contractual obligations, expressed through loyalty as well as service and payments, undergird the autonomy and the power of the state. Compliance is seen to be threatened by people not considered to be fully part of the group, as would hold for many who cross borders. As a result, territorial restrictions on eligibility are attempted, especially through controls on the size, direction, and composition of population flows. Equally essential are social and psychological delimitations, expressed through a host of "othering" postures and practices.

In recent decades, exclusionary policies—including harsher border restrictions, internment, and expulsion—have increased around the world (Kobelinsky and Makaremi 2008). Few events are as profound as those of September 11, 2001. So identifiable has "9/11" become that the entire world has come to use this distinctly US format, rather than the 11-9 standard used in virtually all countries except the United States. Far more momentous than the violence of the day itself have been its implications for security, migration, and borders. As a modern equivalent of epochal BC/AD divide, 9/11 comes with new rules, a "new normal" averred in its aftermath. It thrust "securitization" and similar terms into our lexicon.

Today immigration has been framed as the central national security crisis (Lovato 2008), and immigrants as culpable, cunning, even criminal. Essentialized as "illegals," people on the move lose their names and faces and, progressively, even their very nature as human. By casting immigrants in this way, governments also deflect responsibility for the phenomenon itself, including its roots as well as complexities (Chavez 2001; Inda 2006). Simultaneously, solutions to the looming crises have increasingly been framed as technological, with immense expenditures directed to ever more sophisticated surveillance and interdiction. As security becomes more central to foreign policy and pervading domestic concerns, it also moves beyond criticism, much less curtailment. Alluring as sophisticated technological solutions may appear, however, they are ultimately inadequate responses to something that remains a deeply sociological, economic, and demographic phenomenon.

Breaks in a Broken System

In a time of uncertainty, economically as well as internationally, and in a world of differences in views as well as values, common sense would suggest that understanding and trust lie at the core of all matters of mutual concern, particularly those as difficult as migration and borders. To date, however, xenophobia and enforcement prevail—both at and within borders. As yet, there has been only limited support for socially inclusive policies in countries whose populations have diverse origins. Nor have we had careful assessment of how well the largely unilateral border policies of the United States work together with those of its southern and northern neighbors, much less of alternative multilateral approaches.

Heavy enforcement has chilling effects on families and communities everywhere it has come to predominate. It has also had another tragic consequence, that of helping to shift public consensus toward immigration as a problem, rather than a contributor to life in the United States. After the heavy hand that emerged in Arizona in 2010, and with even more draconian copycat versions of Arizona's SB1070 spreading to other state legislatures, it appears that enforcement may continue to undercut prospects for addressing migration and borders holistically, much less for achieving comprehensive reform anytime soon.

The buildup of a massive dragnet was not an explicit goal during the campaign that resulted in the election of President Barack Obama, but rather seems to have emerged as part of a strategy for achieving broader reforms—an approach that seriously backfired (Wessler 2010). While little bipartisan accord materialized, the growing enforcement structure has come to be increasingly indiscriminate in its pursuit and expulsion of noncitizens, with little regard for their ties to the United States or immigration status.

On the US–Canada border, Integrated Border Enforcement Teams (IBETs) sometimes collect or disseminate intelligence through local joint management teams, sometimes even focusing on transboundary issues and solutions specific to a region. But their functionality relates largely to how well the sides know each other, and the weight of efforts and financing has not led to many such interactions to date. The prevailing controls on the northern border are counterproductive in many other ways as well, including decreasing trade and tourism, diminishing cross-border community and cultural arrangements, and the potential for extending exclusion.

By early 2010, high costs and ineffectiveness were also leading the Obama administration to reconsider the high-tech "virtual fence" under construction on the US-Mexico border. The project had been pushed forward with little consultation with either those with the most knowledge or with the most at stake, including border patrol agents themselves, much less local communities, environmental groups, and the Mexican government.

Reports of significant decline in the size of the unauthorized population in the United States (Hoefer, Rytina, and Baker 2010; Muzaffar and Bergeron 2010) represent further evidence of the value of nondualistic and longer-term thinking with respect to borders and migration. Us/them and either/or thinking deepens separation and reinforces differences—hardly the kind of developments on which satisfactory long-term relationships are fostered.

At a time when the integrity of bioregions, as well as the health of the planet, has become a paramount concern, the environmental implications of the militarization of migration policy and massive bordering practices are cause for alarm. Within the prospective global security matrix being projected through the expansive homeland security network, US borders are to be "reinvented." Articulated first in the North American Security and Prosperity Initiative, the projected goal envisions protection of all US borders—a full 7,500 miles of land borders and another 95,000 miles of shoreline and navigable rivers. Clearly the goal is unattainable, even if it is sensible. The Secure Border Initiative (SBI) includes construction of both old (physical) and virtual walls.

From an environmental standpoint, the impact on shared protected areas may be disastrous. Porous fences that have long allowed species migration are being replaced by solid walls in sensitive wilderness areas in southern Arizona, like Organ Pipe Cactus National Monument and Buenos Aires National Wildlife Refuge, where border issues are taking up to 85% of park administration time. At present, ecological health is being sacrificed for questionable border enforcement, and it remains unclear whether and how environmental protection can work with new border security directives.

Borderblur

The magnitude of global migration, extending into almost all parts of the world and meriting major research attention, provides us with substantial knowledge from which to proceed. This helps to balance a common misperception that immigrants are "bad" for the economy and for the environment as well. The economic, cultural, and social developments we have noted represent a wealth of potentials—such as encouraging systematic investment of remittances in communities and countries of origin, and creating other mutually beneficial avenues for genuine international development.

For some things, we still know relatively little. For example, might migration become a force for greater preservation of land as well as cultural resources, including for future generations? Maya communities across North America, from Boston to British Columbia, are becoming increasingly involved in environmental preservation and restoration efforts in communities from which they are descended. Awareness of environmental problems as well as effective responses increases with greater media coverage, environmental education that children get through schooling, and exposure to recycling and similar efforts in settings that tend to be more affluent than home communities.

Equally promising is the presence of immigrants and their descendants in emerging food production patterns that have followed the mounting critique and even modification of industrial agriculture. Local food movements enable people with agrarian knowledge and skills—whether rooted in Mesoamerica or the Mekong—to contribute to more healthful and nutritious alternatives. In some communities, from Iowa to the Pacific Northwest, land trusts and cooperative structures are even helping to slow the disappearance of small-scale or family farming.

Around the world today people increasingly live a multi-sited existence. An era of global economic integration, with rapid developments in transportation and communication, enables and even requires moving and living in multiple localities. Nowhere is this more evident than in the Americas, where migration is dominated by proximity to the United States, even as discontinuous social and economic spaces have become a norm for many. Notably, this includes indigenous peoples, particularly from Mesoamerica, including Oaxacans (Stephen 2007), Yucateco Maya (Adler 2007; Cornelius, Fitzgerald, and Fischer 2007), Maya from Guatemala (Loucky and Moors 2000), and beyond (Fox and Rivera 2004; Smith 2005). Communication technologies, reinforced by transport options, allow people to maintain social, business, even religious connections across distances that span borders and barriers but also eras themselves.

For many, movement has become as ubiquitous as—and symbolized by—cell phones and computerized travel arrangements. With migration no longer a once-in-a-lifetime move, people develop a resulting sense of belonging to several places and perhaps much less of the fixity and consequence that tended to accompany people of prior generations as they embarked on long voyages by sea or journeys by land. This transnational dimension is as much in the imaginary as in the actual. It also involves carriers and narratives in flows that are not in one direction alone. Migrants bear as well as highlight symbols of "having arrived," but they also return, or remit, in many ways to places and peoples significant earlier in their lives.

Just as it is impossible to contain people within borders, so, too, their histories as well as futures span borders. Bicultural individuals, families, and communities bear witness to what bears remembering in any attempt to manage or solve immigration: that just as borders may persist in the mind, they need not exist as permanent physical features either.

Immigrants themselves foster their own integration in a host of novel ways that enable them to convey appropriate and beneficial contributions to neighborhoods and wider society, and to assume responsibilities for themselves and eventually as citizens. Immigrants everywhere seek and create opportunities for upward mobility, not only for economic betterment, but also because these represent a crucial avenue for integration. Such pragmatic efforts and holistic understandings become even more sustainable as newcomers and more established residents alike coordinate efforts together.

To Be(long) or Not to Be(long):
From Bordered Lands to Common Ground

Perhaps one day the world, our world, won't be upside down, and then any newborn human being will be welcome. Saying, "Welcome. Come.

Come in. Enter. The entire earth will be your kingdom. Your legs will be your passport, valid forever."

—Eduardo Galeano

Borders appear to contradict core human values such as liberty, equality, and democracy, producing instead alienation and devastation on the material and emotional lives of immigrants, as described previously. It would make sense, therefore, to rethink the purpose of borders and to design them to be more humane and inclusive.

Ironically, hemispheric blurring of borders for commodities and corporations since NAFTA was ratified in 1994 has not extended to labor migration. To the contrary, enforcement has grown on both of the US borders. The seeming contradiction is, in fact, a reflection of growing precariousness that has accompanied the rise of neoliberal policies in much of the world and shifted the onus of survival economically, civically, and healthwise to the individual.

Not surprisingly, prevention and interdiction have yet to yield a safer world. Fortunately, humanitarian precepts have not been completely overridden, so considerable potential remains for building policies on understanding of human rights and principles for coexistence. An anthropological perspective is grounded in holistic and long-term perspective, something that unfortunately is not characteristic of prevailing thinking and structures associated with borders. We come to see that while social boundaries are universal, even transcendental, state boundaries are neither ancient nor inevitable, as reconfigurations with the fall of colonial empires or the Soviet Union reveal. This calls for challenging not only of the legitimacy of current nation-state borders but also their logic. Exploring how humans can and do use social and physical spaces while mindful of shared fate, rights, and potential benefits is among the greatest contributions we can foresee as border and immigration studies continue to evolve.

Acknowledging commonalities as well as diversity in borders offers considerable potential for insights and directions amid the profound challenges at hand. Border and migration "problems" are revealed as hardly unique to the United States, if they are problems at all. Comparative and cross-national evidence sheds light on effective paths toward citizenship concepts, multiculturalism, and effective immigration reform in an age of mounting disruptions and mobilities.

Border concerns of the future are also increasingly less likely to be national alone because global connections are now more powerful and more fragile than ever, even as crises that emerge extend ever more rapidly. Unprecedented ecological devastation and resource inequities will provoke ever more serious policy deliberations. The decisions and policies that emerge have enormous consequences. They will strongly determine prospects for either conflict and disposability, or affirmation of social good and universal rights.

5

Criminalizing Migrants, Containing Migration

I get paid to be paranoid, and so do you.
——Federal security director at Baltimore airport, speaking to
security workers (quoted in the *New York Times,* November 23, 2010)

"Comprehensive immigration reform"—the heralded goal for much of
the past few years—has turned out to be mainly comprehensive enforcement, even during the Barack Obama administration. Immigration and
Customs Enforcement (ICE), established in 2003, grew to encompass about
10% of the $55 billion allocated to the Department of Homeland Security
in FY2010. Besides multiplication of agents at borders and increasingly intrusive searches at airports, ICE procedures extend deeper and wider across
the country. Actual or feared tactics include home entries by militarized
agents without the consent of owners, racial profiling, pursuit in homes and
workplaces of people who have not evaded a deportation order or committed a crime, warrantless searches and seizures, use of excessive force, and
random arrests based on appearance and native language (National Network
for Immigrant and Refugee Rights 2010). Changes allowing "collateral" arrests of suspected violators of civil immigration laws, deputizing local police
in immigration raids, and motivating other patterns of unlawful behavior
have alarmed not only civil liberties experts but also local police, who fear
that such Fourth Amendment violations undermine their central mission
of crime prevention (Immigration Justice Clinic 2009; Lendman 2009).
      Initially promising reform of George W. Bush–era tactics that in-
creasingly resembled those of a police state to many people, the Obama

administration has continued and even amplified many of the harshest Bush policies. Far from being a paragon of immigration reform, as many supporters had hoped, the Obama administration trumpeted its role in setting new records for deportations. "The laws we have are not sufficient to meet the demands of the twenty-first century," claimed Homeland Security Secretary Janet Napolitano in October 2010, when announcing that a record 392,000 immigrants had been deported in fiscal 2010 (Frontline 2011). Cited as proof that tighter immigration enforcement was working, the agency was quick to assert that even firmer efforts lay ahead.

Hidden within those numbers were numerous cases suggesting that major expansion of deportations was largely a matter of politics, not logic or fairness, which can only be seen as miscarriages of justice. In a recent case, a man from Montenegro, who had been struggling to remain in the United States, where he had lived for the past 16 years, was ordered to be deported because he was late by 40 minutes for a hearing whose venue had been switched—a hearing that had been continued since a decade earlier. In another case, a young man who had lived almost his entire life in Texas was deported to Bangladesh because he made a mistake and told the border official a wrong immigration status while returning from Mexico without his green card, at a border he had crossed many times before (Wessler 2010). He has paid dearly for being nervous and has not been allowed to return to the United States, where his parents and fiancée live.

Compelling local police to enforce immigration laws dampens willingness of members of immigrant communities to come forward to report crimes and safety concerns. Secure Communities, the signature program that the Department of Homeland Security runs through its ICE division, checks the fingerprints of everyone booked into local jails against a national immigration database. Projected to be nationwide in every jail by 2013, the program has drawn criticism from law enforcement authorities as well as groups concerned with civil liberties. While promoted as a program that targets only serious criminals, nearly 80% of those deported as a result of Secure Communities have no criminal conviction. There is wide potential for mismatches in a database that includes fingerprints of anyone who has encountered immigration officers for any reason. How communities are safer when even a routine traffic violation can result in arrest and deportation proceedings remains open to question.

Coupled with evisceration of due process (for example, detainees are not guaranteed legal counsel), elimination of discretion at the hands of immigration judges, and cuts in benefits even for legal immigrants, deportation continues unabated even as a path to citizenship has become invisible.

Although quotas for deportation have been denied, deputizing local law enforcement as immigration agents, under the Immigration Authority Section 287g program (which evolved from the earlier Illegal Immigration Reform and Immigrant Responsibility Act of 1996), has been part of a widening enforcement through "inherent authority." This has included granting states immigration authority in 2002, vastly expanding the Secure Communities program and increasingly justifying highway roadblocks to check for driver's licenses. Similarly, through Operation Streamline, detainees are shuffled through criminal proceedings in groups, with little chance for individual hearings or opportunities for appeal.

The immigrant detention system that lies at the core of the enforcement regime has come under growing criticism for illogical, and even inhumane, procedures and conditions. Some of the most scathing condemnation has been directed at Service Processing Centers (SPCs) owned and operated by ICE, as well as privately run Contract Detention Facilities (CDFs) and Intergovernmental Service Agreement Facilities (National Immigration Law Center 2009).

Institutionalized Hostility, Part I:
The US Immigrant Detention System

Ridding a country of "undesirable" immigrants today requires massive institutional effort, and the US immigrant detention system is the most adept. This system not only violates human rights in many cases, but also justifies it in the name of national security. The mainstream media adds fuel to the fire by promoting a climate of fear and insisting that immigrants do not deserve rights. What are some of the human rights to which immigrants are entitled by international law?

Every immigrant and asylum-seeker in the United States, except those detained at the border, has a right to a custody assessment, a detention review, and options for release by an immigration judge. In practice, however, an individual immigration officer decides whether or not to release the detainee as well as the conditions of release such as the amount of bond to be posted. This practice not only concentrates enormous power in the hands of individual ICE officers, it lacks supervision, does not conform to international human rights standards, and amounts to arbitrary detention (Amnesty International 2009).

Freedom from arbitrary arrest and detention is also a fundamental human right. Detention is arbitrary if it continues beyond the period for which a government can provide appropriate justification. Many immigrants in the United States spend months, sometimes years languishing in arbitrary detention. According to one study, asylum-seekers spend an average of 10 months in detention, the longest period being 3.5 years (Physicians for Human Rights 2003).

Legitimate grounds for detention include verifying identity, protecting national security, and preventing a person deemed to be a flight risk from absconding. All other reasons violate Article 9 of the Universal Declaration of Human Rights and Article 9 of the International Covenant on Civil and Political Rights (Amnesty International 2009). Furthermore, international human rights law opposes the use of detention as a means of controlling unauthorized migration, except as a last resort.

International law also grants the detainee the right to challenge his or her detention, to challenge the decision to deport, and to have access to speedy judicial review as well as access to legal counsel and interpretation services. International law also requires access to medical care; exercise; the ability to communicate with the outside world including consulates, lawyers, and family; and protection from torture and cruel, inhumane, or degrading treatment.

Western governments have also agreed to respect the principle of *nonrefoulement,* which opposes the return of refugees and asylum-seekers to situations with a high risk of torture or other abuses (Amnesty International 2009). The US government has not yet signed the International Convention on the Protection of the Rights of All Migrant Workers and Members of Their Families, a document formulated in July 2003.

If an immigrant or asylum-seeker can demonstrate that she or he is not a threat to national security, is not dangerous to people or property, and is not a flight risk, then that person may apply for release on bond before an immigration judge. However, reports indicate that judges are not releasing people on bond. In 2006, immigration judges in the United States denied bond in 14,750 cases; in 2007 the number of cases increased to 22,254; and in the first half of 2008, the number of cases was already 21,842 (Amnesty International 2009). Even when a judge sets a bond, it is often so high that detainees are either unable to pay it or are forced into tremendous debt. Nationwide, the average immigration bond is $5,941, while the average in New York is $9,831. Although it is not automatic, those arrested inside the United States qualify for release on a minimum bond of $1,500 and may request a review by an immigration judge.

Another problem is personal bias on the part of judges. One judge told Amnesty International that he always sets bonds at $25,000 for Chinese nationals, assumed by him to have been smuggled in. Similarly, personal bias was confirmed by the findings of a study carried out in New York City which showed that the amount of the bond is likely to be lower if an immigrant is represented by a lawyer. Even when a judge has ordered someone's release, ICE has the authority to "automatically stay" a judge's decision, which means that individuals remain in detention until the Board of Immigration Appeals (BIA) decides whether the judge set bond properly. Amnesty International (2009) reports that ICE routinely denies bond so as to later invoke their power of automatic stay.

Another human rights violation is mandatory detention, which is imposed on thousands of immigrants every year, including those who have lived in the United States for most of their lives. They are placed behind bars for minor, nonviolent crimes committed long ago and are not entitled to an individual custody assessment or detention review before deportation proceedings are initiated. This practice amounts to arbitrary detention as defined previously. In 1996 the US government expanded the categories of deportable crimes for which a resident immigrant could be subjected to mandatory detention. Categories include the suspicion of being a national security or terrorist threat, being charged with two "crimes of moral turpitude," being charged with an "aggravated felony," being charged with a firearms offense, or being charged with a controlled substance violation (Amnesty International 2009).

Moral turpitude and aggravated felony are not clear-cut crimes, and as a result, many people are held in mandatory detention for years while immigration courts try to decide whether stealing bus transfers or signing traffic tickets with a false name deserves deportation. Amnesty International (2009) reports that at least 117 individuals have been subjected to mandatory detention for crimes that ultimately were proved not to be aggravated felony and therefore not deportable offenses.

Amnesty International has also documented more than 100 cases in the past 10 years of US citizens and legal permanent residents being placed incorrectly in mandatory detention and deportation proceedings while they tried to prove their citizenship. Proving citizenship is not as easy as it seems because detainees are often denied access to necessary documents. To make matters worse, the burden of proof is on the detainee. Courts often allow ICE attorneys to postpone and reschedule hearings while they try to procure the documents, leaving the immigrant in detention. Some individuals volunteer for deportation to avoid prolonging the agony, and some judges accept this decision without examining the evidence, resulting in unjust deportations. Immigration lawyers also report that deportations in which the government does not meet its burden of proof, a violation of the right to due process, are commonplace, especially among individuals without legal representation (Amnesty International 2009).

Asylum-seekers form a category of inmates who cannot be deported and languish in detention indefinitely either because their home countries will not accept their return or do not have diplomatic ties with the United States (Amnesty International 2009). This situation happens despite the US Supreme Court ruling that if a deportee is held more than 90 days, ICE must conduct a custody review to determine flight risk or the national security threat of the individual if released. Asylum-seekers, who have already been subjected to torture in their home countries, suffer the most from US detention because they feel that they must choose between tolerating abuse in US prisons and being persecuted in their own country (Guskin and Wilson 2007).

In violation of the US Supreme Court ruling, custody reviews are not being conducted regularly, an Amnesty International finding that is corroborated by the Department of Homeland Security, Office of the Inspector General. The combination of poor record-keeping and failure to conduct timely custody reviews by ICE, added to the detainees' lack of access to information and communication, have resulted in prolonged detention. It is possible to be released from detention by filing a writ of habeas corpus in a federal court, but most detainees have no access to legal counsel and, by themselves, lack the knowledge to pursue or navigate such a complex process.

To add insult to injury, the physical environment of prison facilities is deplorable and fails to meet international human rights standards or even ICE guidelines. In September 2008 ICE published 41 new performance-based standards of detention to take full effect by January 2010 (Amnesty International 2009). However, these new standards are not legally enforceable and prescribe no sanctions for violations. Prison conditions are so appalling, they have inspired hunger strikes by inmates (Moreno Gonzales 2009).

A common practice across the nation is to warehouse immigrants and asylum-seekers, cheek by jowl, with violent criminals (Amnesty International 2009). This practice places immigrants at risk of physical harm. Even worse, the use of physical restraints, such as shackling, is often excessive. Sometimes attack dogs are used to terrorize detainees, and sometimes they are held in solitary confinement (Guskin and Wilson 2007).

One horrifying example is a woman who was nine months pregnant and arrested for driving without a license. When she went into labor, she was taken to the hospital where she was shackled to the bed, both before and after delivery, except for visits to the bathroom. After giving birth, her husband was allowed to collect the baby, but she was returned to prison and was not allowed any communication with her husband, family, or friends (Amnesty International 2009).

Statistics kept by ICE show that 74 people have died while in custody over the past five years because medical staff and prison guards failed to respond to medical emergencies. Regulations state that detainees should be allowed at least one hour a day of physical exercise in the open air, weather permitting, but these standards have not been followed, according to a Human Rights Watch report (Guskin and Wilson 2007). Some detainees have been subjected to verbal, physical, and sexual abuse while in detention (Amnesty International 2009).

Another serious problem is detainees' lack of knowledge about their rights. Although a study by Syracuse University showed that asylum-seekers are five times more likely to receive asylum if they have legal representation, detainees are routinely denied contact with the outside world, denied access to materials that are crucial to their claims for release, and denied access to legal counsel. US Department of Justice statistics show that 58% of individuals in deportation proceedings and 84% of immigrants in detention do not have legal representation (Amnesty International 2009; Guskin and Wilson 2007).

It is not surprising, then, that they are also denied access to other forms of information, such as access to telephones. Detainees reported to Amnesty International that there were often only two to three telephones for 40 to 50 detainees. Even worse, detainees are often kept in prisons located far away, sometimes thousands of miles away, from family and attorneys, as well as being subject to frequent transfers to prisons all across the country (Amnesty International 2009; Guskin and Wilson 2007). It goes without saying that long-distance separation from one's attorney is a prescription for failure in immigration court, not to mention the financial cost of communication.

Equally tragic is the human cost of long separations from family, especially from young children. There is a story of a detainee in Yuba County, California, with a US citizen wife and a two-year-old citizen daughter who drive three and a half hours each way to visit him every week for 45 minutes. His daughter's pleas to "Daddy, come out" are heart-wrenching. To add further to his humiliation, his wife has been forced to apply for welfare to support herself and their daughter because he can no longer provide for his family. This example shows how much the detention system costs the state because it deprives families of their chief wage earner and forces them to seek public assistance.

Perhaps the greatest outrage is that the undocumented are not criminals, contrary to public opinion. Entering and residing in the United States without documentation is not a federal crime or felony; it is a civil offense, a misdemeanor, similar to a traffic violation (Martinez 2009a; Riley 2008). Precisely because they are not criminals, immigrants can be deprived of fundamental rights of due process and basic procedural fairness guaranteed to criminals. Ironically, immigrants not being criminals allows US immigration authorities to arrest, detain, and deport them without providing them a lawyer or a day in court.

Institutionalized Hostility, Part II: The US Prison Industry

The US prison industry is an offspring of the military-industrial complex and is thriving in the midst of the Great Recession. It is no accident that the rise in immigrant detention has paralleled the growth of the US prison industry. The United States houses 25% of the world's prisoners while having only 5% of the world's population and imprisons people at the rate of 756 inmates per 100,000 residents, five times the worldwide average of 158 per 100,000 residents (Webb 2009). These statistics show that the United States has the highest incarceration rates on Earth. America's prisons are bursting at the seams, their newest inmates being immigrants, although the prisons are populated mainly by petty drug dealers, minor drug users, the mentally ill, and violent criminals.

What is the connection between the US immigrant detention system and the US prison industry? Equating undocumented immigrants with terrorists and drug traffickers in the minds of US citizens has convinced the public that the undocumented deserve to be imprisoned without rights of any kind. Accordingly, there has been a rise in rates of immigrant detention in prisons. One side effect is boosting connected industries, such as prison food corporations, prison medical care, prisoner transportation services, and telephone companies within prisons that charge as much as $17.34 for a 15-minute call (Kunichoff 2010).

Whereas undocumented immigrants used to be regarded merely as tax evaders and welfare cheats, today they are categorized as "national security threats" because the political economy of immigration has changed (Barry 2009). This reclassification occurred after the transfer of responsibility for immigration and border control from the Department of Justice (DoJ) to the Department of Homeland Security (DHS), a bureaucracy created in the wake of the attacks on September 11, 2001. This reclassification has served to justify enormous expansion of the security machine. As a result, immigration crackdowns have become a top priority of DHS, although the official goals are to prevent terrorist attacks and to protect the nation.

In testimony to the US Congress in July 2008, Michael Chertoff, then head of DHS, boasted of skyrocketing numbers of arrests, detentions, and deportations. However, a Syracuse University study found that there were fewer terrorism-related or national security offenses during the period after 9/11 than in the mid-1990s (Barry 2009). Arresting and imprisoning undocumented immigrants is not the same thing as eradicating terrorism because there is no logical connection between border enforcement and the prevention of terrorism. For these reasons, immigrant detention can be considered a moral and humanitarian problem (Chomsky 2007). Moreover, the American Civil Liberties Union has sued the Corrections Corporation of America (CCA) for overcrowding and substandard medical care, and there have been 111 reported deaths of detainees (Kunichoff 2010).

Since 2006, immigration detentions have increased 21%, the DHS budget has increased 19% from 2008 to 2009, and the number of ICE prison beds for 2009 is expected to total 33,400 (Barry 2009). Immigration detention in the United States has tripled over the past decade because detention is a popular method of immigration enforcement, with more than 30,000 immigrants being detained each day and more than 3.7 million immigrants having been deported since 1994 (Amnesty International 2009; Kunichoff 2010). Indeed, more immigrants have been deported per year under President Barack Obama than under President George W. Bush.

Redefining undocumented immigrants as dangerous criminals has stimulated a "boom" in the prison industry, one of the fastest-growing sectors of the US economy, expanding explosively even in the face of economic implosion. Building prisons to house the hundreds of thousands of undocumented immigrants apprehended by ICE has become "big business," yielding high profits, especially along the US-Mexico border and particularly in Texas. State and local governments, as well as private prison firms, are competing against each other in this new industry and are making prison construction a centerpiece of their economic development plans as well as a strategy for creating jobs (Barry 2009).

In fact, the Corrections Corporation of America (CCA), one of several private prison firms, reported record profits for the past few years based on contracts with the US Bureau of Prisons, ICE, and the US Marshals Service (USMS), which provide 40% of its revenue (Kunichoff 2010). The job of the government agencies is to stock the new prisons with inmates, which explains why CCA's "clientele" consists almost entirely of undocumented immigrants, sometimes entire families of the undocumented.

Government agencies have contracted with about 350 state and county prisons nationwide to house immigrants awaiting "removal" proceedings, with about 67% of such detainees being held there at the cost of $95 per person per day (Amnesty International 2009). Furthermore, the use of immigration detention in the United States continues to rise, despite evidence that alternatives to detention, which cost as little as $12 per day per person, have a 91% success rate in producing court appearances.

Private prison firms boast proudly to Wall Street bankers and potential investors of rising earnings, ranging from 9% to 29%, while their CEOs assure investors that they need not worry about the recent decline in border crossings because there are still 11 million undocumented workers living in the country, and prison occupancy should remain high with rising unemployment in the United States (Barry 2009). CCA has made record profits every year since 2003, generating revenue of $1.67 billion for 2009; the company's stock more than doubled between 2004 and 2008 from $12.15 to $26.86 per share (Kunichoff 2010).

The Technology of Governing Immigration

Michel Foucault's (1991) illuminating insights into the "arts of government" have inspired interdisciplinary studies of "governmentality" (Behdad 2005; Inda 2006; Ngai 2004, among others), the institutional processes that make people more governable. This research examines the modern workings of power and the crafting of institutions designed to regulate and control the behavior of entire populations. In Foucault's eyes, "government" is made up not only of expert knowledge but also of bureaucratic strategies and manipulative practices, including a technology of governing that one might call "governing through crime" (Inda 2006).

Governing through crime consists of the use of punishment to guide conduct. In fact, governing-through-crime technology in matters of immigration allows governments to formulate rules for immigrants that would not be tolerated by citizens and to avoid discussions of human rights and global inequality (Ngai 2004). The idea of governing through crime also suggests that illegal immigration is not a state of nature but a product of immigration law, the result of immigrants being transformed into criminals by the stroke of a pen.

Another strategy of governing through crime has been to make more byzantine the bureaucratic machinery for policing migration (Behdad 2005).

For instance, the prison industry has been expanded, national borders have become increasingly militarized, and the power of state bureaucracies such as the Federal Bureau of Investigation (FBI), the DHS, the Central Intelligence Agency (CIA), and the National Security Agency (NSA) has been magnified several-fold. Moreover, detailed technologies of observation and control have been refined, and state-of-the-art technology has been added.

The aim of this disciplinary apparatus is, at once, to establish control and to instill in the visitor, potential immigrant, or potential citizen a sense of being under perpetual surveillance (Behdad 2005). It is a system depicted brilliantly in George Orwell's *1984*. This structure of technological monitoring, observation, and display of power makes subjects not only visible at all times, it makes them vulnerable, fearful, docile, and passive. More importantly, it encourages and legitimates a culture of vigilantism among citizens.

The primary goal of this surveillance structure (Jeremy Bentham's Panopticon is a classic example) is to produce self-regulation. In other words, fear should turn immigrants into agents of their own regulation (Behdad 2005). A secondary goal is to make immigrants perpetually aware of their visibility while the power of immigration remains invisible at all times. However, this panopticon is still an imperfect system. In spite of the wealth of seismic monitors and magnetic sensors buried in the ground, low-light television monitors, remote-imaging infrared scopes, night vision goggles, and bright lights along the border fence, this high-tech system has failed to prevent border crossing. In the same way that imprisonment does not reduce the crime rate but actually produces recidivism, any system of immigration regulation that fails to regulate is not failure.

Instead, the system is a "revolving door," based on "benign neglect" (Behdad 2005), that turns a blind eye to cheap, docile laborers entering the country and delivers an elastic supply of disposable labor to satisfy the needs of industry (Chomsky 2007). The system also allows immigrants to be treated as criminals while being exploited in the secondary labor market and serving as scapegoats for the nation's problems (Bacon 2008; Chomsky 2007). A revolving door also facilitates more border crossing and justifies more surveillance of immigrants, who are "anti-citizens" and must be managed through "anti-citizenship technologies" that reshape them, in behavior, if not in body, into citizen-like beings (Inda 2006).

In other words, governing through crime guarantees a permanent underclass of workers, placing them at the mercy of their employers while denying them protection (Chomsky 2007). Simply put, the art of government has produced a reserve army of workers without rights. Worst of all, criminalization also forces them to lead shadowed lives, as fugitives, in constant fear of being apprehended and deported, because economic rights are not respected. Similarly, the concept of "structural violence," developed by anthropologist Paul Farmer (2003), can illuminate the governing of immigrants as an art form. The idea of structural violence explains the social processes and institutions that produce and reproduce extreme forms of inequality and marginalization. For instance, extreme poverty, the denial of basic medical care, and other forms of oppression that are often experienced as violence and injustice are routinely doled out to immigrants worldwide.

Conflating US Immigration With Crime and Terrorism

Beginning in the 1980s and 1990s, anti-immigrant laws were fused with antidrug laws in the United States, seriously curtailing fundamental due process rights and eliminating basic forms of procedural fairness for immigrants. For instance, these hybrid laws allowed mandatory detention, abolished administrative review of procedures, and restricted judicial review of mistakes made in immigration decisions (Kurzban 2008). The marriage of immigration laws with anticrime laws also succeeded in undermining immigrant rights by means of legislation and in boosting rates of immigrant detention in the US prison industry. Not surprisingly, these mergers have produced huge racial disparities in the criminal justice system.

The best example is the Anti-Drug Abuse Act of 1986, which treated any drug offense listed in the federal schedule for drug classifications as a basis for denying admission into the United States. Someone who would have been fined previously for a small quantity of marijuana, either in the United States or in his or her home country, would now be deported or not allowed into the United States. In addition, the law did not differentiate between simple users of drugs or major drug traffickers. Nor did it give dispensation to someone married to a US citizen or with US-born children.

Similarly, the Omnibus Anti-Drug Abuse Act of 1988 made aggravated felony another basis for deportation and also eliminated all rights of anyone who committed a crime, including legal permanent residents living in the United States for a long time. The law defined "aggravated felons" as drug and weapons traffickers and murderers and made them ineligible for certain types of immigration relief. In addition, the Violent Crime Control and Law Enforcement Act of 1994 expanded restrictions on aggravated felons and allowed, for the first time, a summary form of removal for certain nonresident aggravated felons (Kurzban 2008). This law eliminated the due process rights of "criminal aliens," who could be deported in a summary proceeding ordered by an immigration officer, not an immigration judge.

That same year, lawmakers also used a technical amendment to expand the definition of "aggravated felonies" to include ordinary felonies, making them one and the same.

Although not explicitly an anticrime law, the Illegal Immigration Reform and Immigrant Responsibility Act (IIRIRA) of 1996 was equally effective in demonizing immigrants. It permitted, for the first time in US history, mandatory detention of people who posed no threat to society and were not likely to flee. It also permitted, for the first time, summary removal at the border, making border officials judge, jury, and executioner all rolled into one (Kurzban 2008).

In addition, IIRIRA made it impossible even for long-term, legal, permanent residents to challenge in federal court any wrongful, arbitrary, or discretionary decision made against them, including imprisonment and deportation, by eliminating the right of immigration officers and immigration judges to provide immigration relief and then protecting them from judicial review of their mistakes and biases, for which they cannot be sued (Chavez 2008; Kurzban 2008). This law also allowed immigration authorities to imprison any noncitizen, without bond, for as long as it takes to complete immigration proceedings, separating them from their US citizen families for months or years and then deporting them forever, a process also protected from judicial review (Kunichoff 2010).

The coup de grace, however, was the Uniting and Strengthening America by Providing Appropriate Tools Required to Intercept and Obstruct Terrorism (USA PATRIOT) Act, passed on October 26, 2001, which joined the fear of immigrants with fear of terrorists. This law unleashed spying on citizens and noncitizens alike, eroding their civil rights. It also expanded the range of discretionary powers granted to law enforcement and immigration authorities to detain and deport immigrants (Kurzban 2008). It made it impossible for anyone charged with an immigration violation, including mistakes, to contest the charge in federal court, to know the basis of the charge, or to review the final order for deportation. Coupled with the REAL ID Act of 2005, which proposed a system of national identity cards, the USA PATRIOT Act essentially abolished the writ of habeas corpus in matters of immigration.

The abolition of the writ of habeas corpus was extended even further by the Military Commissions Act of 2006, which empowered the US president to detain noncitizens indefinitely and in secret locations, to subject them to torture, and to prevent them from bringing a writ of habeas corpus, as long as the president labeled them "alien enemy combatants" (Kurzban 2008). Furthermore, it expanded protection of the discretionary decisions made by immigration authorities from judicial review, including the illegal revocation of visas.

The lumping together of immigrants and terrorists creates a perfect one-size-fits-all solution to deal with an "all purpose alien threat," and allows the right-leaning media to agitate for even more anti-immigrant legislation (Chavez 2008). Indeed, the marriage of xenophobic immigration laws with crime and terrorism has convinced the US public that immigrants threaten not only their prosperity but also their national security. In addition, the new border enforcement policies form a frontal attack on the judiciary, as they abolish the remnants of judicial review by denying courts of appeal the right to review motions and prevent district courts from reviewing denial of citizenship applications (Kurzban 2008). Furthermore, protection of the discretionary decisions made by immigration authorities from judicial review, including the illegal revocation of visas, has been expanded.

Racial Inequality in
US Immigration Policies and Practices

The blatant contrast between the cold reception given to Haitians and the warm welcome extended to Cubans illustrates beautifully not only the problem of racial inequality in the treatment of immigrants but how the technology of governing works. When the United States became more involved in the affairs of Haiti, Haitians began migrating to America beginning in the late 1950s. However, they did not receive much public attention until the late 1970s and early 1980s when thousands of Haitian boat people fled the brutal dictatorship of Francois "Papa Doc" Duvalier in unseaworthy vessels headed for Miami (Stepick 1998).

Boats leaving Haiti often capsized at sea because they were overloaded with desperate individuals who paid huge sums of money to be packed like sardines into the homemade vessels. Not surprisingly, many people drowned at sea, their black bodies washing ashore on Florida beaches. Boat people lucky enough not to have drowned were intercepted at sea by the US Coast Guard and returned to Haiti (Portes and Stepick 1993; Samuels and Charles 2009). This practice applied not only to adult men and women but to children as young as two years old.

For years, thousands of Haitian asylum applications piled up without being acted upon by US immigration—until 1978, when a blanket policy was formulated, declaring Haitians to be "economic refugees." In compliance with this policy, new arrivals were detained, interviewed at the rate of

40 interviews per day, denied work permits, and then processed for deportation. Those who had applied for asylum while already in residence were given a 30-minute asylum hearing, including time spent in language translation, then denied asylum and processed for deportation (Chomsky 2007).

In September 1981 President Reagan, who characterized Haitian immigrants as a "serious national problem," reached an unprecedented agreement with President Duvalier to allow the US Coast Guard to patrol Haitian waters and return all boats to Haiti before reaching US territory (Chomsky 2007). By late 1990, 23,000 Haitians had been stopped at sea, and only eight were granted asylum; even those who provided evidence of torture were rejected. In September 1991 the military coup that toppled Haitian President Aristide stimulated another mass exodus of Haitians. Extreme political repression and human rights violations had made them desperate enough to risk life and limb at sea.

With hundreds dying at sea, human rights groups and even members of the US Congress protested the inhumane treatment, and a federal judge was inspired to order President George H.W. Bush to stop sending Haitians back. He refused, sending them instead to the US Naval Base in Guantánamo, Cuba. Six months later, the camp was overflowing with Haitians, so he resumed the old policy of stopping boats at sea and returning them to Haiti. In the 1990s, most of the US Haitian population were to be found in the states of New York and Florida, about 150,000 each, with a smaller population in Boston, Massachusetts (Stepick 1998). The population in Florida is younger and consists mostly of new arrivals.

In 2002 US Attorney General John Ashcroft, under orders from President George W. Bush, formulated a no-release detention policy, applied exclusively to Haitians, on the grounds that the release of Haitians would threaten US national security. This policy included those who had already been granted asylum by immigration judges and those who had convinced asylum officers they had legitimate cases. When confronted with the absence of logic in this policy, Ashcroft replied that it was important for Haitians to know they would not be released from detention if they came here, illustrating the harsh treatment of Haitians both inside and outside the United States.

Given that one US administration after another has discriminated against Haitians, the ironic and tragic story of Joseph Danticat should come as no surprise. Danticat was an 81-year-old Haitian pastor and uncle of the award-winning Haitian American novelist Edwidge Danticat, who has been awarded a MacArthur Genius Grant. Joseph Danticat died while in immigration detention in Miami because immigration authorities had confiscated his life-supporting medication. He was also denied telephone communication and family visits while he was dying (Danticat 2008).

On many previous occasions he had used a valid multiple-entry tourist visa to visit family members in New York. However, in October 2004 his church and home in a poor neighborhood in Haiti were attacked by armed gangs, and his life was threatened. He managed to escape into temporary hiding and then flew to Miami, where his niece, Edwidge, lived. When he passed through immigration, his tourist visa was stamped and approved, but when asked how long he intended to stay he made the mistake of telling the immigration officer that he wanted to apply for political asylum because he feared for his life in Haiti (Danticat 2008).

Danticat paid dearly for this mistake because he was promptly arrested and sent to Krome Detention Center, a squalid prison located on the outskirts of Miami where he became fatally ill. He was arrested, held as a virtual prisoner, and abused by immigration authorities; he died tragically, because he entered the country legally, while being Haitian. Sadly, he was only one of hundreds of thousands of Haitians treated in this way. Fortunately, not all die. Ironically, if Danticat had been Cuban instead of Haitian, he would have qualified automatically for asylum through the "wet foot, dry foot" policy and welcomed. Under this policy, Cubans picked up at sea would be returned to Cuba, while those who touched US soil with their feet would be admitted to the United States.

In contrast to the harsh treatment of Haitians described previously, let us consider the warm welcome given to Cubans (Stepick 1998). They began arriving in the United States in several waves after the rise of Fidel Castro in Cuba in January 1959. Between 1959 and 1962, 200,000 Cubans arrived, and between 1965 and 1973, when the first wave ended, 260,000 more arrived on "Freedom Flights" from Havana to Miami (Rampersad 2009). By 1980 the United States had embraced 800,000 Cubans (Guskin and Wilson 2007), and today there are 1.3 million Cubans in the country.

From the beginning, Cubans were classified as "political refugees," meaning "refugee from communism," while Haitians have been treated merely as runaways. Indeed, it was not until 1980 that President Carter passed the Refugee Act, which, for the first time, conformed with UN standards of equal treatment for all people confronting political persecution (Chomsky 2007; Rampersad 2009). This law eliminated special treatment for people from communist countries and set a limit of 1,000 for Cuba.

The Cuban Adjustment Act was passed in 1966, granting special legal status to the first wave of Cubans who, not coincidentally, were mainly white or near white, and professionals, businesspeople, and members of the government or the military in pre-Castro Cuba. As such, they arrived as a ready-made elite (Stepick, Grenier, Castro, and Dunn 2003). Legal permanent resident status was granted almost automatically to those who had been in the United States for two years (changed to one year in 1980), and they also received $1.4 billion in federal assistance to facilitate their settlement (Chomsky 2007).

The preferential treatment and generous assimilation policies extended to Cubans have generally continued to the present day (Guskin and Wilson 2007), although the US government was less welcoming to the 125,000 Cubans who came, in the second wave, on the Mariel Boatlift in 1980, because the Marielitos were mostly poor, black or mulatto, and some were mentally ill or criminals. In contrast the US government has conducted a systematic campaign to keep Haitians out (Stepick 1998).

Under the Bill Clinton presidency, which began in January 1993, Haitians continued to be rejected and Cubans continued to be embraced. In response to the third wave of Cuban rafters who fled Cuba following the collapse of the Soviet Union in 1990, President Clinton initially reversed the harsh Bush policy of Haitian repatriation by sending about 21,000 to the camps in Guantánamo (Chomsky 2007). However, in August 1994 President Clinton was confronted with a mass exodus of over 31,000 Cubans (Rampersad 2009).

Instead of admitting them to the United States, he ordered them to be intercepted at sea and sent to Guantánamo to join the Haitians, bringing the camp population to about 50,000. This gave the appearance of equal treatment of the two groups. However, within a month, Haiti was occupied by US troops and an overwhelming majority of Haitians were sent back to Haiti, against vocal protests by immigrant and human rights organizations. Meanwhile, hundreds of unaccompanied Haitian children were still in Camp Guantánamo, children with relatives in the United States but none left in Haiti. Nevertheless, they were sent back to Haiti, destitute and homeless, to fend for themselves in the streets.

On the heels of repatriating Haitians, President Clinton signed the US-Cuban Agreement of September 1994, admitting into the United States 21,700 Cubans who had been held in Guantánamo (Rampersad 2009). In addition, he approved the fourth wave of legal migrants by agreeing to admit no less than 20,000 Cubans annually, not including the immediate relatives of US citizens, resulting in the admission of 17,937 in 1995 and 26,466 in 1996. At the same time, President Clinton formulated the new Cuban policy nicknamed "wet foot, dry foot" (Chomsky 2007; Guskin and Wilson 2007).

Differences in the treatment of Cubans and Haitians have not been confined to US immigration policy and practices but extend into social relations in Miami. Cuban exiles, mostly white, are resented not only by Haitians for the preferential treatment they receive, but by African Americans who believe that immigrants have derailed African Americans from their journey to the promised land. While government policies have enabled some African Americans to become middle-class entrepreneurs and to defect from the inner city to the suburbs, their social mobility has been eclipsed by that of Cuban exiles (Portes and Stepick 1993). Cubans have risen meteorically in local politics and government, propelled by their success in small business in the inner city and the professions (Stepick, Grenier, Castro, and Dunn 2003).

In self-defense, Haitians and poor African Americans have joined forces, sometimes, in racial solidarity against the racism and the power of Cubans but, at other times, have been split by Haitian culture, regarded by some African Americans as ignorant and backward. Class differences within the Haitian and African American communities in Miami have also produced balkanization. Thus, the tension between Cubans, Haitians, and African Americans in Miami has been and continues to be threefold: color, class, and culture (Portes and Stepick 1993). Not surprisingly, Miami was the only US city in the 1980s to experience three riots, each one triggered by the killing of a black individual by police, many of whom are Latino.

In response to accusations of police brutality, the Miami police department riveted its attention on containing future riots and other forms of social control. In contrast, the local business elite and politicians (white and Latino) turned away from civil rights issues and focused on developing black entrepreneurship with government assistance. As a result, political representation and economic conditions improved with the limited growth of the black middle and professional classes in the 1980s and 1990s. However, life was decidedly worse for poor African Americans, as the rates of poverty and unemployment intensified and the standard of living among black Miamians plummeted to the lowest among the nation's 50 largest cities (Stepick, Grenier, Castro, and Dunn 2003, 74). The coup de grâce came in the 2000 elections when thousands of votes from predominantly black precincts were not counted (Stepick, Grenier, Castro, and Dunn 2003, 76).

Racism and anti-immigrant sentiment have been a leitmotif of US history. Anti-immigrant rhetoric has weaved its way through the US social fabric since the birth of the nation, so much so that the anti-immigrant narrative may be considered a national ritual of purification (Behdad 2005;

Navarro 2009; Ngai 2004). Laws matching this narrative are also a time-honored tradition in US immigration history, deflecting attention away from the fact that as long as there are desperate job-seekers who have been dispossessed of their livelihood in their homeland on one side of the border and businesses eager to exploit cheap labor on the other side, fences, whether high- or low-tech, will not keep them out. And, as long as the US government provides only 1% of the legal immigrant slots needed each year, low-skill migrants will continue to come through the back door. History also tells us that providing more opportunities for people to migrate to the United States legally has produced the best results (Riley 2008). In the next chapter, we look at how immigrant-receiving countries, apart from the United States, have addressed the issue of migration and the lessons that might be learned from them.

6

Learning From Others, Living With Others

REFUGEES
—Caption beneath a sketch of Mary, Joseph, and baby Jesus
fleeing to Egypt, on the concrete wall that encircles Bethlehem

In March 2006, thousands of migrant workers—mostly from India, Pakistan, and Bangladesh—staged a protest against unpaid wages, squalid living conditions, and their indentured status in Dubai, where they labored on some of the most grandiose construction projects ever conceived. That same month, hundreds of thousands of immigrants took to the streets in cities coast to coast in North America, asserting their place as hard workers and solid community members in a country they had come to love and to be part of for many years. Just two years later, in both places and elsewhere in the world, growing numbers were being rounded up and deported, for lack of "papers." They included people with citizen children, and many with little knowledge of their unplanned destinations, places they may have left many years earlier, sometimes in the arms of parents.

Migration is replete with the good, the bad, and the ugly. Immigration policies reflect global as well as national concerns. Yet they are also very acutely felt and personally important to individuals, each one a man, woman, or child, and to many others linked to them. The way immigration policy comes to be determined, then, goes far beyond political considerations. It has profound implications for people, families, friends, and communities. Learning about best practices, as well as the worst, is essential.

107

Nowhere is it more valuable to consider perceptions and procedures that prevail elsewhere than in a country like the United States, given our proclivity for looking no further than what is immediate, comfortable, and insular.

Around the world, claims and counterclaims mix with an alarming rise in preemptive, even vicious, actions toward people who are either on the move or recently arrived in cities or countries different from their places of origin. The incompatibility of Islam and European values is argued on one side of the Atlantic, the requirement that English be the official language on the other. The advisability of denoting places for hiring day laborers is pursued in some US cities, while predawn roundups are conducted elsewhere by immigration authorities in full-body armor. Millions languish in refugee camps or at borders, prevented from finding safe haven, and sometimes also from returning home. Even the UN High Commissioner for Refugees has deliberated policies of forced repatriation to prevent internally displaced people from crossing borders and qualifying for the legal status of refugee. The fact that popular media often seems to be directly linked to incendiary rhetoric suggests that anxiety is widespread and that hostility often lies not far beneath the surface.

Nativism and xenophobia are nothing new in human history, but neither are efforts to understand human need and pursue common interest. If the past is prologue to the present, then we can foresee that ill treatment of immigrants will continue before there is a subsiding of sentiments worldwide that today favor keeping people "in their place." Yet while examples of hostility, harm, and nonsolutions abound, two things merit closer consideration: (1) the ways that current policies fail to address, or unwittingly exacerbate, problems, and (2) cases and approaches that are more effective.

The various ways that the reality of human mobility is being reimagined through exemplary policies and practices present the subject for this chapter. We turn first to why an approach that encompasses comparative empirical evidence is essential. We then examine the extent to which communities and countries worldwide are facing challenges similar to those racking the United States. In those examples, we see a variety of responses to the highly contentious and complicated sets of issues that surround migration and immigration. Following a somewhat geographical consideration, we address some of the chief policy avenues that emerge as relatively less discriminatory, and potentially more effective, than others. By learning from others, the United States may come to have greater success in any comprehensive approach it may yet venture.

Paradoxes and Blind Spots

Perception and reality are often fuzzy, with clarity sometimes coming long after events or crises arise. As we have seen, many people are propelled to migrate involuntarily, at least in part, and more and more have been targeted by states as being real or imaginary threats. Others are subjected to deception and predation by human smugglers and new permutations of debt servitude after undertaking their increasingly hazardous journeys (Bacon 2008; Bhattacharyya 2005; Marfleet 2006). Such paradoxes speak to the complexities inherent in determining migration policies and the need for a more informed approach.

Disconnect between fact and fiction is, of course, part of life, as people attempt to make sense of events and continue over time to infuse and confuse meaning and memory. Governments, too, weigh and waver while trying to mobilize. Governments also strive to forge a commonality among people and governments worldwide, as crises accelerate along with flows of information and people. The unfortunate consequences of blindspots include even greater problems that come with overreactions and nonsolutions. We can, instead, examine the validity of common claims in light of existing studies as well as comparative evidence of policies based on different assumptions and objectives.

For example, health and education costs are frequently cited as among the most egregious costs associated with undocumented immigrants. In the United States, some people maintain that federal laws mandating that all school-age children have access to public education (though not extending to higher education), or that everyone be treated if they show up in emergency rooms, represent open doors for flooding the system and driving up costs of schooling as well as health care. In fact, problems are highly localized, and magnified where immigrants are concentrated. Furthermore, the case of health care suggests that undocumented immigrants are a small percentage of the uninsured, and their fears of deportation mean they are less likely to use even basic health care to which they may be entitled. The result is that they may be gravely ill before they show up in emergency rooms, hardly the most effective situation with respect to either health outcomes or costs.

Mismatch between presumptions and fact is not unique to longer-term residents of any one place. People in flux may also have limited understandings and unrealistic expectations. Migration and settlement are complicated by frequent disconnects between plans and what is possible, improbable, or proscribed. Human behavior—whether decisions of individuals, politics and vested interests, or policing of states—may have multiple, overlapping, or even contradictory motives, along with results. People in any sending community can recount evidence that both confirms and contradicts prevailing thinking about risks and benefits associated with migration to the United States. "*Se fue pero regresó muerto*" (he left, but returned in a coffin), one might hear in a village anywhere in Central America, for example, or such lament as "*con el norte, ya no hacemos eso*" (with migration to the north, we no longer do that [tradition]). Research and public attention are often grounded in what we know, or think we know, from evidence and understanding of earlier patterns. However, we also know that the unforeseen can significantly affect decisions of different players, as well as developments in varied communities.

The planned as well as unplanned characteristics of growing destinations and durations, as well as of border and immigration policies, call for reexamining economic self-interest assumptions and affirming family well-being and human security incentives. As we will see in the growth of transnational dimensions of migration, there is ample reason to believe that broad social good more than individual motivations are both common to and significant in decisions and developments. This is particularly so within the migration complex or "migration culture" that has come to powerfully connect Central and North America, as it has numerous countries to other places around the world.

In the absence of knowledge, ignorance—and its close partner, fear of the unknown—can become sources of the most invidious of prejudice. In light of decades of research and practice (Massey, Durand, and Malone 2002; Foner 2005; Loucky, Armstrong, and Estrada 2006; Marfleet 2006; Messina and Lahav 2006; Castles and Miller 2009), a rethinking of prevailing assumptions about migration and immigrants is in order. Visualizing people as new neighbors and valuable partners in cities, towns, and rural places throughout the world enables people to perceive others in terms of interconnectedness and common interest, instead of as different and as "other." As, and because, we maintain such vision and commitment to our democratic potential together, our societies become ever more vibrant and long-lasting.

A further disconnect exists between migrant lived experiences and public policy. The divide is huge between the worlds occupied by people living in new communities and countries and those of most native-born or longer-term residents. Legal, language, and economic differences dampen the human tendency to approach or engage freely with those who are different.

Authorities—whether employers, police, teachers, or service providers—have considerable power to influence lives and livelihoods, all the more so for people whose circumstances are insecure. As a result, undocumented people tend to live "shadowed lives" (Chavez 1998), not as fully participative or constructive as they could be.

The long interest of anthropology and other social sciences in the dynamics and human implications of transnational migration provide great capacity to contribute to migration reform. No longer stuck in a tradition of seeing cultures as distinct entities, anthropologists have for decades been emphasizing the interconnectedness of a global world. Giving attention to how individuals and cultures construct difference, while sometimes also bridging differences, illuminates ways by which discourse and policy may perpetuate hegemonic ideals (which can include nationhood and identity) while disempowering the other. Research into lived experiences of migrants and commonalities across migration flows can also assist in the development of more sensible and humane migration policies.

Migration and the Politics of Inequality

Migration everywhere engenders a complex web of issues and challenges at multiple levels, from local to global. Disruption is sometimes associated with natural disasters, at times sudden, at times predictable. But migration is nearly always also deeply rooted in inequalities. Looking beyond numbers and rhetoric reveals hidden structures of disempowerment and control, through which resource differentials are enforced, even magnified, by hierarchies that are political and financial as well as racial.

Ironically, immigrants, among those most affected by a pernicious pairing of the politics of fear with the politics of inequality, are routinely blamed for negative economic trends, particularly depression of wages. How numbers and incorporation of immigrants affect wages, particularly of native workers in sectors deemed "low-skill," is a valid concern, as are such questions as how flexible labor accords like guest-worker programs may affect nonimmigrants. We have seen that extending labor protections, capacity to choose, and opportunities for jointly planning are nearly always of benefit to the widest number.

A related claim is that inequality increases with higher levels of immigration. Gaps in income have been widening in the United States and throughout the world, in conjunction with the disruptive imposition of neoliberal policies. Rather than being the cause, immigrants are often also losing ground overall. Today many take longer to achieve upward mobility compared to earlier generations, and few efforts have been made to address economic inequalities, or to include immigrants in the limited redistributive policies that have been attempted.

By recognizing the existence of gross and growing inequity, we come to see people on the move as not only emigrating for opportunities to make a living but also as people dispossessed. Dispossession is not just a tribulation suffered by Haitians or others leaving increasingly inhospitable lands. It is also the experience of vast numbers in places like the United States, where 80% of the increases in income since 1980 have gone to the top 1%.

Nonetheless, because inequities are largely human in origin, therein also lies the promise. People on the move not only challenge thinking and policies, they ultimately represent tremendous hope. In large part, this is because of their labor potential and youthfulness. Castles (2010) and others remind us that a global political economy based on massive exploitation of labor backed by military power of a sole superpower or two cannot persist. The dualism inherent in a mobile workforce benefitting elites and a world of barriers and controls for the rest has given rise to the contemporary global crisis. When things get tougher, migrants everywhere are largely choosing to remain in destination countries, even when facing job loss and shrinking incomes. There, as well as in other destinations, the resilience of collective actions and creative livelihood strategies at both individual and community levels represents a powerful impetus for new economic centers and developments that are multiple, flexible, and more democratic.

A critical, comparative perspective has never been needed as much as today. Together, what has not worked, what has been overlooked, and what has indeed worked give us a chance, in turn, to better understand what might work or at least what might be changed. Our country certainly can benefit from learning about the experiences of other places, four of which we consider here.

Cosmopolitan Canada

Canada has earned considerable praise for its long history of advocating humanitarian principles in its refugee and immigration policies, as well as its strong commitment to being a multicultural nation. How is it that the maple leaf has become a symbol of multicultural pride, even as the Stars and Stripes evoke images of bullying and bunkers? Is it simply a function of how basically "nice" Canadians are? Does Canada represent a country that effectively incorporates people from various backgrounds, a model the United States might emulate?

To begin with, religious and language rights have been acknowledged and affirmed since Canada was founded. They are encoded in its Constitution and the Treaty of Paris that formally ended the fighting between Britain and France in 1763. Still, as in the United States, naturalization in Canada was historically tightly restricted to European immigrants, to preserve the "character" of the population. Not until immigration reform in 1966 was overtly racist language eliminated, opening the way for recruitment of workers from the Caribbean and Mexico.

In contrast, the Seasonal Agricultural Workers Program (SAWP), created in 1966 in Canada, like the former *bracero* program in the United States, was designed to provide cheaper and more controllable labor, while conveying the appearance of careful federal management of migration (Basok 2002; Mize and Swords 2011). It is sometimes considered a "model for managed migration" because, as a government-to-government program, it is structured to ensure high return rates of workers (Preibisch 2010, 410). Accordingly, it has become a popular policy formula. As in the United States, seasonal recruitment undercuts efforts to mobilize for better working and living conditions.

The Canadian SAWP does include worker protections and benefits that were, and continue to be, largely absent in US programs. Yet, as in the United States, in Canada, "a web of labor controls . . . force the calculus of complacency, desperation, and acquiescence to trump personal safety and caring for one's health" (Mize and Swords 2011, 215). Such nationalist convergence is hardly grounds for well-being. Workers who are tied to a single employer fear deportation or repatriation if they express complaints, depend on grower requests or callbacks, and are unlikely to request or even utilize contracted benefits.

This is also true of the Temporary Foreign Workers Program (TFWP), created in 2002, as an extension of SAWP. As an employer/demand-driven program, TFWP is intended to manage migration flows and provide Canadian employers with quick and easy access to workers, particularly those with low skill. It essentially deregulates labor markets, providing employers with greater flexibility and control over their workforce, especially in terms of restricting mobility and exercising the time-honored threat of deportation. Not surprisingly, the temporary foreign worker (TFW) population in Canada has leaped from 101,174 in 2002 to 282,194 in 2009, far outnumbering economic migrants (Smart 2011).

What the SAWP and TFWP programs have in common is the exploitation of worker vulnerability which, it is hoped, will deliver a docile and timely labor force. Both programs aim to import units of labor, not people, and may even be characterized as systems of indenture (Preibisch 2010, 413). Indeed, the dramatic rise in the temporary worker population in Canada has raised concerns about the potential for their abuse as well as the abuse of undocumented workers who have no employment mobility and face enormous barriers to permanent residence, access being restricted to provincial nominee programs. It has also enhanced the likelihood for TFWs to go underground (as in the United States) when their contracts expire (four years maximum).

In addition, the shift of responsibility from government to market institutions for recruiting temporary migrant workers is no cause for celebration. Labor brokers tend to target the land-poor or landless in countries with an enormous wage gap with Canada, who are more likely to accept lower wages and work longer hours than Canadians and tolerate substandard living conditions (Preibisch 2010). Nevertheless, there have been some labor gains: labor unions such as the United Food and Commercial Workers (UFCW) and the Agriculture Workers Alliance (AWA) have emerged to enhance workers' ability to exercise their rights. Indeed, migrant workers were a key campaign issue for UFCW. In addition, UFCW's Agriculture Workers Alliance Centers expanded from one to 11 over a decade. In short, migrant workers have become unionized, and labor organizations are increasingly addressing questions of human mobility.

The surge in TFWs has even led the Canadian government to revise TFWP regulations, effective April 1, 2011, with the aim of protecting workers. Changes include reducing the validity of the "labor market opinion" from one year to six months; banning bad employers for two years; and allowing TFWs to stay for a maximum of four years, after which they must leave Canada and not return to work for at least four years. At the other extreme of Canada's human capital model of migration is the "designer immigrants" strategy, calculated to attract millionaire migrants (Smart 2011). The Business Immigration Programme, created in 1982, aimed at investors, entrepreneurs, and the self-employed, requires a minimal capital injection of CAD $800,000. However, the volume of low-skill workers in Canada far exceeds those with high skills.

Recent years have also seen growing discontent. Chief among the complaints is that federal policies allow thousands of unannounced immigrants to come to Canada with scant review of their skills or possible criminal background. In 2009 and 2010, when cargo ships landed on the coast of British Columbia with hundreds of Tamil from Sri Lanka on board, charges raged about lax standards toward potential Tamil Tigers terrorists on the one hand, heavy-handed treatment that doubted the veracity and undermined the rights of refugees on the other (Walia 2010). Congestion in the "M.T.V." cities (Montreal, Toronto, and Vancouver), where about two-thirds of new immigrants concentrate, stirs further concern. Furthermore, as security has come to dominate US border and migration policies, Canada has been pressured to "harmonize" its own policies with those of its more powerful neighbor to the south (Alper and Loucky 2009).

Nor has Canada been immune from the worldwide erosion of support for refugee and immigrant rights. By 2009 there was a backlog of more than 60,000 applications for political asylum, leading many to assert that Canada's open-door policy was leading to a large number of fraudulent claims. Immigration Minister Jason Kenney even asserted that the country would work to bring in more refugees designated by the UN High Commissioner for Refugees, in part to counter "fake" claims and the costs associated with them, including for social assistance to claimants awaiting hearings. The assertion is that immigrants are knowledgeable about Canada's relative generosity, and they take advantage of long processing times and various levels of appeal to string out a claim until it or another remedy is granted, such as compassionate grounds based on years in residence or having family members. In turn, the claim is that valid petitions may also be delayed, at cost to *bona fide* refugees. Such complaints are not unlike those heard elsewhere, of course, including from small communities in the United States that have had to bear burgeoning costs associated with rapid growth in immigrant students in schools, many with limited proficiency in English.

Still, Canadians today widely adhere to multiculturalism as a goal, something affirmed in Canada's official stance as a bilingual nation. Multiculturalism is also encouraged through immigration policy. Canada has an immigration rate second only to Australia (as measured by proportion of population that is foreign-born). It has more than twice as many legal immigrants as the United States, and welcomes 250,000 immigrants a year, three times more than in the 1980s (Todd 2010). Canada has also been a leader in addressing social group status and gender-related abuses in asylum claims.

Most Canadians express strong appreciation for what immigrants mean, including acknowledging that newcomers are needed in a country as large as theirs (Alper and Loucky 2006). College students from other countries are routinely permitted to count their years of study toward landed residence status, should they decide to remain in Canada. By contrast, international students have in recent years been choosing destinations other than the United States, some at least because of the greater welcome they perceive in other countries. Rates of interracial dating and marriage are among the highest in the world, so much so that few today even give this an afterthought. Metropolitan areas suggest what other urban areas of the world might look like, or at least aspire to, in years ahead. In metropolitan Vancouver, for example, 40% of the 2.1 million residents—and an astounding 70% of the student bodies of the three largest universities—belong to a "visible minority."

Lacking a large undocumented population means Canada has been able to avoid some of the conflict experienced in the United States. But instead of seeing a threat, a business leader from Manitoba sees opportunity, when referring to the estimated 11 million undocumented immigrants in the United States: "I'm sure many of those people would make perfectly wonderful citizens of Canada. I think we should go and get them" (DeParle 2010). The implication may be that needs and understanding tend to be local and regional, so choices that include those constituencies are likely to be more reasonable than generic federal policies.

Lessons From Down Under

Australia is in many ways like the United States—having immigrant origins, a drastically reduced and impoverished indigenous population, and fears about unsettled masses nearby. Like other countries in the West, Australia has also subjected immigration to strict legal and administrative control. Historically Australia was established as a British colony when, in 1788, convicts were sent to provide labor for producing raw materials such as wheat, wool, and minerals. By the mid-nineteenth century, as the supply of British workers declined, workers were imported from elsewhere in the British Empire such as China, India, and the islands of the South Pacific. This, in turn, provoked the adoption of a White Australia Policy in 1901, amid violence directed at Chinese and other Asian workers, and in response to strong antipathy of the white Australian labor movement toward the entry of nonwhite workers. The policy so restricted Australian population growth, however, that the government, by 1945, began to recruit more white families. Immigrants from the Baltic and Slavic regions predominated at first, before sources shifted to southern Europe, especially Italy and Greece. Only when the White Australia Policy was abandoned in 1973 did Australia begin again to admit non-Europeans.

Recent policies aimed at social inclusion are a new development for Australia. For instance, in 1989, Australia produced a document, the National

Agenda for a Multicultural Australia, which declared "the right of all Australians to enjoy equal life chances, participate fully in society," so that Australia's potential could be fully developed (Valtonen 2008, 68). Australians also seem to be increasingly aware of the positive economic benefits of migration, including reduction of the burden of an aging population as well as increased capacity in the global marketplace (Gray and Agllias 2010). Efforts like the government's Living in Harmony Initiative, and those of the Centre for Research on Social Inclusion at Macquarie University, aim to educate about conflictive histories and cultural differences, as part of initiatives to improve social cohesion, intercultural cooperation, and local community sustainability.

As Europe Goes . . .

At the peak of the Industrial Revolution, those seeking to escape conscription into British factories and the horrors of industrial production undertook transatlantic migration, resulting in 66% of immigrants to the United States originating from Britain between 1800 and 1860 (Castles and Miller 2003). Before World War II laborers from Ireland and Jews fleeing the pogroms of Russia were imported to Britain because natural population growth was insufficient to meet industrial labor needs. In other words, direct recruitment by firms, governments, labor contractors, and traffickers, which connects the workforce with the industries needing their labor, is an age-old practice that has served as a stimulus package for migration.

Between 1945 and 1973 most Western European countries solved their postwar labor shortages by using direct labor recruitment to supply workers for their expanding economies. After World War II the British government imported 90,000 male workers from refugee camps and also from Italy through a program called the European Voluntary Worker (EVW). These workers were tied to specific jobs, had no family reunion rights, and were subject to deportation for disobedience. Belgium imported workers from Italy for its coal mines and iron and steel industries. France also established the National Immigration Office in 1945 to increase the declining French population and to import workers from southern Europe as well as 150,000 seasonal farm workers per year from Spain (Castles and Miller 2009).

By 1970 France was also flooded by large-scale immigration from North Africa (Algeria [600,000], Morocco [140,000], and Tunisia [90,000]), West Africa (Senegal, Mali, and Mauritania), and overseas departments such as

Martinique and Guadeloupe (Castles and Miller 2003). Although they were all French citizens, they provoked racial violence and the formation of extreme-right political parties. In the case of the Netherlands, 300,000 people migrated there from Indonesia (the former Dutch East Indies) between 1945 and the early 1960s without much opposition. However, after 1965, black immigrants from Aruba, Curaçao, and Surinam, former Dutch colonies in the Caribbean, aroused opposition.

Foreign labor was equally indispensable to German industrialization, the largest numbers coming from Poland, followed by Italy, Belgium, and the Netherlands. In the mid-1950s, the Federal Republic of Germany (FRG) entered into binational agreements with Italy, Spain, Greece, Turkey, Morocco, Portugal, Tunisia, and Yugoslavia, which increased the number of foreign workers in Germany from 95,000 in 1956 to 2.6 million in 1973 (Castles and Miller 2009).

The German labor recruitment system is the most instructive because it was the most highly developed and the most contradictory. Germany initially recruited only single workers and denied them workers' and civil rights based on the legal distinction between citizen and foreigner. It also banned family reunion and maintained the illusion that foreign workers could be discarded at will when they outlived their usefulness. The German state perceived migrant workers to be units of labor rather than human beings. However, it soon discovered that it was impossible to prevent family reunion, the birth of children, or settlement.

Most interesting of all is the fact that between 1945 and 1973 the highest economic growth rates were experienced by countries with extremely high immigration rates, such as the Federal Republic of Germany, Switzerland, France, and Australia, which suggests strongly that labor migration was indispensable for their economic expansion (Castles and Miller 2003). Massive flows of capital, goods, and laborers were responsible for industrial development and the eventual economic dominance of the United States (Sassen 2007). These flows began, in the 1800s, as a transatlantic economic system binding several European nations to the United States in a feedback loop, with mass migrations from Europe to the United States. When the United States passed laws and entered into international agreements designed to open its own and other economies to the free flow of capital, goods, services, and information in the 1960s and 1970s, it was merely continuing a strategy that began more than a century earlier.

The political and demographic makeup of Europe has changed dramatically over the past quarter century, but only recently has it had to deal with the numbers who have settled as well as with limited efforts toward integration. Germany was one of the first countries to recognize the unanticipated effects of active recruitment of guest workers, particularly from Turkey, beginning in the 1970s (Castles and Miller 2009). The inertia of network dynamics and anchoring associated with family settlement is not easily reversed. France, the Netherlands, the United Kingdom, and even humanitarian-minded Scandinavia have all experienced a growing backlash against immigrants, perceived as too many and too different in countries previously less diverse in composition. Arguments and restrictions are particularly acute with regard to Muslims, but also Roma (gypsies) from eastern Europe, both characterized as poorly educated and lacking skills to compete in modern industrial society, if not also harboring thoughts and behaviors antithetical to Western values (Bawer 2006; Daley 2010; Hill 2010b). Birth rate differentials raise the same concerns in Europe as are voiced in the United States regarding immigrants from Latin America.

This backlash has been expressed in many different ways, including but not limited to ethnocentrism, nationalist attitudes, nativist attitudes, opposition to equal treatment of immigrants, denial of civil rights, hostility, and voting for anti-immigrant political parties (Gijsberts, Hagendoorn, and Scheepers 2004). For instance, in reaction to a perceived flood of immigrants, parties of the extreme right, such as the Freedom Party in Austria, the Vlaams Blok in Belgium, the National Alliance in Italy, the People's Party in Denmark, and the National Republican Movement and the Front National in France, have emerged and received support in countries of the European Union, based on calls for the preservation of national "purity" and anti-immigrant political platforms denouncing tolerance, political correctness, and multiculturalism (Guibernau 2007).

One survey compared nationalist attitudes and the desire to exclude immigrants in 22 countries, dividing them into three different types: (1) long-standing immigration countries such as the United States, Canada, Australia, and New Zealand; (2) western European countries; and (3) former socialist states of central and eastern Europe (Coenders, Gijsberts, and Scheepers 2004a). The researchers found that resistance to immigrants was highest in eastern European countries (77%), followed by western European countries (63.2%), then long-standing immigration countries (62.5%), and finally Japan (52.4%) (Coenders, Gijsberts, Hagendoorn, and Scheepers 2004a). Furthermore, Latvians, Hungarians, and Bulgarians were the most resistant to immigrants, followed by former East Germans.

Every country in the survey favored exclusion except for Ireland (25.7%), which is long known for its commitment to human rights. Interestingly, there was a sharp contrast between resistance to immigrants and the willingness to allow refugees, with most countries favoring refugees, except for Slovenia and Latvia. Also, regular attendees of church were less resistant to immigrants, while women were more resistant than men. Those with the lowest incomes and least education, particularly manual laborers, the self-employed, and the unemployed, were the most resistant to immigrants. Not surprisingly, very strong resistance to immigrants was related to declining national economies (Coenders, Gijsberts, Hagendoorn, and Scheepers 2004b).

Before today's stridency over new immigrants, then, Europe had a relatively good record of integrating ethnic minorities and immigrants. Economic downturns, however, give new vigor to any undercurrent of dissension. "It's the economy, stupid," is a refrain that has variants in many languages. Boom-and-bust cycles are reflected in the global recession of 2008, and echo the rise and fall of civilizations for millennia. Distinctions between developed and developing countries also blur during times when jobs, or lack of jobs, are the primary drivers of movement. Spain, with the fifth-largest economy in Europe, witnessed heady growth in the decade before the collapse, including huge housing developments for many of the 4 million immigrants who had settled in Spain, many employed in construction. As unemployment shot above 20% nationally, and 40% or more among youth in some provinces, immigrants became familiar scapegoats and many returned to their home countries.

Europe's woes continue to be headlines, as once-booming economies like those of Ireland, Italy, and Greece have gone into freefall. Yet European leaders were also grappling with how to envision a new era that was not hinged on carbon or on continuing transfer of wealth to the uber-rich, unlike the increasingly attenuated trickle-down, asset-driven, and debt-driven economy in the United States.

So while European integration had for several decades been hailed as proof of the benefits, and inevitability, of blurred borders and a nonstatist future, by the twenty-first century disharmony and potential disintegration were evident. Accolades to multiculturalism waned in the face of evidence that integration was not always coming easily, while terrorist acts in Britain, Spain, the Netherlands, and elsewhere suggested that some immigrants and their descendants were not even strongly supportive of the idea. Stricter integration policies began to appear, including federally mandated language courses in Germany and civic integration exams for prospective immigrants in the Netherlands (Migration Policy Institute 2009), as well as recent proposals to ban the construction of mosques in Switzerland and public veiling in France.

But even the present rigidity and animosities do not equate simply to racism. Not unlike small communities in the United States, small countries in Europe have legitimate concerns that huge or sudden influxes can be overwhelming. Populism and xenophobia find fertile ground amid perceptions that some newcomers not only cannot "fit in" well, but consciously choose not to. Nonetheless, centers for newcomer protection and support (*acojido*) are found throughout Spain, and shop window signs that "*auslanders* [outsiders] need not apply" have come down in Austria following passage of antidiscrimination laws. In much of Europe, minorities and even immigrants, after a waiting period, receive workfare supports and rarely sink to the miserable conditions that persist in the United States, especially for descendants of African migrants forced into slavery centuries ago. Sealing borders and stopping immigration is impossible, because of geography as well as the crucial economic benefits that immigrants provide an aging continent. Ultimately, Europe faces an equally noisy and messy, but perhaps more integrated, future as the United States. It is also one that is inevitable, except for an even more unacceptably conflictive apartheid alternative.

Caribbean Intraregional Migration

The vast literature on Caribbean migration has been focused almost exclusively on movement out of the region to places like North America and Europe. More than likely, this focus is due to the concerns of policymakers and the public in receiving countries. One million migrants left the Caribbean for Europe, and 3.5 million Caribbean migrants settled in North America over the past 40 years (Valtonen 1996). Nevertheless, despite the lack of academic interest, migration among different islands within the Caribbean has been a long-established pattern dating back to Emancipation in 1834, with half a million migrants moving over the past 40 years. The movements consist partly of seasonal labor circulation and partly of unskilled laborers seeking better opportunities not available in their homeland.

For our purposes here, we focus on intraregional migration within the English-speaking Caribbean, while being mindful of the constant movement of people from Haiti to the Dominican Republic, from the Dominican Republic to Puerto Rico, and from Guyana to Suriname, as well as elsewhere in the Caribbean. In the Anglophone Caribbean, the movement is typically from the poorest countries to the less poor—for example, from underdeveloped countries with stagnant agricultural sectors such as Barbados, Grenada, St. Vincent and the Grenadines, and Guyana to more industrialized

economies such as that of Trinidad, where 6.6% of the population are foreign-born (Valtonen 1996). Although there has been continuous immigration since 1834 Trinidad has proved particularly attractive during periods
of economic boom, such as when US military bases opened during World
War II, and during the oil booms of the 1970s and 1990s.

Surprisingly, immigrants from neighboring islands are well received in
Trinidad, in contrast to the cold reception of immigrants by other receiving
countries. What might account for their exceptional social integration? Most
of all, a similar history of British colonization, Afro-Caribbean culture, and
race is shared by English-speaking Caribbean immigrants to Trinidad, who
have been embraced and have blended with the local population (Valtonen
1996). In a way, their situation resembles that of Canadian immigrants to
the United States. In addition, working-class newcomers and working-class
Trinidadians have poverty in common, the differences between them being
eclipsed by rigid class divisions among Trinidadians themselves.

Although unskilled, what enabled the "small islanders" to survive periods of serious unemployment was their occupational flexibility. For instance, they accepted menial work as day laborers, domestic servants, and
even prostitutes. They also squatted on government land (a common practice accepted by the government), which provided shelter, food, and income
from market gardening, fishing, or raising animals. Their willingness to do
any and every kind of work gave them a distinct advantage over locals in
the job market. This is especially useful in countries with no unemployment
insurance (Valtonen 1996).

However, there is a growing generation gap between the original migrants and their children and grandchildren, born and raised in Trinidad and
Tobago, who face large-scale unemployment. They have neither acquired
the education for knowledge-based work nor skills necessary for a capital-
intensive, petroleum-based, industrial economy. Instead, many prefer to
remain destitute or to turn to crime and drug trafficking, having absorbed
the work ethic of their Trinidadian peers (Valtonen 1996). The policies of
Trinidad and Tobago regarding health care, social services, and schooling
are quite generous, extending to everyone who lives in the country, with
eligibility based on length of residence, not nationality. However, the beneficiaries of these policies are the elderly, not the youngsters who must produce income to survive.

Moreover, the picture in Trinidad is not quite as rosy as at first glance.
In contrast to the warm welcome extended to Afro-Caribbean immigrants,
there is growing hostility toward Chinese construction workers, which lends
support to the notion that similarity of history, race, and culture contribute

to the social integration of immigrants. These Chinese guest workers were imported by the Trinidad and Tobago government in contractual agreements with Beijing construction corporations under the auspices of the government of China. Local trade unions believe that the Chinese workers are taking away jobs from locals and have inspired calls to "send them back" and "beat them up."

Chinese workers were imported because they have a reputation for working long, hard hours and completing projects within budget and on time (Pickford-Gordon 2009). However, although viewed by authorities as the answer to their prayers for efficient construction in Trinidad and Tobago, the Chinese workers were being exploited to the hilt—working under appalling conditions, poorly fed, and housed in substandard quarters, much like fellow guest workers in other countries. Indeed, one worker died on the job, and many were marching in downtown Port of Spain, the capital city, to protest their situation, demanding outstanding wages, better treatment generally, medical care for the sick, and to return home. In response, riot police were assigned to control the protesters.

Lessons From One Caribbean Transnational Family

The story of the Price transnational family who emigrated from the Caribbean to the United States illustrates how strong kin ties that straddle different countries and different cities can keep a family together across vast distances (Ho 1993). Globalizing kinship is not a new challenge for Caribbean people, who for centuries have practiced large, kin-based support networks. Women are the protagonists in this drama, involving the active exchange of children, child care, food, housing, goods, services, communications, travel, and personnel.

The women in the Price family launched the migration process by moving first from Trinidad to New York, then later to Los Angeles and Miami. Building bases in several locations, a multilayered, complex kin circuit, spanning two countries and several cities, has enabled the Price family as a whole to exploit resources in many locations, making it less vulnerable to any single economy. The family strategy of activating multiple links also enhanced the symbolic unity of the family. For example, sharing an apartment in New York and, later, renting several apartments in the same building in Los Angeles; eating their meals together; and sharing responsibility for the care of the Price children enabled individual members to pool their resources.

When no single location offered enough in the way of resources to satisfy basic needs, family links were activated in as many different places as possible, at different times. For instance, Grandma Pearl moved from New York to Los Angeles to serve as the caretaker for all the Price children and assist with other household duties in Los Angeles. Child-minding is an old Caribbean custom in which children are cared for by female relatives or close friends and not necessarily by biological parents. Child-minding in the United States is simply transplanting this practice overseas.

The exchange of children becomes a form of human currency, on both a symbolic and a physical level, cementing relationships between family members separated by distance more firmly than other types of reciprocity (Ho 1993). It is indispensable for the peace of mind of young working mothers who migrate from the Caribbean and lack child care in the destination country. In other words, children become building blocks in transnational family systems. For example, the Price children spend alternate summers in New York and Los Angeles and, occasionally, in Trinidad.

Moreover, the movement of children is not a one-way street. Some children are left behind in the Caribbean, others who have migrated are sent back for schooling because the schools in the home country are perceived to be of a higher caliber and the children are thought to perform better away from the racial tensions and urban violence of the United States. After finishing primary and secondary school in the Caribbean, they then move back to North America or Europe for their higher education. In other words, schooling is a two-way transnational family project, the comings and goings of these children being orchestrated by the women of the family.

Follow the Money:
Transnational Connections and Transformed Communities

Geography, types of work, modes of incorporation, and historical period contribute to significant contrasts in the migration experiences of different countries and regions. This is also only a brief accounting of selected cases (it would be possible to pick nearly any country and find a migration story). Nonetheless, we can discern consistencies in determinants, dynamics, and implications of migration. Several of the more salient relate to the kinship ties described previously; economic transactions, notably remittances; flexible labor arrangements, either attempted or anticipated; and legal remedies, which are frequently denied yet prospectively intriguing.

The transnational nature of the lives of millions is evident in the substantial financial and social remittances that return to families from those who have migrated to jobs elsewhere. Remittances have become a mainstay of the economies of many developing countries and for tens of millions of households in them. Cash remittances reaching developing countries dwarfed official development assistance by 2007 (Gabriel 2008). Considerable research documents how earnings sent by family members from jobs in cities or working abroad lead to higher living standards, material acquisitions and often more conspicuous consumption, and an impetus for further mobility.

Remittances sent home by emigrants worldwide rose from $70 billion to $230 billion between 1998 and 2005 (Sassen 2007). In 2006, 20 million households in Latin America and the Caribbean received $60 billion in remittances (Oppenheimer 2007). Salvadorans sent home more than $3 billion, which made up 20% of the GDP of El Salvador (Rogers and Dada 2007). Migrants from the Dominican Republic sent home $2.8 billion, a substantial increase over $1.8 billion sent in 2001. According to the Inter-American Development Bank, this amount exceeded that of official development aid and private capital investment combined (Shoer-Roth 2007). In Bangladesh, remittances sent home by emigrants in the Middle East, Japan, and parts of Europe represented one-third of foreign exchange.

In fact, remittances from migrants make up the primary or secondary source of external capital for many home governments, so much so that these economies have been characterized as "remittance economies." In other words, remittances are the most stable and largest source of foreign exchange, rivaling export manufacture and tourism in earnings for much of the developing world. For example, tourism in Nicaragua generated only $239 million in 2006, whereas remittances totaled $1 billion (Rogers and Dada 2007). National debt burdens have also forced many governments to depend on remittances sent home by migrants.

Remittances not only provide vital lines of support for those left behind, they also act as an economic engine, serving as a financial booster shot for the local economy. For example, dairy and cattle farming, fishing, and growing rice, coconut, and bananas are the traditional occupations in the town of Cabrera in the Dominican Republic, which have not created new jobs or brought prosperity (Shoer-Roth 2007). In contrast, remittances have both revitalized public infrastructure and transformed the town: land for sale and house construction (built with money earned abroad) are visible everywhere; grocery stores are bursting with shoppers armed with cash. Beyond the face value of cash, remittances enhance purchasing power: lenders will approve loans without collateral, and groceries can be bought on credit.

Expatriates who remain connected to their homeland also contribute to communities by donating computers to schools, by helping to rebuild churches and hospitals, and by providing medical supplies, equipment, and so on (Shoer-Roth 2007). There is also a new telecommunications center, an investment agency, a credit corporation, a currency exchange office, and an attorney's office. Although most remittances are used for daily expenses, some recipients have invested in small businesses, such as buying sports vehicles to rent to tourists or remodeling an old shopping center.

However, evidence also points to growing disparities between those who leave and those who stay behind (Binford 2003; Cohen 2001; Hugo 1996; Moran-Taylor 2008). Often there is a steep rise in land prices and increasing concentration in the hands of those who benefit from earnings from abroad. Remittances may also lead to acceleration of environmental degradation that may have helped propel people to migrate in the first place. People with shrinking access to land may use it more intensively, while those in transnational circuits often use more industrial pesticides and fertilizers, even as production of new cash crops contributes to erosion of a different kind: that of traditional ethnobotanical knowledge.

In the attention to dramatic changes in housing, purchases of vehicles, and other forms of visible consumption, productive potential and venture investing associated with remittances have been somewhat overlooked. Evidence is growing that trade and entrepreneurial activity are stimulated by international migration, along with investments both in productive ventures as well as in education and professional training, all of which can, in turn, benefit community development and infrastructure (Cohen and Rodriguez 2005).

The recent global economic crisis has reduced work opportunities not only in developed countries but in the United States. Decreases in remittances to Mexico, Guatemala, and elsewhere have also been widely reported. Remittances are likely to decrease further, not just during such downturns, but as successive generations become more distanced by time and place from homelands of parents and grandparents. Still, flows are likely to continue and to mature rather than disappear altogether, in light of the complex layering of social, cultural, and economic processes that produce permanent contemporary migration from local to international levels (Castles and Miller 2009).

In particular, policies and practices designed to reduce migration are doomed to failure if they do not take into account the economic forces and relations of power that uproot people (Bacon 2008; Ngai 2004). In our opinion, policymakers rely too heavily on econometric models to explain migration, using rational choice theory and market variables to estimate the cost-benefit calculations of solitary individuals. They fail to perceive migration as a dynamic social process involving households, social networks, and a "culture of migration" (Hagan 2008). Such models can deflect attention from migration's complexity and trick policymakers into the simplistic notion that it can be turned on and off with a switch.

Brain Drain or Brain Gain?

Recruitment of workers on a temporary basis to keep economies moving has become a common rationale—in the United States throughout the twentieth century, in Europe since the 1960s and 1970s, and in the Middle East and Asia more recently. Created for economic ends, such arrangements have also usually proven ineffective in the long term, because they tend to treat workers solely in economic terms, while they are first and foremost people with social needs and cultural attributes.

Temporary work arrangements are not categorically impractical, inhumane, or contrary to the desires of many workers for employment options that are not disruptive to family and community affiliations. However, they must be critiqued in light of how they often arise, concomitant with erosion of the social contract and "casualization" of labor. Flexible labor arrangements are proposed as a way to ensure business demands for an environment that is "safe and secure" which, not coincidentally, was a phrase used in the lead-up to the Arizona laws targeting immigrants in 2010. A system of wage differentials has great potential to become a persistent separate-and-unequal economic arrangement, and to lead to "unsafe and insecure" conditions for workers afraid to speak out in the face of danger or discrimination.

Exodus of the best and the brightest has long been another lament of sending communities and countries. An overall increase in skills among migrants worldwide is indicated by a 69% rise in college-educated migrants in Western countries between 1990 and 2000 (Cornelius, Espenshade, and Salehyan 2001; DeParle 2007). In contrast to the obstacles put up by the United States, countries like Canada, Hong Kong, Australia, New Zealand, and Britain provide work visas, paths to legalization, and tax breaks for skilled migrants. Not all destinations, however, take effective advantage of the bounty represented in immigrant populations. In the United States, for example, at least one in five college-educated immigrants remain stuck in unskilled jobs (Batalova and Fix 2008).

Because there is a high demand for skilled guest workers, it is commonly assumed that educated immigrants receive high salaries and good treatment, but this assumption is false. Many highly skilled engineers in the high-tech industry are recruited and hired by temporary employment agencies, not directly by the companies themselves, as "guest workers" in "modern sweatshops" on H1-B visas (Bacon 2008). In general, wages for H1-B workers are 20% to 30% below prevailing rates. The experience of these engineers often mirrors that of their unskilled counterparts: working seven days a week without overtime pay, being cheated out of wages, being charged enormous rents for housing, having their passports confiscated, and being threatened with deportation when they complain about ill treatment.

Many are freshly minted graduates who are desperate to find a job and regard the H1-B visa as a ticket to permanent residence and family reunification. Although they are allowed to apply for a green card while on the temporary visa, once they obtain one, they often lose their jobs because they have lost their vulnerability, the source of appeal to employers (Bacon 2008). The high demand for skilled engineers comes from electronics giants in the Silicon Valley and elsewhere in the United States. For instance, Bill Gates, the head of Microsoft Corporation, is an ardent supporter of the H1-B visa system, claiming that US engineering schools are not producing enough graduates. Apart from not paying their fair share of corporate taxes to help fund the US educational system, the practice by giant computer firms of hiring engineers from overseas also undermines job prospects for US engineers of color, who are rare to begin with, and reduces motivation for entering the field.

The migration of highly educated workers out of their homelands, "the brain drain," is the result of increasing Westernization in advanced educational systems everywhere. However, this trend might be reversing. One study reports that many skilled immigrants are leaving the United States and returning to India and China (Wadhwa 2009). A main reason for leaving was visa problems; many came to the United States as graduate students, and others entered on H1-B visas. They were frustrated with living in immigration limbo, the long wait to convert their temporary visas to permanent residence sometimes being longer than a decade. For instance, more than 1 million applicants were in the queue for the annual 120,000 permanent resident slots in late 2006. Skilled immigrants also complained that US life was too difficult—language and cultural barriers, missing their family and friends at home, and caring for children or aging parents in the United States without servants. Most of all, there was growing demand for their skills in their homelands where they were offered more options, enjoyed a higher quality of life, and believed family values were better.

Legal Remedies

Among the best ways to promote integration are long-term government policies, most importantly that of birthright citizenship granted to children born within a country (*jus soli*). In contrast to some countries, like Germany, the Fourth Amendment in the United States confers naturalization to children of immigrants, effectively limiting the designation of "foreigner"—and the subjugation that often accompanies it—to a single generation. Legal status provides tangible affiliation, but also healing of misperceptions associated with damaging, even hateful, characterizations of things (and people) as "illegal." Time, of course, plays a critical role in indirectly favoring integration. Sudden pace and substantial scope, such as a rapid influx of newcomers to a small community, magnifies their presence as well as potential for misportrayal in the media or in electoral campaigns.

Contrast this with strategies to manage and secure borders, in the United States as elsewhere, which are increasingly projected as efficient redesigns of travel and tracking, enabling efficient and effective governing through risk reduction. The complex and costly architecture of control may not, however, have its intended results (Muller 2010). The politics of borders do not lend themselves easily to logical design of safety for citizens or to ready compliance by people whose identities and mobility are under question.

As the social and political incorporation of immigrants has become a pressing concern worldwide, the concepts of citizenship, and the rights and duties it entails, have been ever more contested. Commonsense notions that being a citizen involves voting and taxes no longer seem so obvious when the world's finite resources are increasingly up for grabs, leaving growing numbers of people dispossessed materially and legally. The roles and agency of people, many of them on the move in terms of geography as well as careers, have become a central focus along with the structures in which they operate. While mechanisms for sorting and control become more prominent, they are also challenged as never before. People are asserting identities as plural and nations as constituted by peoples, not just nation-states. As the inviolability of the nation-state is questioned, serious consideration is turning to notions like democratic citizenship (involving participants in community), flexible citizenship (Ong 1999), local citizenship (associated with where one dwells), and even pragmatic citizenship (Reed-Danahay and Brettell 2008).

Rights to belong may still lag behind realities associated with global labor and resource demands, but human beings are demanding a legitimate place in the present, not just relegation to the past or the margins. The challenge—for the European Union, as for the United States and many other countries—is to foster a sense of belonging among people who have not had a sense of shared culture. Transnational discourse highlights enduring ties to former homes, but also hybridity and fluidity as adaptive responses to displacement and changing conditions. While discomforting to established beneficiaries and frameworks, these assertions are both substantive and imminent.

States can shape, rather than resist, the evolution of citizenship practices. Mexico, for example, recognizes the inevitability and benefits arising from emigration of its citizens, as well as the clout of its northern neighbor. Through government and economic institutions that encourage retention of the affective, as well as the financial, Mexico—and countries like Colombia and the Philippines, as well—encourage perpetuation of investments and cooperation across borders.

Ultimately the defense of immigrant rights is a defense of standards for others. Rulings, like that in the United States in early 2009, that immigrants have no constitutional right to representation during deportation hearings, cast a pall on hopes for reducing a climate of intimidation and exclusion. Workplace raids that terrorize people into accepting low pay and miserable work conditions do little except undercut that of documented workers as well. Restoring proportionality frees people to better serve society, while also freeing resources for dealing with real crime and need. At the same time, broader pan-ethnic and cross-border engagement can provide tangible means for improving conditions at home, in both their former and present senses. As many have observed (Castles and Miller 2009; Foner 2005), far from being in opposition, transnational participation goes hand in hand with emerging loyalties and involvement. Experiences and skills from one context frequently transfer well to others. Far from leading to divided loyalties and confusion, continuing respect for origins—and even dual nationality—encourage stronger appreciation for, and even naturalization in, one's new country.

7

E Pluribus Unum

Parvinder and Habib are street beggars. They beg in different areas of New York.

Habib begs just as long as Parvinder but only collects $4 to $5 every day.

Parvinder brings home a suitcase FULL of $20 notes, drives a Mercedes, lives in a mortgage-free house, and has a lot of money to spend.

Habib says to Parvinder, "I work just as long and hard as you do, but how do you bring home a suitcase full of $20 notes every day?"

Parvinder says, "Look at your sign. What does it say?"

Habib's sign reads, "I have no work, a wife, and six kids to support."

Parvinder says, "No wonder you only get $4 to $5."

Habib says, "So what does your sign say?"

Parvinder shows Habib his sign.

It reads, "I only need another $20 to move back to Pakistan."

The United States. *E pluribus unum.* Land of immigrants. One people. It's a familiar narrative, but one that includes innumerable stories of hardship and unfairness, times of dislocation and exclusion, and accounts of resilience and struggle. The past is often prelude for the present. The course of US history, then, provides valuable insights into the lived experiences of people worldwide, people whose lives are tough or becoming tougher and, increasingly, in flux. So what is arguably the operative motto today, "Proud of its immigrant past, hostile to its immigrant present," may actually be a persistent theme.

131

That alarm about people who are new, in transit, or seemingly different becomes more vociferous amid worsening economic and environmental conditions is not surprising. As disruptions widen, and people seek out explanations and resolution, they often direct worries and justification outward: there are too many of "them," they're taking our jobs, they don't fit in, they're not like earlier immigrants (read: our own ancestors). Ultimately many of the arguments and misunderstandings that persist today are not just about immigration and border policies. They form in response to perceptions of diminishing control, personal and collective. Insecurities that arise amid rapid or multiple changes are also subject to manipulation, through the media or for political gain. Repeated framing of immigration as a "broken system" prefigures that policy will be more prosecutorial and draconian, while ensuring funding to achieve "results."

In calmer moments we can realize that however much we assert or hope for a simple answer to something as fundamental and complex as migration, it will ultimately be wrong, or at least incomplete. However popular tougher measures appear, they will fail without an understanding of the forces that determine or motivate human movement. Through thoughtful civic dialogue we can come to see how the American immigrant narrative is not altogether ideal or mythical. It includes recurrent exemplars of success, and of dreams and careers of relative newcomers who are often not unlike those of native-born or long-term residents. Newcomers remind us that strengths are as inherently human as disruptions are predictable. Affirming the humanity of people on the move supports their capacity to express and attain dignity as members of communities and society. Moreover, that shared understanding enables us to fashion more constructive and equitable social policies in response to the realities and potentialities of a changing population.

Mesoamericans in Middle America

Rural Iowa provides a sobering example of the ramifications of tougher borders, including within the United States. Surrounded by farmland and dominated by a large meat-processing plant, the town of Postville in recent years had come to see itself as "homeland to the world." Food processing is notoriously filthy, dangerous, and poorly paid. Not surprisingly the workforce in recent years has largely come from Latin America, particularly people of Maya descent from Guatemala, and others from southern Mexico. They joined residents from Russia, Ukraine, Somalia, Bosnia, and Palau who had, in turn, arrived after German and Irish settlers moved into lands of the Iowa and Fox nations.

How Maya from Mesoamerica came to be in a town of little more than 2,000 in the heartland of the Midwest, and why so few remain today, are questions that extend geopolitics more than 1,000 miles southward and macroeconomics decades into the past. For millennia, the highlands and lowlands of Central America have been farmed through shared work efforts and diverse production strategies, including domestication of a variety of foods such as maize (corn). Carefully transmitted stewardship practices sustained communities for centuries. Today, however, people of Maya descent are found throughout the continent, far beyond their Mesoamerican homeland.

A visit to almost any community in Central America or Mexico today reveals much about the root causes of migration, as well as the impact of remittances and continuing dislocations associated with dependent economies and separated families. The Maya—who include over 20 ethnic-linguistic groups, spread across hundreds of villages and towns—are among the most deeply affected by geopolitical conflict and subsequent globalized economic policies. A brutal counterinsurgency war and its persistent impacts compelled many to leave traditional communities in order to secure livelihoods in distant places. The resulting diaspora is emblematic not only of the ferocity of violence that enveloped the highlands but also of the deep wounds on economic viability and social harmony in the years since. Maya people have become dispersed across the continent (Loucky and Moors 2001; Tobar 2005; Foxen 2007) to large cities like Los Angeles and Houston, as well as to innumerable smaller places in between, like Postville.

On May 12, 2008, in the largest workplace raid against undocumented workers in decades, dozens of agents of Immigration and Customs Enforcement (ICE), backed by helicopters, arrested 389 workers at the meat-packing plant in Postville. Three of every four arrested were from Guatemala, most of them Maya. Chained and shackled together, they were quickly processed in groups of 10, charged with felony "aggravated identity theft" for using Social Security numbers not assigned to them, found guilty, and sentenced to five-month detention before being summarily deported. Many ended up serving their prison time in other states, marking the start of continuing separation from spouse and children. Refusal to accept this procedure would have meant indefinite imprisonment before trial, followed by even longer sentences, and inevitable deportation. Workers had virtually no time to consider options, little legal representation, and poor understanding of the proceedings, particularly the case for those with limited comprehension of English and even Spanish. Most returned to their highland Guatemala communities humiliated and owing thousands of dollars, borrowed to make the journey north. Several dozen women were released from prison to care for children, but not permitted to resume jobs; nearly all were required to wear heavy ankle monitors (Argueta 2010; Jonas 2010).

Postville was one of the first cases of what has become standard procedure. Termed "Operation Streamline," what had before been treated as a civil violation is increasingly being prosecuted criminally as a felony. Hardly any of the arrestees in Postville had a prior record, even for a misdemeanor. To the contrary they had been repeatedly praised by community members and church leaders for their neighborliness and for how they had helped revive a town that had been in serious economic decline.

Postville remains devastated—commerce halted, former neighbors and coworkers gone, and dozens of US-born children effectively orphaned by ICE. An outpouring of support from teachers, members of the community, and beyond has helped the remaining women and children, but years are passing in which families remain broken and separated. Rather than a model for the rest of the country, a human tragedy resulted from the effort to respond forcefully to public concern that immigration is out of control. In the end, Postville epitomizes what can happen without resolution of a fundamentally contradictory message: help wanted, and keep out.

DREAM Act or Dreams Hacked?

Another cautionary tale about misdirection in existing approaches to immigration involves children and how they are, or are not, valued and accorded rights. Today there are in the United States about 1.5 million minors who were born beyond its borders and lack legal documentation. Many have lived most of their lives in the United States and are generally indistinguishable from other youth, except for their lack of status. In addition, some 4 million to 5 million children of unauthorized immigrants are US citizens by birth. Together they represent a sizeable population at considerable risk when exclusionary practices are on the rise.

The contemporary global reality is one in which numerous families, whole communities, sometimes even entire countries, have become interconnected in multiple, geographically dispersed, and long-standing ways. Human movement and fluidity have been and are increasingly compelled by global as well as individual forces. Linkages of movement and exchange usually continue across more borders than just those demarcating US national territory. Inherent as well is the inertia of transborder movement within a "culture of migration" that has come to envelop large portions of humanity. Various directions are followed, places are settled, and families get established. With national citizenship usually connoted on the basis of geography—the country where you took your first breath—hundreds of millions of people worldwide reside beyond that place. Many of them are young, some even moved beyond their birthplace while infants, carried as so many have been over generations and eras by parents to what eventually became new homes. Except for being in the United States without authorization, these young people are integral to families, schools, and communities nationwide. Many have distinguished themselves academically or through other achievements. They are American youth in every respect except for papers.

Incorporating unauthorized youth is the intent of the Development, Relief, and Education of Alien Minors (DREAM) Act, legislation that would enable undocumented youth who have grown up in the United States to achieve conditional legal status, and eventually be able to apply for citizenship, if they attend college or serve in the military.

The present and future contributions of these young people were recognized through broad bipartisan support in the development of the initiative, including early sponsorship by Senator Orrin Hatch (R-Utah). The DREAM Act is a sensible response to unnecessary divisions as well as unfulfilled prospects. Notably, national as well as cross-national evidence demonstrates irrefutably that capable and hard-working young people represent substantially higher earnings over the course of their working lives, as well as high rates of movement into business and home-ownership. Incomprehensibly, even a measure that would incorporate some of the best and the brightest failed in the US Senate in the waning days of 2010, amid a governance climate that paired nativism with partisan absolutism. Like many immigration issues, unsubstantiated claims were raised. Some thought taxpayer money would fund scholarships, others feared it would allow families access to public benefits, still others claimed it would result in mass "amnesty."

Essentially the DREAM Act got caught in the controversies that churn about legalization, in which more innuendo and misinformation are generated than clarity about practical procedures and plausible benefits. Numerous proposals for comprehensive reform have been derailed by inclusion of a path to legalization. Such has been the level of misinformation and political misrepresentation; the logic of acknowledging contemporary cultural and demographic reality has been disregarded. Just as the Secure America and Orderly Immigration Act of 2005, cosponsored by Senators Ted Kennedy and John McCain, was never voted on, the Comprehensive Immigration Reform Act (CIRA) failed in the House the following year. In turn, CIRA failed in the Senate in 2007, amid characterizations that it was a blanket "amnesty" program that would reward lawbreakers with citizen-ship. In the case of the DREAM Act, concern for the welfare and human potential of the youth themselves was largely lost in the din, though many of the youth themselves are determined to not be silent about what is both sensible and just.

Children are the future. That truism has emerged because it is so. Chil-dren, younger people, are also very much the present. Youth are thoroughly part of, affected by, and contributors to today's world of mobilities. They have youthfulness, all kinds of techno–communications capabilities and other emerging skills, representing immeasurable sources and resources of hope. They are central to social continuity, to sustaining community well-being as well as that of each person. Epics of migration, along with innu-merable experiences of families and small groups in motion, suggest that as societies change their demographics, they would do well to support the young, whether of one place, or of many.

Common Sense Versus Common Nonsense

Many people support and others seem unfazed by tougher enforcement. The "Republic of Arizona" was declared, said some, through "pioneering" laws in 2010. Immigration scrutiny was extended substantially beyond what had long prevailed, as immigration checks at routine traffic stops and other monitoring was mandated. Even more discriminatory proposals emerge among the scores that have been proposed or passed in recent years, usu-ally at state or even municipal levels, to address immigration concerns. By 2011, bills or laws in Georgia and elsewhere extended the reach of immigra-tion checks to others as well. When signing a law requiring police to arrest anyone suspected of being in the country without legal status, and making it a crime to knowingly rent to or transport anyone lacking legal status, the governor of Alabama, Robert Bentley, went so far as to praise how "it is the toughest bill in the country."

Requiring law enforcement to conduct immigration or identity checks along with myriad public safety tasks makes little sense, particularly when we need to use all of our resources most effectively. Imagine the added de-mands on police or sheriffs of having to determine whether a person has committed a crime (such as crossing the border without papers) or a civil violation (overstaying a legal visa), or may simply be a US citizen without identification. Deeper implications surround criminalizing even more peo-ple, including in a part of the continent—the Southwest—where human movement has for centuries been part of a fundamentally transborder reality.

The role of law enforcement, like other emergency services, is community safety, not implementing foreign policy or border control. Deputizing law enforcement for immigration duties does more than just open the way for racial profiling and violations of equal protection. It can be dangerously counterproductive. Relationships of trust are fundamental to providing protection. Provoking fear and pushing people further into the shadows in turn deters them from reporting crimes, which is hardly conducive to public safety. Enforcement of immigration statutes is not the same thing as enforcement of civil and criminal law. Dragnets and immigration checks, like lockdowns and walls, create headlines, but ultimately they are irresponsibly ineffective and expensive. By 2011, increasing numbers of communities and states ranging from Massachusetts to California—along with many police agencies—were withdrawing from Safe Communities and similar programs that rationalized policing the immigration status of residents as essential to stopping terrorism (Preston 2011). Criticizing such approaches as overly broad and possibly deterrents to reporting crimes, some communities were opting instead for public safety through community dialogue and other steps toward promoting, rather than rending, communities.

Another obvious problem relates to freedom from arbitrary detention, a fundamental constitutional right and a central feature of international law that has increasingly been denied in the United States. On any given day in 2011, more than 33,000 immigrants throughout the country were detained on civil immigration charges. Those detained could be held indefinitely and denied access to legal representation. Detainees included people arrested in immigration sweeps or stopped through traffic and law enforcement operations, as well as asylum-seekers and even longtime lawful permanent residents. Fortunately, in spite of the secrecy and chilling effect of such increasingly widespread practices, terrible conditions of incarceration and harmful physical and mental health consequences are coming under increasing scrutiny.

The Department of Homeland Security has authority to review each detention and to release those who pose no danger or flight risk. Although that authority has largely been overlooked, the legal as well as economic and social ramifications of current practice provide growing support for applying appropriate and existing legal standards for determining whether detention is warranted. Individual case review would ensure that fewer people are subject to costly and unnecessary detention, isolation, and further family and community disruption. Fortunately as well, investigative reports and critical policy assessments are creating opportunities for challenging the legitimacy of measures that threaten to become routine, and for highlighting legal and sensible alternatives.

Challenges to Comprehensive Immigration Reform

Postville, DREAM legislation, and divisive intranational gatekeeping notwithstanding, amid such adverse or hesitant transitions we can discern reasonable paths forward. Numerous challenges arise, however.

One of the problems is simply the sheer complexity of issues and inflexibility of constituencies, some of whom have long-established positions. Migration and immigration are intensely emotional topics. While the immigrant experience is shared by, or resonates with, many people, an equal number either do not understand or care to understand it. Some people are understandably resentful at being vilified because they worry about their own employment prospects. Others see the country or culture as under threat, particularly by "illegal" migration.

The sheer number of unauthorized immigrants in the United States—estimated at 10 to 11 million—is of obvious concern. Perception that a blanket amnesty would have untold demographic and fiscal implications, while undermining respect for the law, unites many against any such provisions. How could fraud be avoided? What kinds of "sorting" might be optimal? Critics point to the Special Agricultural Worker (SAW) provisions in 1986, which required proof of employment on farms for 90 days or more between May 1, 1984, and May 1, 1986, as part of application for temporary residency and, in turn, more permanent options. Not only was such documentation unavailable to people who had been paid under the table, document fabrication operations quickly sprung up to sell false paperwork.

Critics point also to the results and aftermath of the Immigration Reform and Control Act of 1986 (IRCA). Through IRCA, 3.1 million people eventually adjusted their status. Yet it also had a major and largely unanticipated result, essentially changing what had mostly been a circular movement, at least for Mexican workers, into a more permanent migration (Casteñeda 2007; Alba 2010). So while IRCA was successful in legalizing many, it was also faulty as labor certifications were so easy to falsify and undocumented hiring continued apace, even as trust in the system eroded.

Existing avenues for reform are also faulty. The system for proportioning legal visas remains archaic. Hundreds of thousands worldwide have been waiting, sometimes for years, for legal permission to enter the United States. In the case of Mexico the annual limit of 15,820 family-sponsored visas per country translates to nearly 1 million (961,744) on the waiting list today with waits of up to 60 years. Effectively precluding legal entry, including that of many with spouses or children in the United States, the system leaves individuals with few options other than attempting entry without authorization. Reducing bureaucratic bottlenecks would lessen that problem, but the entire system of apportioning and queuing—including fixed country rates regardless of population size, the legacies of outdated European-source priorities—needs massive overhaul. It would also be sensible to acknowledge those in the queues through prioritization in entry policies and reward them for their patience.

A further problem that has complicated policy reform for years is how to balance potentially countervailing aims of order and inclusion. This contradiction surfaced during earlier debate over the Immigration Reform and Control Act (IRCA), with acrimony continuing long after its passage in 1986, with some asserting it achieved neither real reform nor control. Making clearer separation between enforcement and legalization functions of the long-standing Immigration and Naturalization Service (INS) was initiated with organizational differentiation into three bureaus in 2003. Nonetheless, absorbing all three within the Department of Homeland Security continues a securitization emphasis, as does the recent growth of subnational enforcement laws and effort.

Further impediments to immigration reform come with well-funded campaigns of misinformation. Claims of massive abuse of public resources or disloyalty by immigrants contribute to rising resentments, and while unsubstantiated, they are also difficult to refute, particularly amid the alarm that rises with effective innuendo. As long as legalization measures continue to be characterized as giving "amnesty" to lawbreakers, tougher enforcement is likely, with little or no attention to more reasoned responses. Political and powerful interests may both push goals other than what is best for society, much less for immigrants. Some sectors continue to benefit from hiring compliant, and therefore more exploitable, undocumented labor. Institutional interests also tend to harden, and in turn neutralize, useful public discourse.

Yet another obstacle rests in the fact that the promise of immigration reform has been floated so long, without resolution, that neither citizens nor immigrants remain very optimistic. Instead, a demoralizing and increasingly untenable climate has settled in. With growing prominence of enforcement mechanisms, people in immigrant communities continue to live and work even further in the shadows. The litany of anti-immigrant mechanisms includes greatly tightened border restrictions, deputizing of local law enforcement to do immigration enforcement, racial profiling, whole-scale abrogation of rights under international law for people to apply for political asylum, and a surge of lengthy and costly incarcerations. The intense campaign of raids and deportations has so clogged immigration courts that the

American Bar Association has even proposed an independent court system to better address rights as well as effectiveness.

Effective immigration policy is not likely to gain much momentum as long as economic concerns weigh heavy, which is even more the case when such concerns are magnified or distorted, as they can be amid the climate of perpetual electioneering that has come to exist in the United States. Tragically this lack of momentum means continuing deterioration of life for already-vulnerable individuals and families. Unfortunately, society as a whole is also harmed. Local communities and the country as a whole now benefit only fractionally from the energy of workers and the potential that emerges with better education and training. Meanwhile, other US workers are routinely disadvantaged as well by downward wages and conditions associated with informal work arrangements. Rising tensions further compound what might otherwise remain only minor problems.

Integration Is Integral

When people see the humanity in each other, understanding and respect generally follow. Never has this been more important than in an interconnected, accelerated world. As our species has come, increasingly, to have sobering portent for the biosphere, our unprecedented mobilities and circulation can help determine any number of scenarios. Human migration is a fact and a certainty. It involves the noblest motives, and sometimes also the most egregious barriers. Thinking of humane migration brings in discourse about rights along with benefits. Moving and relocating involve considerable knowledge and skills. New relationships add to healthy community dynamics. Uncertainties about emerging cultural and demographic mixes do appear, but they tend to dissipate, as people become more informed and less susceptible to manipulation. Through civic engagement, people also hear and come to appreciate multiple points of view.

The global mix that comprises the United States, however contested in the judgment of its members, has persisted—although unevenly—in large measure because of the determination of those dislocated as well as those already settled in communities. The failure of countries to adopt principles of social integration as essential ingredients of national immigration policy is a prime reason that many new immigrants are not being welcomed or accepted; this is true in the United States as elsewhere (Fix 2007). An element as critical as immigrant integration remains conspicuously and inexplicably absent from proposals for immigration policy reform, or is at best muted.

Instead, much effort has been directed to "keeping people out," however unsuccessfully. By default, the task of immigrant incorporation has been left largely to families, churches, nongovernmental organizations, and occasionally to state and local governments.

Policies of integration must address the realities and benefits of diversity. Vocal alarmism about invasions or a creeping cult of multiculturalism (Chavez 2008; Tancredo 2006) perpetuates fears and reinforces a code of uniformity, while eroding public comfort with and commitment to newcomers and change as part of normal community development. In contrast, the hallmark of a forward-looking country of varying peoples is the adoption of explicit policies that affirm different languages, religions, and cultures, and thereby also addresses issues of discord and discrimination.

Simply put, multiculturalism requires countries not only to formulate policies but also to develop programs and practices to implement them. Canada, for example, devotes significant financial as well as educational resources to encouraging a perspective of inclusivity and appreciation of diversity, including through community services available to all residents. In contrast to the laissez-faire approach practiced by the United States, countries including Australia, Sweden, and Canada practice state intervention in the form of explicit multicultural policies. These not only encourage toleration of cultural difference but also create structural changes in social institutions and collective behavior (Valtonen 2008). Canada and the Netherlands, for example, have national (as well as some municipal) offices for immigrant and refugee integration (Fix 2007). Helping newcomers fit in remains far more peripheral, uneven, and reactive in the United States, despite clear evidence of its benefits.

One source of tension between newcomers and established residents in the United States relates to patterns of immigrant settlement, which, beginning in the 1990s, began shifting away from gateway cities with long histories of immigration to emerging gateways, small towns, and parts of the country unaccustomed to new arrivals (Godziak and Martin 2005). The Midwest and South, in particular, are new destinations; nationwide, more immigrants in metropolitan areas now live in suburbs rather than cities (Singer 2011). There are often few established institutions for integration or established pathways for cross-cultural communication. Immigrants who are both from new areas and in new areas, therefore, challenge more traditional perceptions, including a black-white dichotomy that has long characterized US race relations. Many people are particularly unsure where Latinos "fit" in the racial hierarchy. Conflicts between Latino immigrants and African Americans are not uncommon, as tensions grow amid competition for jobs and housing near the bottom of the occupational ladder and in lower-cost housing.

Despite the challenges and persistent boundaries, there are hints that a new integration model is emerging, dictated largely by the US economy's increasing dependence on immigrant labor and recognition of its functional interdependence (Hirschman and Massey 2008). Immigrants have injected new blood into declining industries, for example, sometimes keeping them in business and surrounding communities viable. Lower immigrant wages have helped to keep consumer prices down. Immigrants have breathed new life into churches almost bereft of congregations. They are a mainstay of agriculture, as well as a range of caring professions including child care and elder care. Not surprisingly, there is a growing recognition of the necessity of addressing immigrants' needs as well as contributions, which is visible in the hiring of immigrants, including Spanish-speaking staff, in many public institutions such as hospitals.

This new trend is particularly encouraging, if only because of incontrovertible evidence of the benefits of immigration. US Census data show not only that the skills and income levels of foreign workers span a broad spectrum but, more important, how immigrants have played a central role in the economic growth of cities over the past two decades (Preston 2010). Between 1990 and 2008 the highest rate of growth was in cities like Atlanta, Denver, and Phoenix, all with large numbers of immigrants possessing a mix of skills and performing white-collar and blue-collar jobs. In St. Louis, for example, the arrival of Bosnians and Chinese restored thriving commerce to formerly blighted streets; many similar cases are found from coast to coast. The arrival and integration of immigrant groups is what feeds the core of many US cities, along with spaces in between.

People, as well as countries, sometimes head in a direction different from others. The twenty-first-century United States has in many respects been such a case, whether it is remaining as a last bastion that denies health care for all, or having a laissez-faire approach to integration paired with marked exclusion and further uprooting (Jiménez 2011). Far from an active, coordinated immigration policy, we have efforts of limited reach that promote belonging, along with policies that are so restrictive as to sacrifice future descendants along with rationality. Insufficient concern has been directed to youth, to intercultural and multilingual learning, and to both the perniciousness and resolution of generational poverty. These are community and educational matters. They are all also long-term investments in human resources, and therefore in a country's future.

As population movements have become global in scope, policies of integration that are multinational as well as national must be pursued. Only then can issues of workable relations between groups and access to opportunities be effectively addressed. It remains to be seen whether the United States will embrace its cross-cultural potential, domestically and abroad, and whether principles of liberty and justice will prevail. Destiny certainly will, and it is one that can be both innovative and inclusive.

Contours of Sane and Humane Migration Policy

Recent US immigration policy has seemed to lurch back and forth between reactionary mobilizations and thoughtful efforts to strive for more humanitarian results. For at least three decades, platforms and blueprints have grappled with this kind of bifurcation. So, although self-evidently critical, comprehensive reform remains elusive, despite reaching for the practical while guided by the ethical.

Fortunately, even though imagining a national community of multiple origins is, today, largely relegated to historical accounts, numerous positive practices and enlightened perspectives exist within and beyond the United States. These provide valuable guides for how direction could shift from exclusion to inclusion and, in turn, from narrowly secure communities to those that are healthy and open. No one, of course, can presume to answer all the divergent, and often hostile, questions surrounding immigration. Nor is a formulaic, cookbook approach satisfactory. Still, certain components that emerge repeatedly in research and through voices of reason are worth noting and supporting.

First, any foundation for immigration reform lies in acknowledging facts on the ground, and the need to fully include all parties involved. A functional border between the United States and Mexico, just as that between Europe and Africa, is only possible through the full participation of expertise from all sides, particularly of migrants themselves.

Second, opportunities for shifting emphasis from securitization to commonalities of goals and commitment should be identified. Real security can go hand in hand with human rights, rather than being assumed to be mutually exclusive. Enforcement should conform to human experience and common sense; it should follow, not drive, policy. In a few short years, the Department of Homeland Security has become a massive agency in size and budget. Burgeoning spending, including for essentially idle agents along the US-Canada border, hardly guarantees greater security. Just as we have come to see nuclear arsenals as obsolete, wrapping immigration in security fears and militarization is similarly misdirected. Understanding and trust, more than ranks of personnel, contribute to a sense of safety and shared prospects at the local level. As trust builds within and across multiple communities, and between law enforcement and neighborhoods, a country also becomes safer. The key is affirming the positive strengths inherent in demographic shifts and multicultural developments, as much as addressing discomforts that arise.

Since most cross-border migration is motivated by economics, and much internal movement as well, policies should also build on the innovation, rise in human capital, and workers' determination that come with immigration (Papademetriou and Sumption 2011). In addition to labor issues, policies must encompass international trade agreements, as these propel much of today's global disruption. Cross-border employment and equity development hold great promise for enabling people to minimize or even avoid migration; such arrangements also fit what the majority of people desire worldwide. Even though they benefit home communities as much as they do native labor in places that are currently migration destinations, US policy has been largely inflexible in responding to their potential. Similarly, the United States lags in advocating other labor arrangements that are equitable and flexible, including some in the Philippines and, to some extent, in Canada. Skill-focused programs that provide streamlined ways to move toward permanent residency would also enable the United States to continue to attract talented workers. The existing visa system can and must be revised so the numbers fit economic needs, without undermining employment of native-born workers.

In addition, the desire and the need for people to belong must be legally confirmed. Legalization does more than just encourage further social contributions; it also promotes significant economic benefits, including tax revenues along with entrepreneurial vigor. A clear path to permanent residence must be established for those currently undocumented, for refugees and asylees, and for multistatus families. The legalization process should prioritize the rights for minor children. Immediate attention must be directed to the traumatic and tremendously counterproductive policies that allow separation of parents from children, through deportation of parents of US-citizen children. Encouraging family integrity and child well-being is in the best interests of everyone.

A fifth element of essential immigration reform relates to civic engagement and education. It behooves us to promote a variety of ways for everyone to learn not only about the prevalence and inevitability of migration, but also what citizenship connotes and what comes with it as it is extended to all members of society. Opportunities to interact with others represent occasions for learning another language, and untold further knowledge. We become better able to relate to people in all their varieties and capacities. It is especially critical to thoroughly involve, and invest in, younger people. Instead of remaining afterthoughts in a flawed system, youth should be a priority in a reformed system. Migration flows tend to be youthful with respect to ages of participants. Their potential contributions along with proven competence hold unforeseen benefits for society overall, as well as for youth themselves (Suárez-Orozco, Suárez-Orozco, and Todorova 2008).

Despite recent legislative paralysis about immigration, the executive branch and its agencies can take a more prominent lead. One sensible directive would be to direct the Bureau for Citizenship and Immigration Services (BCIS) to enable undocumented immigrants who are immediate relatives of citizens to adjust their status without having to leave the country, thereby keeping many families intact. Similarly, granting relief from deportation to young people who would qualify for the DREAM Act, until such time as that stalled bill is passed, would draw in rather than eject a remarkable pool of talent. Relocating efforts for worker protections and reducing labor trafficking to the Department of Labor, and out of Homeland Security, would reverse the enforcement image that dampens workers' willingness to speak up. The federal government can also support governors, local officials, and law enforcement professionals in ending Secure Communities, which unintentionally affects noncriminals and minor offenders much more widely than dangerous felons.

American Mosaic

Although immigration is the purview of the federal government, when that responsibility has not resulted in a viable process—one that incorporates people who are newcomers as well as native-born, while including some combination of border security, flexible labor arrangements, and legalization—all states become potential border states, stepping in to fill the perceived void. By learning from experiences within and beyond the United States, and by drawing on bodies of knowledge from anthropology as well as history and other disciplines, we can achieve the positive immigration reform that is of greatest benefit to all.

Stereotypes of "lawbreakers" and "freeloaders" are as shortsighted as they are wrong. A vast quantity of evidence, historical and cross-cultural, reveals how people on the move generally share remarkable characteristics. In the United States, as elsewhere, migrants are among the most able, strongly determined, and resilient people in their communities. They tend to be younger and healthier. Rarely are they the poorest of the poor, for whom the journey is often precluded by cost as well as arduousness. They may be suddenly or forcibly uprooted, but even then, people consider as carefully as possible their alternatives. Deliberations are usually thoughtful and most likely made within the context of a family or other social support network. Their children—our children—are central to long-term social and economic health, whether of communities or of countries.

The challenges associated with every stage of migration call forth considerable personal and interpersonal strength. One of the great ironies of migration is how people often must separate in order ultimately (and with good fortune) to reunite. Potential impacts and harms for migrants, just as for family members, are usually not lost on those who leave nor on those left behind. The regrettable choice may be rationalized by plans for a relatively short sojourn, even though this often extends into years or permanence. Still, large numbers do return, as is evident today in return migration and transnational circularity. But this is also true historically, including in the return from the Americas in centuries past of many people to Italy, northern Spain, and elsewhere, despite the considerable difficulties and dangers of transoceanic travel. The decisions—sometimes dramatic, always of consequence—produce new opportunities ranging from development of new skills to deepening resolve and resilience in the face of hardships or deferred rewards.

Who, then, are today's immigrants? They include individuals, families, even entire communities and countries whose prosperity—much less self-sufficiency—continues to recede amid global economic turmoil. Whether facing repression or retrogression, some have literally risked "dying to live." Some have become high school and college valedictorians. Yet they also continue to be rashly characterized as different, less worthy, and inassimilable— as Germans, Italians, Irish, and others were in earlier decades.

It is worth noting the accomplishments of those who have come before. They include notables who have changed not just the United States but also the world. Imagine the world without Google, which is plausible, had immigration authorities denied entry to or deported cofounder Sergey Mikhaylovich Brin. Similarly, Yahoo!, one of the most trafficked cybernetworks today, was cocreated by Jerry Yang, who at the age of 10 migrated from Taiwan to San Jose, California. Baseball fans will never forget Fernando Valenzuela, the young man from Sonora, Mexico, who became a media icon, generating "Fernandomania" while making history with the Los Angeles Dodgers as the only player in major league history to win the Rookie of the Year, Cy Young, and Silver Slugger awards along with a World Series championship in the same season, in 1981. In the entertainment world, Sidney Poitier, of Bahamian origins, became the first black person to win an Academy Award for Best Actor (in 1963) before continuing to be a top box-office star. In 2009 he was awarded the Presidential Medal of Freedom, the highest civilian honor in the United States, by President Barack Obama, himself the son of a man from Kenya. Anthropology itself has been heavily influenced by migration, and not only as a major topic of research. German-born Franz Boas became known as the father of American anthropology. His immigrant and Jewish background certainly contributed to his fearless testimony to Congress in 1911, at the height of eugenics and nativism, that no immigrants are inherently better than others—in effect, that oval heads don't mean more smarts than rounder ones.

It turns out, in fact, that "new" immigrants are a lot like earlier ones. They tend to be young, healthy, and innovative. They build practical skills and resiliency through hard work as well as through experiences of hardship. They are well-qualified intellectually and motivationally.

Ultimately, of course, people on the move are also us—our ancestors and our children, many of whom are likely to be increasingly buffeted about by future economic and environmental challenges. The United States has much to gain by allowing immigrants, particularly young immigrants, to "unleash their great potential to the benefit of all Americans" (Suárez-Orozco, Suárez-Orozco, and Todorova 2008, 377), not the least because of their productive roles in a global economy and in solving looming inter-generational problems (Myers 2007). Demographics will increasingly work in favor of immigration, given the growth of the Latino voting population and entry of new younger voters overall, many of whom tend to be open-minded about diversity and social issues. Imagine what can come through embracing rather than denying reality. We would do well not only to affirm commonalities but also to emulate communities and countries that are already committing to their newest members.

The United States has much to gain by working with, rather than against, migration. Essentially, we can apply principles that societies have long used to promote social harmony, community well-being, and positive solutions to shared problems. The result would be far better than the prognoses to come through continuing policies of exclusion. Unless, and until, climate change and environmental degradation are reversed, a tougher world seems unavoidable. Communities and countries that pursue social integration of those currently living shadowed lives are the most likely to make progress toward effectively addressing the other enormous challenges that humanity faces.

8

Right to Move, Right to Be

. . . liberty and justice for all.
—Pledge of Allegiance, United States of America

Whoever doesn't have, isn't.
—Eduardo Galeano (2000, 26)

Movement is basic to human experience. It lies at the core of a foraging life that characterized the course of most of human history, and it continues today to characterize the lives of people on every continent. The pervasive integration intrinsic to a global economy is predicated on movement—of goods and capital, but also of people, both physically and of what they make and think. Whether immediate or repetitive, short-term or prolonged, migration helps ensure life just as it shapes everyone's relationships. Migration, in other words, is far more than just a political matter or a question of controlling flows.

Understanding the profound roles played by migration and determining the multiplicity and synergies of the moves and flows that continue to emerge are essential for determining what it means to be human. Modern lives have become an amalgam of mobilities, associated with resources and requirements of a digital age as well as rapid intercontinental travel. Literature and discourse of all kinds address the suddenness and scope of changes, in myriad localities, as in the world overall. As implications of such a world continue to unfold, philosophies and politics bound to notions of fixity and stasis appear increasingly limited, conceptually and pragmatically. What is needed is deeper appreciation for the anthropology of migration, which means awareness not only of the realities of historical and spatial patterns but also the rights to human movement.

Be Here Now, Be There Soon

Migration is such a ubiquitous feature of human evolution and lives today that it is reasonable to see it as firmly embedded in our human nature. From hominid migration out of Africa to the emergence of transnational migration alongside regular and internal movements, our history is that of a colonizing species. Anthropologists surmise that movement is now reflected in human biology, with the propensity for migration evident as a variation in brains, bodies, or even genome. Such species behavior may, in fact, be as notable as any other characteristics in patterns and determinants of migration across human populations.

One of the more pernicious myths about immigration is that decisions and journeys are determined exclusively by individual migrants themselves. Another is that immigrants today are not like many in the past; the Pilgrims and one's own ancestors are frequently cited as evidence. The result is that responsibility and blame focus on those who move, with removal becoming the solution. Reasons for migration are not hard to discern. They include "pushes"—for example, persecution, warfare, and lack of jobs—as well as the "pulls" of dreams and opportunities. Contemporary global realities, however, buffet and propel people as never before. Discerning involuntary from voluntary migrants—which is at the crux of asylum and hardship determinations—becomes increasingly difficult as worldwide capital penetration and conflicts unleash powerful forces for people to move. As economies are restructured, jobs are outsourced, and traditional agriculture and local economies are undermined by global forces, migration is a logical outcome of the resulting dispossession and displacement.

Reality and fairness require us to recognize that multiple actors, not migrants by themselves, produce migration flows. These include countries, many of which have had pro-immigration policies in the past intended to further their development, or whose military operations trigger dislocation of people and exodus of refugees. Multinational corporations are powerful determinants of migration, as modes of production are increasingly internationalized. Imposition of structural adjustment and austerity measures by the International Monetary Fund and other financial institutions also drive many poor people to seek new strategies for survival that include domestic and cross-border migration. Finally, trade agreements based on international flows of capital and information are accompanied as well by international circulation of labor, from professionals to entry-level workers.

Besides economic crises, mass migrations are triggered by natural disasters; further dislocation is likely with expanding conflicts over resources, deepening divisions, and subsequent new and unresolved grievances. Equally critical is the profound global demographic shift associated with aging populations and shrinking labor forces in the United States, Europe, and Japan. The crisis would be even greater in many industrial and postindustrial countries, in fact, without the entry of younger, productive immigrants. What we see today, then, is a brave new world in which "irregular" (including undocumented) forms of international migration are hardly unexpected.

Against such a background, the current climate for immigration policies and cross-border practices seems incongruous, especially the attempts of more developed countries to close borders and criminalize migration. More puzzling still is the virtual absence of acknowledgment that immigration is a logical set of trade-offs—many positive, some negative. Foreign investment, multisource manufacturing, and changing consumer demands all play roles in producing and reinforcing migration in a global age. Migration is neither simply the result of poverty nor of decisions by individuals in isolation. Recognizing the many key actors in receiving and sending countries, and factoring in powerful interaction effects, is fundamental to any hope for effective immigration policies.

Movement is part of the histories of most peoples and countries. Feeling safe and seeking opportunities for secure futures are fundamental to human experience. Economic links that have grown global foster even greater mass migration. The capacity for flexibility and creativity expressed through movement, however, clashes with the stasis and domination associated with exertion of state power and influence. Reconciling universal human needs for security with the security concerns of states becomes ever more crucial as the rising pace of forced migration is met with increasingly exclusionary and punitive responses. These take on an entirely new light when the ethical dimension is acknowledged. Rights to movement seem especially valid in times of hardship or looming danger. Notably, the morality of migration is implicit in many of the most prescient views of what is right and just, whether proverb ("It is in the shelter of each other that we live"—Irish) or proclamation ("Either we learn to live together as brothers, or we will die together as fools"—Martin Luther King Jr.).

Emergence of a contemporary world, in which circularity complicates a world of places, calls for rethinking space and its resources. The wisdom of common interest is basic to societies and religious traditions of every kind. It is also central to the long-term, biocentric perspective emerging as a shared tenet of a new millennium (Hawken 2007). Territoriality is not likely to fade quickly or entirely, but neither are geopolitical empires and global economic systems as immutable as they appeared only a few years ago. The reality of worldwide movement can provoke increasing rejection stoked by the historic burden of racism (Marfleet 2006; Harris 1995). Alternatively, realization that a system predicated on growth has led to neither global harmony nor ecological health can promote greater understanding of how closely associated forced migration and regimes of exclusions have been to globalizing processes. In turn may come a shift in focus to affirming possibilities for how we may dwell, peaceably and well, together.

War, Refugees, and Migration

Wars, refugees, and asylum-seekers, as well as the humanitarian crises that follow in the wake of forced migration, serve as litmus tests of our human capacity to live together in harmony. In 1951 the UN Convention Relating to the Status of Refugees defined a "refugee" as a person residing outside the country of his or her nationality, who is unable or unwilling to return because of a "well-founded fear of persecution on account of race, religion, nationality, membership in a particular social group, or political opinion." Of the world's 190 nation-states, 140 signed the Convention or its protocol in 1967. Member states agreed to protect refugees and to respect the principle of *non-refoulement,* which means not returning refugees to a country where they may be persecuted. However, many countries are becoming reluctant to accept refugees, even as the number of refugees and asylum seekers has grown exponentially since the mid-1980s (Castles and Miller 2009).

Refugee policies formulated in the West, such as the 1951 UN Convention, presumed a world engaged in the Cold War. They were designed to welcome individuals fleeing communism and to serve as powerful propaganda for the West (Castles and Miller 2009). Unfortunately, the only people who fit this Cold War template were those fleeing Cuba and Southeast Asia, and defectors from the former Soviet Union and its satellites. Furthermore, the UN Convention addressed only individual persecution, not streams of refugees numbering in the thousands, hundreds of thousands, and millions, which grew dramatically after the collapse of the Soviet Union in 1991. The UN Convention was also ill-equipped to deal with vast flows of refugees moving directly to Europe and North America in the 1980s, stimulated by anticolonial struggles in Africa, resistance to US-backed military dictatorships in Latin America, and proxy wars to eradicate communism in Asia (Castles and Miller 2003). In fact, the global refugee population increased from 2.4 million in 1975 to a peak of 18.2 million in 1993, after the Cold War ended.

Most refugees originate from countries torn by war, violence, and chaos, such as Afghanistan (2.6 million in 2000), Iraq (572,000), Burundi (524,000), Sierra Leone (487,000), Sudan (468,000), Somalia (452,000), Bosnia (383,000), Angola (351,000), Eritrea (346,000), and Croatia (340,000) (Castles and Miller 2003). Between 1975 and 2000 the United States accepted more than 2 million refugees for permanent resettlement— more than the rest of the world put together, 1.3 million of these refugees originating in Southeast Asia (Castles and Miller 2009). However, the United States eventually caved in to anti-immigrant hysteria and passed the Illegal Immigration Reform and Immigrant Responsibility Act in 1996, which reshaped asylum policy and refugee rights (Castles and Miller 2003). In fact, the act dismantled refugee resettlement altogether after the terrorist attacks on September 11, 2001, and resumed later only on a microscopic scale.

For its part, Canada accepted about 200,000 refugees from Southeast Asia between 1975 and 1995, resettling on average 21,000 refugees per year during the 1980s. However, unlike the United States, which receives most of its refugees from Latin America, refugees to Canada came mainly from the Indian subcontinent and China, with approval rates of refugee claims being highest for Sri Lanka. In 2006, 30,000 refugees and asylum-seekers were admitted to Canada, among them people from Colombia (5,000), Mexico (3,900), Afghanistan (3,000), and China (2,700) (Castles and Miller 2009). Australia's Humanitarian Programme resettled about 12,000 per year from the early 1990s, but anti-immigrant hysteria also brought this program to a halt.

The refugee situation has grown far worse since 2000, because war, violence, and chaos have deepened and expanded worldwide to include many more places, Pakistan among them. Beginning in summer 2008, warfare between the Pakistani military and Taliban militants intensified in the frontier provinces of North West Pakistan, a minimally governed tribal area bordering Afghanistan (Stuteville 2009). The region has served as a Taliban stronghold and alleged headquarters of al-Qaeda. Pressure from the United States for Pakistan to exercise greater control over the Taliban most likely triggered the escalation in fighting, although the Pakistani government denied this vehemently. Since August 2008, attacks by US drones (pilotless aircraft) armed with bombs have killed hundreds of people in Pakistan, mostly civilians (Al Jazeera English 2009). Civilian Pakistanis have also been caught in the crossfire between the army and the insurgents.

The result has been casualties, injuries, and massive displacement of people. The *Washington Post* (Witte 2009) estimates that more than 2 million civilians have fled the violence, seeking shelter in camps such as Jellozai, Pakistan's largest camp for internally displaced people, located outside of Peshawar, where 43,000 people are housed in tents in an area less than one square mile. There are eleven such camps, where life is a challenge because of overcrowding, poor drainage, insufficient food, and lack of privacy, despite the attempt by UNHCR to provide white tarp "purdah walls" around families to give some semblance of privacy (Stuteville 2009). There is also no schooling for children and nothing for adults to do, although those who have attempted to go home have found their homes destroyed.

According to Al Jazeera English (2009), at least 834,000 civilians from the Swat and Buner districts of Pakistan have registered with the UNHCR as displaced persons after leaving their homes to escape the fighting and as columns of cars, trucks, and horse-drawn carts streamed out of the town of Mingora, packed with people and their possessions. The escalating numbers of refugees and asylum-seekers worldwide have spawned humanitarian crises of gargantuan proportions, making it necessary for the UNHCR to take on responsibilities as a humanitarian relief organization, although the burden is shared by other organizations like the International Red Cross, the World Food Programme, UNICEF, and NGOs such as OXFAM, Doctors Without Borders, and CARE International, among others. Not surprisingly, UN High Commissioner for Refugees Antonio Gutierrez told Al Jazeera that the magnitude of the refugee crisis is overwhelming, requiring massive humanitarian aid to avert disaster.

In Europe, policies and practices have shifted from a position of welcoming Cold War refugees to excluding third-world refugees, as politicians of the extreme right capitalize on popular anti-immigrant sentiments and call for stricter border control as well as immigrant detention and deportation. Following electoral victories of extremist politicians, laws were enacted to restrict access to refugee and asylum status. As a result the number of officially recognized refugees worldwide has fallen since 1995, not because of gains in human rights but because of strong limits on official recognition (Castles and Miller 2003). Those lucky enough to be recognized officially as refugees enjoy a clear legal status, which is a great advantage because they become eligible to receive the protection of the UN High Commissioner for Refugees, a very powerful global institution.

If Corporations Can Be Persons, People Must Come First

Inequality has a long and tragic history, one that continues to unfold amid the global power shifts of the twentieth and twenty-first centuries. Dickens's noting of "the best of times . . . the worst of times" is an apt characteristic of the contemporary era. Wealth has been amassed as never before, but there have also never been so many disenfranchised. The need to move is just one set of responses occasioned by rising uncertainty, quickening pace, and the inability to maintain raised or desirable living standards.

Social justice and environmental justice merge in these times. More than just a function of population growth, the immense impact of our species on Earth is magnified through unprecedented, hugely wasteful, and generally harmful concentrations of wealth and power. As the global economy shifts toward ever-greater inequity, vast numbers of people have become increasingly pressured and pauperized. Dispossession abounds: *los olvidades. . . . o povo* . . . the shrinking middle class. Yet while commodities and capital have become liquid, human beings by the hundreds of millions continue to enjoy far less freedom, including the freedom to move. Often through little fault of their own, they bear much of the brunt of diminishing resources, visible in declining physical as well as environmental health. The dispossessed are also both complicit and controlled, inasmuch as their labor has become commoditized and their conformity compromised.

If an increasingly exclusionary migration climate accompanies a worsening planetary climate, people on the move face still greater threats. When prospects grow dimmer, work becomes less reliable, savings scarcer, socially adaptive practices underminded. People may lack time or money to engage in healthy shared activities; moreover, they may lose sight of what observation and reflection might otherwise engender: that which we would take for granted that all people deserve.

So it is essential that we learn not only about framings and philosophies that justify inequities, or policies like trade accords that dramatically shift profits and power to vested interests not aligned with the public sector (Bhattacharyya 2005; Binford 2009; Marfleet 2006). We must also actively discern how people work to increase food self-sufficiency and overall viability (Sumner 2007).

Cooperation and conflict, cultural continuity as well as change, remain in a rather amazing cosmic dance. Humanity has a track record for working cooperatively to sustain itself in tough times—to sacrifice for, rather than to sacrifice others. We see this in proverbs as well as cultural histories. We can examine how growing insecurity is not only of such tremendous concern to so many, but also how people experience this mainly in the context of groups—families, communities, cultures. Groups have generally been supportive, or are at least potentially so.

Genuine long-term answers require expanding, rather than contracting, options. They require more than just exposing scapegoating and reiterating harmful implications of past and current policies, though both are important. Solutions to migration challenges also require avenues for secure migration, fair adjudication of asylum claims, assurances of family reunification, and inclusion of migrants as creative and crucial players in all decisions that affect them. We can no longer assume or afford to think that the norm is citizen versus foreigner. Not only are such dichotomies increasingly blurred through work, travel, and allegiances that span borders, but democratic ideals also support a modicum of rights of participation to all. Planetary crises only heighten the need to address these issues.

Rights to Move in a Tougher World

One of the toughest challenges testing our ability to dwell together peacefully is migration in response to climate fluctuations. While nothing new, these are now increasing exponentially. Archaeologists have discovered that to escape drought in grasslands, people in today's Middle East long ago migrated to valleys along the Nile, Tigris, and Euphrates rivers where they built early civilizations through organizing dense population settlements and managing scarce resources in a limited space. Anthropologists have also documented contemporary movement of pastoralists and their herds of animals to water sources and grazing lands, not only as part of seasonal routine but increasingly in response to drought. Similarly, in the 1930s there was massive migration out of the US Midwest to escape starvation in a dust bowl generated by prolonged drought coupled with unsustainable agricultural practices (Egan 2006).

There may already be 50 million "climate refugees" by 2010, and a mind-boggling 200 million predicted by 2050, dislocated by changes in monsoon and other rainfall systems, flooding, droughts of unprecedented severity and duration, and rises in sea level (Myers 2005). Conversely, places that are inhospitable to human settlement today might become more resident-friendly in the future. Temperature rises might make parts of the planet more habitable, increase some crop yields, and even bring greater rainfall to some deserts. But even such positive changes in climate would entail population movements.

Scenarios of regional and global climate change, environmental deterioration, availability of food and water, and overall livability have gone from sobering to grim in just a few years. Numerous news reports suggest that the world is seeing its first climate refugees (Battisti and Naylor 2009; Brahic 2009). Environmentally induced mass disruptions are becoming standard fare for the Weather Channel's *Storm Stories* and similar programming that follows devastation and exodus following hurricanes, volcanic explosions, and prolonged droughts. While the scope and pace may be unprecedented, archaeology suggests that valuable lessons can be learned from the past. Abandoned Anasazi, Maya, and Khmer cities reveal that human migration has often followed vagaries in climate, particularly when people have over-extended carrying capacities and neglected stewardship practices.

Anthropogenic impacts on the earth's climate include rising global temperatures, accelerated melting of polar ice and high-altitude glaciers, and further changes in weather patterns. Should sea levels rise even one to two meters, which many scientists consider a very conservative estimate (Dyer 2010; Gillis 2010), huge swaths of coastal zones would be inundated, displacing tens of millions of people on every continent. Faster erosion of beaches, marshes, and mangrove and island barriers is likely, along with saline contamination of freshwater sources.

Rising sea levels are already producing climate refugees in vulnerable coastal areas. By 2009, residents of Tuluun, islands northeast of Papua New Guinea, were forced to move in the wake of waves that washed away homes and left food gardens devastated by saltwater. That same year, the entire government of the Maldives convened underwater, with scuba gear, to alert the world to a desperate situation in which their entire low-lying country is likely to disappear in just a few decades if sea levels continue to rise. Far to the north, Inuit communities along the coast of Alaska are preparing evacuation plans as rising temperatures radically reduce sea ice that once protected their communities in winter and supported migratory patterns of animals on which their subsistence is based.

The flooding in the Indus River basin in mid-2010 was a catastrophe of biblical proportions, affecting 20 million people, and a portent of things to come. At one point, about one-fifth of Pakistan's total land area was under water. One village received in only four days a tenfold increase in their mean annual rainfall. Nearly 2 billion people ultimately depend on the waters of Himalaya glaciers that are melting at alarming rates, some losing as much as eight meters in height per year.

The floods submerged 17 million acres of Pakistan's most fertile farmland, washed away massive amounts of grain, and killed 200,000 livestock. Lost crops included cotton, rice, sugar cane, wheat, and animal feed. Four million Pakistanis were left with food shortages, with the UN World Food Program estimating that, at one point, 70% of Pakistan's population, residing mainly in the countryside, lacked access to proper nutrition. Furthermore, the UN World Health Organization reported that the flooding forced 10 million people to drink unsafe water, a preface to outbreaks of cholera.

Flooding in the immediate future, and desiccation in the longer term, is a scenario playing out elsewhere as well. Hydrologists report that glaciers in the Andes have lost over 20% of their volume since 1970. Some hydrologists project that virtually all of the more than 700 glaciers in the entire range will disappear by mid-century, an alarming portent for the 80 million people and vital global biodiversity that depend on that water supply.

As increasing frequency and intensity of climate disasters exacerbate displacement, associated social conflicts and policy challenges are also unavoidable in what is likely to be unprecedented forced migration in the not-too-distant future (Davison 2007). What is still largely a hidden crisis is unlikely to remain so for long. Darfur, Rwanda, and Palestine are only a sampling of recent human rights tragedies that are in large measure rooted in environmental crises (Klare 2001).

Paradoxically and ironically, the people least responsible for changes in climate and environmental integrity are among the worst victims. A prime example is Bangladesh, which has been called the "ground zero of global warming" (Dyer 2010, 56). Greenhouse gas emissions are among the lowest in the world, with carbon dioxide emissions per capita averaging just 1/30 of the industrial world. Yet low elevation and tropical location, compounded by poverty and the fact that agriculture is the principal source of livelihood, expose the people of Bangladesh to multiple adverse impacts of climate change. Rising sea levels, damage from cyclones during the monsoon season, increasing salinity through intrusion of seawater, and erosion of river levees are already leading to deepening health crises and food insecurity.

A further irony is that environmental declines may have even greater migratory implications stemming from greater conservation efforts. Protected area designations, for example, often displace populations or preclude their use of natural resources, ignoring how human beings, particularly indigenous peoples, have long been part of natural environments (Dowie 2010). Similarly, hundreds of millions are "development refugees"; only war displaces more people than development projects (Cernea 1999).

Although the question of the degree to which climate change is human-instigated is a political one, present shifts occur in a context altogether different than when shorelines changed in earlier times. Long ago, foraging peoples could move easily, whereas the majority of humanity today is urban.

Some of the largest cities are coastal, especially in Asia but also including London, Miami, and Lagos, and it is hard to see where huge numbers of displaced (many who already live in mega-slums) would go even if societies could adjust to faster changes the warmer it gets.

Natural disasters raise questions of social justice and human rights, such as what constitutes a "climate refugee"? Whether people displaced by environmental causes are defined and classified as migrants or refugees is no trivial matter since its definition determines the obligations of the international community in accordance with international law (International Organization for Migration 2008). A case in point is the UN 1951 Convention on Refugees, which limits the definition of "refugees" to persons fleeing political persecution and excludes those fleeing environmental forces. The Convention also limits the definition to those crossing national borders and the right of return after the persecution stops.

There is strong resistance in the international community to expanding the definition of "refugee" to include victims of environmental events. As a result, the definition of a "climate refugee" is the subject of heated debate among human rights lawyers. In the absence of a legal definition, "forced climate migrants"—the term favored by the International Organization for Migration—have no access to basic services, except for those provided by the UN High Commissioner for Refugees (UNHCR), which is already overwhelmed as a global institution. Nor is there a database of information about them. In other words, forced climate migrants fall through the cracks of both immigration and refugee policy. The collective refusal to confront the scale of the problem suggests that forced climate migrants will not be classified as refugees anytime soon.

Current discomfort over terms like "environmental refugee" is exacerbated by worries that legal guarantees or humanitarian provisions may be increasingly unrealistic given migration projections in a no-longer-distant future. Whatever the terminology, however, the probability of greater numbers, wider geographies, and multiple needs is impossible to ignore. We would do well to remember the sentiments expressed by John F. Kennedy in 1962, which can be easily paraphrased to include people forced to move: "Those who make peaceful revolution impossible will make violent revolution inevitable."

The world is no longer locked in a cold war; what looms instead is a very hot war. Potential scenarios include some that are dire and bloody. Eventual trajectories, though, depend as much on cooperation and progress toward equity as they do on science and engineering. All cultures relate examples of human will to survive, even in desperate circumstances.

The diaspora response to disasters in Haiti and Pakistan in 2010 illustrate the tremendous potential within the extensive networks that link people to places and communities to which they maintain ties. Seeing persistence and promise in the movement that is such an essential aspect of humanity can be a powerful ally in our shared work ahead.

Migration as a Human Right

> To consider mobility as morally charged is to acknowledge that the ways in which human mobilities emerge and exist hold consequences that extend beyond the economic or strictly functional.
>
> —Chio (2010, 15)

What a pity the 1948 UN Universal Declaration of Human Rights endorsed the right to leave a country (emigrate), but denied the right to enter a country (immigrate), because human rights constitute one strategy for addressing power inequalities, protecting the poor, and achieving structural change aimed at social justice. It is not only a pity but ironic because the UN declaration supported every person's "right to work, to free choice of employment, to just and favorable conditions of work, and to protection against unemployment" (Cavanagh and Mander 2004). After all, these core rights are the very ones for which migrants struggle, as individuals, in groups, and in large social movements. The struggle for core rights is especially poignant for indigenous peoples who have been displaced from subsistence agriculture, fishing, and other occupations that fall outside the market economy, and whose livelihoods have been destroyed by globalization. Just as food security and water security for all should be treated as basic human rights guaranteed by governments, so should human migration.

Freedom of movement should be a basic human right because migration has been central to the human experience. Today, migration is increasing, often involuntarily and sometimes in a harmful manner, as in the case of forced displacement. Between 1910 and 2000 migration grew almost sixfold, more than half of this increase occurring between 1965 and 2000, during which time 75 million people crossed national borders to settle in the rich countries of Europe and North America. At the same time, there are now 20 million refugees, asylum-seekers, and internally displaced persons, concentrated in countries such as Chad, the Sudan, the Central African Republic, Pakistan, and Afghanistan, to name only a few (Benhabib 2004). Arguing for the right to mobility is not merely adding to the current list of human rights, but honoring that which is already regarded as fundamental, a notion codified in the UN International Convention on Migrants' Rights (Pecoud and de Guchteneire 2007). Indeed, the 2004 UN resolution on migration confirms that migration is beneficial not only to receiving countries but to migrants, their families, and their communities of origin (Nagengast 2009).

What exactly does it mean to propose migration as a human right? First of all, a rights-based approach to the movement of people across state borders provides a dimension of accountability (Nyamu-Musembi 2005). Although civil and political rights are fundamental and form the basis of more popular ideas about human rights in the West, they are not our concern here. Rather, what we emphasize is the achievement of economic and social rights for migrants, ideas articulated in the International Convention on the Protection of the Rights of All Migrant Workers and Their Families, ratified by the UN General Assembly in 1990 and enforced in 2003, which applies to undocumented and documented migrants alike (Martinez 2009a). What are some of the economic and social rights, enumerated in the Convention, to which migrants are entitled? We begin with basic freedoms such as the right to freedom of movement to and from countries of origin (Article 8); the right to life (Article 9); the right to freedom from torture or cruel or inhuman treatment (Article 10); the right to freedom from slavery, servitude or forced labor (Article 11); the right to freedom of thought, expression, conscience, and religion (Articles 12 and 13); the right to privacy (Article 14); and the right to property (Article 15) (Migrants Rights International 1990).

We continue with economic rights such as the right to be treated as equals of nationals in terms of wages and other conditions of work such as overtime, holidays, and so on (Article 25); the right to join any trade union freely (Article 26); the right to be treated as equals of nationals in terms of social security benefits, within limits of the law (Article 27); the right to transfer earnings and savings when their stay in the state of employment has ended (Article 32). Equally important are social rights such as the right to information of their rights within the Convention, the conditions of their admission, and their rights and duties in the state of origin, state of employment, or state of transit (Article 33); the right to emergency medical care (Article 28); the right of the family and children of migrant workers to have access to education (Article 30), to a name, registration of birth, and nationality (Article 29), and to preserve cultural identity (Article 31) (Migrants Rights International 1990).

There is no question that rights of due process are absolutely indispensable: the right to fair and public hearings with guarantees of due process

(Articles 16–20); the right to legal assistance, interpreters, and information in a language that can be understood (Article 16); the right to freedom from arbitrary arrest and detention (Article 16); the right to be presumed innocent until proven guilty (Article 19); the right to freedom from group expulsion (Article 22); the right to diplomatic or consular assistance and protection (Article 23); the right to be recognized everywhere as a person before the law (Article 24); and the right to be treated as equals of nationals in courts and tribunals (Article 18) (Migrants Rights International 1990). The United States and other migrant-receiving countries in the Northern Hemisphere have rejected the ICMW convention, although it has been ratified by Mexico and 34 other migrant-sending countries (Nagengast 2009).

In other words, what we mean by migration as a human right is reforming immigration policy so that it would protect and expand the rights of all workers. One way to do this is to uncouple employment from immigration status. Unless all workers are treated equally under the law, regardless of immigration status, the greater power of employers will always allow them the freedom to exploit and abuse the vulnerable. We can no longer allow the basic needs of the poor and the working poor to be shaped by the whims of market forces, capricious financial investments, punitive privatization, and the restructuring of economic policy (Falk 1999). Nor can we continue to deprive people of basic human rights because their knowledge and skills are arbitrarily assigned a low market value. The struggle for the rights of migrants remains an uphill battle because far too many native-born people in destination countries believe that migrants are not deserving of any rights at all.

Furthermore, there is a fundamental contradiction between claims to border control based on *state* sovereignty and the practice of *universal* human rights. Simply put, there is a tension between universalism and particularism, which poses an ethical dilemma for liberal democracies professing a commitment to both principles (Benhabib 2004). However, if aspirations to a higher moral order are to be achieved, this contradiction must be resolved. This ethical dilemma is precisely why a focus on economic and social rights is imperative, because the ability of organized labor to contest the power of the business and financial sectors in their manipulation of party politics has been undermined by globalization and its side effects, such as transformations in the nature of work (Falk 1999).

Worldwide, poverty levels are skyrocketing while job opportunities are plummeting, leaving millions with no choice but to migrate. This situation makes the emphasis on rights more urgent than ever: legislators, policymakers, pundits, and the general public need to be reminded that migrants have rights, whether the migrants are authorized or undocumented. In fact, entering and residing in a country without authorization is a violation of civil immigration laws, not a criminal offense (Martinez 2009). Given this fact, the immigration issue needs to be reframed as acts of collective civil disobedience, instead of as crimes (Ansley 2005).

Rethinking Citizenship and Belonging

Globalization has reconfigured the institution of citizenship, the emblem of the nation-state, but in so doing has produced a crisis of citizenship. First, there is no blueprint for a legal status that is detached from a nation-state, so decoupling citizenship from the nation-state is out of the question at this time. Nor is there a blueprint for "postnational," "transnational," or "global" citizenship except for the informal "postnational" citizenship enjoyed only by the global elite (Bosniak 2001). Second, the nation-state has been weakened by the global economy, the globalization of arms, globalization of communications technology, transnational cultural networks, and the rise of substate political actors (Benhabib 2004). Simply put, political globalization has lagged behind economic globalization. It seems ironic, however, that nation-states do not seem too worried about losing economic sovereignty to the global marketplace (Falk 1999).

More importantly, citizenship is not a unitary concept and has many meanings and dimensions, including but not limited to legal status, political participation, cultural identity, and entitlement to rights. We know that civil and political rights are more or less impossible without economic, social, and cultural rights and that such rights are interdependent and indivisible (Castles and Davidson 2000). This highlights the logical contradiction between political equality and the absence of economic and social equality (Kabeer 2005; Kivisto and Faist 2007).

In other words, the reason that formal types of citizenship have not delivered on their promises is because of the fundamental contradiction between territorial sovereignty and universal human rights. On the one hand, border control is synonymous with exclusion, which violates a fundamental principle of liberal democracies: that all members of society should be included as citizens. On the other hand, human rights implies practices of inclusion. One way out of this morass is the idea of global justice, which, if it is to be more than a political slogan, requires us to imagine more democratic, inclusive forms of citizenship that allow people to claim not only their civic and political rights but their economic and social rights.

From the perspective of the excluded, civil and political rights—without the economic, social, and cultural rights that give substance to them—are merely empty promises. Sadly, there is still a difference between "state citizenship" (legal) and "democratic citizenship" (Reed-Danahay and Brettell 2008). Moreover, the quest for "substantive citizenship" still requires a struggle to redefine and expand the meanings of citizenship and its rights and duties. In addition, new strategies of citizenship must match the flexibility, fluidity, and mobility of global capital (Ong 1999).

What might substantive citizenship look like? For some, it is a constitutional right to basic food, land, shelter, health care, and education. For others, it is recognition of what Hannah Arendt (1986) calls "the right to have rights." This is the right to be recognized as whole persons, the right to be different, and most of all, the right to dignity and respect (Kabeer 2005). For yet others, it is the ability to exercise some control over their lives and to be free from the tyranny of absolute power. It is also the right to act in solidarity with others in the quest for justice.

Because the idea of justice lies at the heart of the liberal democratic concept of citizenship, substantive citizenship would need to resemble what Seyla Benhabib (2004) calls "just membership." This would entail the admission of refugees and asylum-seekers; porous borders for immigrants, no "denaturalization" (loss of citizenship rights), the "right to have rights" and "to be legal" (entitled to inalienable rights regardless of citizenship), and the right to citizenship for aliens who have fulfilled certain conditions. More rights could easily be added to Benhabib's list: the right of labor to the same freedom of mobility enjoyed by capital and the right to protection from global market forces; the right of indigenous peoples to their ancestral knowledge; the right of humankind to unpolluted environments, and so on. To negotiate their rightful place in new host societies, immigrants must invent new models of citizenship and imagine new human rights claims that match the character of the new global economy. Such changes will require collective struggles of the excluded groups or "citizenship from below."

What might citizenship from below look like? One example is the successful reform of Tennessee state law, a battle won by undocumented Latin American immigrants. Despite their "illegal" status, they acquired state-issued driver's licenses in the US South, where a car is necessary to accomplish the simplest daily tasks such as getting to and from work. They engaged "communities of practice" (Reed-Danahay and Brettell 2008, 21) and "informal practices of citizenship," such as engineering the migration of low-wage workers from Latin America into a multigenerational critical mass. They also converted unlikely bedfellows into patrons and allies in the struggle—for instance, communities of native-born and naturalized Latinos and Latinas, church groups, labor unions, civil rights organizations, agribusiness, chambers of commerce, police chiefs, and the Tennessee Republican Party. They then built social, economic, and cultural networks to enhance economic and social capital and also mobilized collaborations that anchored them strongly to their local communities. Most of all, they framed the issue as one of highway safety, rather than immigrant rights, which appealed to the self-interests of US citizens (Ansley 2005).

In the absence of formal legal rights, the excluded must claim substantive citizenship through strategies of positioning, control, maneuver, and social agency rather than through formal law. In other words, strategies of citizenship must match the flexibility, fluidity, and mobility of global capitalism by emphasizing the art of flexibility. For instance, the *New York Times* reported a rally in Milan, Italy, designed to draw attention to the contributions made by foreign workers to the Italian economy and to organize a nationwide strike urging workers to stay home and boycott shopping for one day (Povoledo 2010). A similar boycott called "A Day Without Immigrants" took place in the United States in 2006, demanding full rights for immigrants. The rally in Milan had been initiated in France, inspired by protests in other European countries and supported in Spain and Greece. Studies have documented immigrant labor becoming indispensable to the Italian economy, especially in the construction industry. In addition, the Bank of Italy reported that foreign residents contributed about 4.5 billion Euros in personal income tax (3% of revenue) and slightly less than 10 billion Euros toward social security (5% of revenue) (Povoledo 2010). Nevertheless, there was a rising tide of xenophobia, particularly among young people between ages 18 and 29, nearly 50% of whom express anti-immigrant hostility (Povoledo 2010).

Although a radical idea, we are advocating freedom of movement for people across international borders equal to that of global capital. This is a radical notion because it would contest the nation-state's divine right to sustain the contradiction of allowing the free flow of capital, goods, information, and services while prohibiting the free flow of people. In fact, open borders would go a long way toward compensating people for government policies that not only glorify the free market but bring tremendous suffering in their wake. Besides, the main benefit of border enforcement is that it allows nation-states to practice what Aihwa Ong (1999) calls "zones of graduated sovereignty." In the evolving relationship between global capitalism and nation-states, governments have retained little sovereignty except for control over their people. By creating different treatment zones, each segment of the population is administered differently by the government: the power elite are embraced warmly while the laboring classes are subjected to technologies of punishment. However, such strategies of discipline are counterproductive in that they are neither sustainable (they contain the seeds of their own destruction) nor smart, given the benefits of migration documented by research.

Open Borders, Anyone?

Let us consider what the world might look like if it became borderless. It is worth recalling that open borders have existed both before and after the emergence of the nation-state. For instance, before 1962, people from the former British Empire were allowed to migrate freely to the United Kingdom (Pecoud and de Guchteneire 2007). The past existence of open borders also suggests that they may offer opportunities and benefits, if we consider migration policies in the long term rather than as knee-jerk reactions to current migration flows. Not only does keeping immigrants out contradict the core values and principles of freedom on which democratic societies rest, embracing immigrants would, in the long run, bring dividends such as new communities based on the values of openness and social justice.

The fear that open borders would open the migration floodgates seems groundless. Open borders might inspire some to move, but a migration tsunami seems unlikely, given that not everyone in sending countries is longing to leave, despite the popular myth. Open borders would also reduce underground economies and enhance contributions to the tax base of governments at all levels by both employers and immigrants. Thus far, policing migrants has failed to stop border crossing, in spite of spending huge sums of money. Instead of arming their borders with sophisticated technologies, raiding immigrant workplaces, depriving immigrants of medical care and schooling, conscripting airlines to serve as border agents, and ultimately detaining and deporting immigrants, nation-states would be better off welcoming those whose labor sustains their economies.

Besides, the right to mobility may not be as utopian as it might seem and has a moral basis. In a globalized and unequal world, the right to free choice of employment (Article 23) and the right to an adequate standard of living (Article 25) cannot be achieved today without moving between countries (Harris 2002). In a world of flows, the right to move is a resource to which all human beings should have access. The denial of the right to work and the right to move to where jobs can be found is directly linked to the perpetuation of poverty (Harris 2002, 119). In an unequal world, migration is an attempt to level the playing field, to allow people to go where the money is and to send remittances where they are needed. Simply put, migration is intended to reduce inequalities between countries.

However, some migration scholars oppose open borders on the following grounds (Castles 2007, 50). First, freedom of movement already exists for the highly skilled, allowing the industrialized world to siphon off the human capital of the underdeveloped world. Second, labor markets in the developed world could not absorb all of the unemployed and underemployed of the underdeveloped world. Third, it would lower wages for low-skill local labor, exacerbating competition and conflict between immigrants and the local workforce, and thereby encouraging racism and violence. In addition, balancing wages would be at very low levels, lowering the standard of living for locals in the destination country. Lastly, open borders would erase the distinction between refugees and migrants, depriving millions of protection from human rights abuses (Castles 2007, 50).

Nevertheless, policies and practices that allow capital, goods, technology, information, services, and culture to roam freely across the planet while placing strict limits on the movement of people are not only contradictory and paradoxical, they fail to recognize the link between inequality, poverty, and international migration. Policies and practices aimed at reducing inequality and poverty would go a long way toward relieving pressures to migrate at their source and provide alternatives to migration. In fact, some argue that relaxing restrictions, even a tiny bit, on the movement of labor could produce dramatic leaps in economic development in poor countries. They further argue that freedom of movement could increase not only equality but GDP worldwide (Pecoud and de Guchteneire 2007, 12).

Affirming Movement as Inherent

Despite the ubiquity of human movement today and in the past, international accords on the right to move are indeterminate with respect to settling outside one's country. The Universal Declaration of Human Rights both reflects and reifies nation-states, so not surprisingly it gives voice to individual rights to leave and return to a country. Less clearly articulated are rights to be taken in somewhere else, or who holds responsibility for adjustments and costs. A further difficulty arises because identity is as mutable as it is fundamental, whereas nationality is relatively recent and frequently also arbitrary.

One avenue for resolution rests on the basis of social reality. Justice-based claims for the right to settle, just as for legalization, have a strong basis in history. As a prime example, decades of demanding and encouraging migration into the United States set in motion a chain of social and economic consequences: growing families, loyalties to new communities, and patterns of economic and cultural links across borders, to name a few. That history, most strongly visible in the Mexican labor force and the growth of the Mexican and Latino population, generates a chain of obligations that are both real and abstract. While some might argue that Mexico is unique, given the convergence of geography and economic linkages to the United States, similar situations exist worldwide.

Injustice can rarely be simply legislated, much less eliminated. Instead, policy grounded in ethical as well as political and utilitarian calculations seems most promising (Blake and Risse 2006; Risse 2008). Just as personal experience can heighten a sense of shared interest and even affection, there is considerable potential for workplace citizenship, a kind of piggybacking on rights of citizens, which demonstrates that migrants serve economic and societal interests.

Earth's changing climate magnifies the imperative for engaging and resolving these critical issues. Humanity simply cannot ignore much longer the pernicious implications of the current conundrum: that whereas governance is organized nationally, the nature of the gravest world dilemmas is transnational.

Can effective domestic and international legal frameworks for determining responsibilities and obligations, rights to move, and compensation be developed effectively and quickly enough? What moral system will emerge to inform policies? How rooted will they be in historical and anthropological realities? How humane? Answers to those questions lie at the very core of our future.

9

No Place Like Home

A man's homeland is wherever he prospers.
—Aristophanes

Sense of place is fundamental to all human beings. As organisms, people are part of ecosystems; like all animals, we seek continuity and security through having food, shelter, companionship, and suitable settings for nurturing young. We develop deep attachment to the places we call home and to those with whom we share it, beginning with places of birth and growth. Sense of belonging deepens through the myriad ways we connect to home and each other—work, raising children, and vulnerabilities to resource crises. This is the basis of shared culture or cultural place. So it is little surprise that people today, as in the past, often have little desire to leave home or homeland, or that many return after being away (Long and Oxfeld 2004). Nor is it remarkable that moving from one place to another is seen as disruptive, sometimes excruciatingly so, especially when the move is involuntary or made under duress.

The permanence of what we now term as "globalization" remains to be seen, but clearly ours is an age of migration. For many, home and culture are increasingly convoluted through unprecedented movement, or mobilities. Global travel, instantaneous transactions of 1.5 billion email users, and 2 million ATMs worldwide are among the most prominent manifestations. Vast extensions, intensities, and abundance exist alongside disruptions unleashed by global shifts in control of wealth that determine life chances. For hundreds of millions today, home is a street, often many streets.

Set in motion by determination and usually also in part by powerful factors beyond their control, people pursue established routes and network connections whenever they can. They move near or far, often or occasionally. Maya migrants seek work in Guatemala City and Cancún, or seek providence in Providence, while Mixteco and Trique families along the entire Pacific coast of Mexico and the United States challenge our notions of where Oaxaca begins or ends (Foxen 2007; Holo 2004). Kin and cultural bonds buffer and shape all phases of migration, contributing to people's safety and success. Destinations become home, shared destinies, new communities.

Where people belong is central to governance as well as citizenship. Identity and affiliation comprise many aspects, however. Policies based solely on nationality are inadequate, then, including border practices geared solely to keeping people out. Broader understanding recognizes rights deemed to be universal, both in common understanding and in international declarations. These are not synonymous with rights nested in the nation-state or available to citizens alone. People have inalienable rights by virtue of being human—primarily the right to exist, to be, to belong. Neither does citizenship accorded by nation-states automatically encompass all who provide benefits through efforts and labor. Clearly, many people without national citizenship contribute to places where they go or live, as well as to communities and countries of origin.

Effective response to what has become a kind of "globalization of immigrant hostility" requires challenging the exclusivity that nation-states have come to claim in the according of rights. The condition of lacking documents can be a huge barrier to feeling secure or having access to things like education and freedom of expression. Surely the fact of being human holds as much validity as a basis for citizenship as membership in a particular nation-state (Brysk and Shafir 2004). This is increasingly acknowledged through speaking of global community and global citizenship. Further economic and environmental turmoil promises to make citizenship questions ever more problematic. The numbers of stateless people, for example, are projected to explode as migratory flows extend wider and longer in the years to come (Berkeley 2009).

The complex and malleable nature of human relations requires reflection, however much headlines may generate a sense of immediacy and emergency. The humanitarian and economic nature of security and humane governance must not be sacrificed by increasingly militarized or privatized security "solutions," seminal events like September 11, 2001, notwithstanding. Genuine security—human security—implies a far different paradigm from securitization. For the United States securitization model is projected through more than 560 US military bases worldwide and is premised on military spending that today equals nearly all other countries combined, complete with bankrupting expenditures under Democrat and Republican administrations alike (Bacevich 2010). As a country becomes a homeland and as cultures become marginalized through exaggerated preparedness for perceived and imagined threats, a strong counterbalance of diversity and morality becomes all the more critical.

Human security envisions safety in a collective and a long-term perspective, and in meeting needs predictably and equitably. It would incorporate principled approaches to business, along with labor and other human rights and environmental priorities (Stiglitz 2010; United Nations Global Compact 2011). It would mean investing in diplomacy that precludes costly wars, protecting people through health care and community development, and providing educational opportunities as broadly as possible. Finally, it would give emphasis to incorporating people into the system rather than to time since their arrival.

Seen in terms of human security, migration is both a human characteristic and a human right. Debate, blurring, and transformation will continue to characterize migration as much as they define modernity. Many journeys, yet also one. Seeing commonalities in trends and embracing possibilities within human migration are keys to helping shape the emerging world.

Governance in a More Humane World

Humane governance is essential to humane migration and must rest on two important principles, the most important of which is the need to control global market forces (Falk 1999). The second principle is to oppose forms of extremism based on mass violence. Reining in economic globalization is imperative because many governments have abdicated their responsibility to the well-being of their people, slashing life-supporting services such as health care and education, among others. Governments have chosen, instead, a headlong pursuit of global capitalism. The operating principles of this capital-driven, deterritorialized world order are determined by the ideas and practices of bankers, currency traders, and corporate chiefs, in collaboration with international financial institutions such as the unholy trinity of the World Bank, the IMF, and the WTO. Today, only 48% of economic entities on the planet are those of nation-states, 52% are corporations

(Cavanagh and Mander 2004). Even the most powerful nation-states seem incapable of opposing corporate ground rules, which often violate market principles. Today, presidents and prime ministers tend to wait for appointments with CEOs at world meetings in Davos or Dubai, rather than the other way around.

Corporations have come to rule the world (Korten 2001; Robbins 2011), through a combination of market power, campaign contributions, advertising, and public relations that help "manufacture consent." Simply put, corporations dictate the rules of trade, finance, and investment that govern the lives of people on this planet. If corporate rule persists, governments will exist only to sustain corporate power, to keep workers docile, and to make them perpetual consumers. Such a world is not sustainable. The unsustainability and inequities that accompany corporate rule appear to be as detrimental to people today as the monarchy was to peasants (Cavanagh and Mander 2004). We must find ways to make governments less obedient to the dictates of financial engineers and more dedicated to protecting their people, particularly the poor and the working class.

To heal our dysfunctional world order, spotlighting and dismantling the unhealthy alliance between governments and corporations should be the first task of any system of humane governance. National governments must assert their sovereignty and resist corporate interference with the political process (Falk 1999). Corporations are notorious for subverting governmental power by replacing democratic political processes with ones that serve corporate interests. For instance, the Halliburton Corporation was awarded more contracts by the US government than any other company for the "reconstruction" of Iraq, when former CEO Dick Cheney served as vice president of the United States. Rewriting laws to suit corporate interests is another way to subvert democracy. A prominent example is the US Supreme Court ruling in 2010 that corporations are equivalent to persons under the law, enabling them to donate unlimited sums of money to reshape public policies in many domains. Furthermore, many existing laws already permit corporations to victimize ordinary people.

The recent global economic meltdown provides us with the perfect opportunity to recall the social contract that binds governments to their people and to rethink policies of all kinds, including migration policies. For example, governments would do well to reassess and renegotiate trade agreements such as NAFTA that not only swelled the bank accounts of corporations but succeeded in transforming millions of Mexican nationals into undocumented immigrants in the United States. Therefore, instead of feeding the juggernaut that transnational corporations have become and their practices of absentee ownership, governments should support human-scaled, locally owned enterprises that still exist in many parts of the world and help them to defy globalization. Government policies should also encourage businesses to be rooted in a place and to discourage them from globetrotting. They should also encourage business practices that are transparent and account-able to all stakeholders, particularly to communities that will feel the sting of decisions made in faraway places.

Humane governance demands human agency which, in turn, is fun-damental to humane migration. People across the planet must rise up to demand their rights as human beings. In nonviolent ways, they must also oppose forms of extremism based on mass violence, the second principle of humane governance. They must form and consolidate a worldwide com-mitment to the global common good, to press for peace, human rights, and environmental preservation. Powerful transnational social movements, grassroots globalism, immersion in the global public domain, and a strong global civil society must emerge for cooperative action at the global level. At the very least, popular myths and deceptions, particularly those about immigrants, must be exposed for the fallacies that they are.

The Internet can serve as an instrument of hope for developing this "grass-roots info-power" (Falk 1999). The Internet is multifaceted in char-acter and can be used for both good and evil. For instance, there are at least as many blogs promoting hate and racism as there are blogs denouncing them. However, for the past 25 years, the Internet has revealed a democratic face and demonstrated a strong potential for electronic empowerment. On many occasions, electronic communities have succeeded in rallying support for projects on human rights and environmental protection. They have also provided counterpoint to the deceptive information of the business world and the corporate media. The important goal, however, is to keep the Inter-net focused on democratic principles so as to design a people-driven politics, the most dramatic and optimistic examples being the Arab Spring rebellions against oppression by dictators in Tunisia and Egypt in the spring of 2011.

Above all, humane governance must resist the temptation to dismiss law and morality as obstacles to capital flight and market operations (Falk 1999). Humane governance must also embrace human values that cannot be quantified—for example, by reducing the human suffering caused by de-structive patterns of production and consumption; building communities that extend beyond the boardrooms of transnational corporations and banks; building communities that respect the economic and social rights of all members; abolishing violence both at home and abroad; and last but not least, promoting economic, political, social and environmental practices that are sustainable.

In the final analysis, a humane world order must strike a balance between the well-being of its people and the success of markets by perfecting humane governance. However, humane governance requires a sea change in nation-state consciousness. Just as the market model subordinates the parts to the whole, thereby creating a borderless financial system, humane governance must emphasize the whole above the parts, subordinating the nation-state to the planet, thereby creating a borderless and seamless architecture of governance.

Challenges of Diversity

> Those French, they have a different word for everything.
> —Steve Martin

Recognizing that diversity and complexity are normative is essential for better understanding the potentialities inherent in a world in flux. Cartesian thought influences Western cultures to treat reality in terms of oppositions or dichotomies. Much is precluded by use of simplistic conceptions like legal versus illegal, people who belong versus those who do not, voluntary versus involuntary migrants. Categorizing people into two sides can even result in a bifurcated society, with diminished possibilities for negotiation or accord between the two groups. Similarly, a border like that between the United States and Mexico comes to be seen as one that not only divides neatly but also requires ever more militarization, even though it has been relatively functional and peaceful for most of its history. In truth, human qualities, social relationships, and accurate diagnoses are far more complex. So, too, are the conditions for full participation.

Philosophers, researchers, and therapists alike realize that cultivating the right perspective is vital for making problem-solving easier. Reducing the immigration issue to cost-benefit assessments and binary choices severely limits beneficial solutions. Instead, agreement on immigration reform requires widening the terms of debate, substantive dialogue, and opening space for those who are frequently left out: immigrants themselves.

New mixes hold great promise for dynamic arrangements and approaches for resolving vexing predicaments. From evidence of "hybrid vigor" in evolution, to the success of Ben and Jerry's plethora of flavors (Page 2007), we can intuit the value of innovative pairings and new understandings. Yet, despite the strengths that emanate from ethnic and cultural diversity, demographic and social trends also produce changes that may be unsettling, or come to be perceived as culture clashes. Greater diversity found in larger communities, in fact, may lead to distrust, less involvement in community projects, and lower expectations of being able to make a difference. As Putnam (2007, 151) concludes from his survey of forty-one US communities, "Diversity, at least in the short run, seems to bring out the turtle in all of us."

This diversity paradox suggests that while tolerance is necessary, it is just a first step. Opportunities for meaningful interaction across lines of ethnicity and origin are essential. In schools, on playgrounds, or through planting gardens together, we not only reinvest in the places we share, we become comfortable with, and even more eager for, diversity. So while immigration policy is largely dictated at the national level, bridging differences and building social capital is local. The simple recipe to "add diversity and stir" (as typically occurs in migration situations) is neither risk-free nor advisable. Focused efforts that encourage people from separate origins to see each other as valued members of a shared group, with shared or syncretistic identity, do much to reduce isolation and separateness without undermining the importance of people's ethnic identities.

Predictable as well as unforeseen benefits have come, and will continue to come, through responses that are holistic, participatory or multilateral, and generative of knowledge and common good. Consensus—or at least a modicum of agreement—about movements of people across the globe is also crucial because escalation of enforcement regimes will almost certainly lead to human suffering and greater turmoil of disagreement. Assessing migration as a significant, but not solitary, dimension of world transformations helps us to see how it entails uneasy tensions and adjustments, but also possibilities for new senses of community and belonging.

New identities have been the focus of debate throughout human history, and especially during the last half-century as world empires dissipated, with new and not-so-new configurations emerging in our age of global migration. Identity will always remain a central concern, all the more amid rapid changes and their implications for social membership and responsibility for others, as well as for order. While excluding is hardly new, neither are longing, cultural and rights claims, and bonds and relationships formed across former divides. Languages, technology, symbols, and cultural markers are no more immobile than people. Contemporary reconceptualizations of inclusion, rooted in historically valued concepts like hospitality and respect, are fundamental to the ethics required in the new millennium.

Far from being an outdated concept or threat, multiculturalism affirms the value of people from diverse backgrounds. Certainly, policies designed to respond to claims and needs of constituent groups must take into account potential inequalities within those groups (Okin 1999). But as arguments over clothing in Europe suggests, it is not a simple matter to say it is oppressive to wear a head scarf, but liberating to wear a miniskirt (Al-Hibri 1999). People on the move—whether recent and older, richer or poorer— are, by and large, talented and motivated, and an inherent part of today's world. Many families, communities, and countries confirm that multiculturalism is a normal human experience. Immigration policy should as well.

A Brave New, Socially Integrated World

Interpersonal relationships are no doubt the greatest, and the most frequently overlooked, resources on which to build effective policy regarding newcomers. The power of relationships is evident even in neurobiology, which reveals literal shaping of brains as humans engage in relationships. We are, in effect, hardwired to connect. Empathic potential is inborn, learning is overwhelmingly through social interaction, and relationships are central to healthy growth and well-being. With psychosocial well-being at stake, the ability not only to adapt to but also to incorporate with others is vital. Mutuality becomes a fundamental challenge for groups of all sizes, whether spouses and partners, or communities and countries. Exclusion and isolation, on the other hand, rarely provide possibilities for engagement of the sort that encourage confident, effective social integration. Evidence is considerable that separation breeds mistrust, and in turn discrimination and conflict (LeVine and Campbell 1972).

Growing personal connections with people of different backgrounds and recognition of commonalities in their own histories provide grounds for greater inclusion. Interfaith and cross-ethnic dialogues are catalysts for working together on issues as big and as complex as immigration. Dignity calls for this, but economics and demographics determine it as well. Seeing beyond rhetoric and political calculations, concerned people everywhere can listen to current as well as historical accounts of immigration in every country. They can also acknowledge failings in current policies. While exploitation and injustice are fixtures of the history of the United States and much of the world, so too are periods when community values and social good have been affirmed.

The irony, of course, is that just as people have voted with their feet through migration, they are also fostering interchange and interdependence through social behavior. Pluralism is increasing almost everywhere as a result of intermarriage. Mixed Latin American families have become so common in places like Los Angeles and Phoenix that new names have been coined, like "*Guatemexicoestadounidenses,*" or "Guatemexiamericans," to describe their children. Youth everywhere appear far less likely to see ethnic differences as obstacles, something clearly evident in the mosaic that has come to characterize fashion and diverse student composition on many campuses.

Racial categories and quotas have, of course, rarely been successful because of the mixing that inevitably occurs. For example, firm distinctions made by the Spanish early in their colonization of the Americas (including separation into Spanish-born, those born in the colonies, Indians, and Africans) quickly morphed into a lengthening list of blended categories, before the untenable racial hierarchy collapsed and gave way to demographic reality. What emerged is a hybrid of hundreds of millions of people, collectively called *mestizo* or *criollo*. What Mexican philosopher José Vasconcelos termed "*la raza cósmica,*" the cosmic race, very much applies to today's world.

Integration has a long history of use in migration research, reflecting how sustained interaction and sense of connectedness between and among newcomers and longer-established residents remains a perpetual challenge. Integration also became a familiar phrase during the campaign for civil rights in the United States, since it implies collective effort both to facilitate transition into society of people hitherto excluded and to mitigate negative impacts of that exclusion. By the 1980s, "diversity" had become the operative term. This was a logical result of deepening appreciation of how inclusion did not mean negating disparate origins, viewpoints, and social patterns.

Migration research confirms that most immigrants adapt to and quickly adopt the values and norms of new settings. Aspirations and achievement usually build on, rather than replace, learning and behaviors grounded in one's origins. Transnational research and longitudinal attention to emerging generations have also demonstrated how educational and employment opportunities strongly determine life chances and, in turn, the likelihood that either integration or social fragmentation will characterize descendants of immigrants (Portes and Rumbaut 2001; Rumbaut and Portes 2001; Suárez-Orozco and Suárez-Orozco 2001).

New realities do challenge assumptions that integration necessarily unfolds as an inevitable result of interaction and mutual change. Assimilation or acculturation are not always perceived as advantageous or a mutual goal. Furthermore, compared with earlier eras, migrants today may come from any region of the world, and they often move with unprecedented frequency and speed. In some countries, communities, and neighborhoods, residents born elsewhere are no longer the exception, but instead have become numerous and customary participants in social and economic life. Those who have experienced forced displacement or persecution encounter even greater challenges for successfully fitting in or settlement.

The prominent place of community studies in anthropology points to the fundamental role that relatively small groupings play in human development and interpersonal relations. In community we find ourselves developing a sense of identity as well as belonging. Cohesiveness helps ensure survival (Wilson 1978), as well as sense of shared consciousness. History and social science both suggest that social cohesion can be strained by group diversity, whether linguistic, cultural, or in appearance. Nonetheless, in contrast to the absolutism of some politicians, like racial-purity proponents before them, we also know that diverse settings (such as modern cities, borders, and many campuses) are also places for some of the most vibrant interchange. It is therefore critical to know which practices facilitate and which inhibit social cohesion, and possibilities for bridging differences and forging optimal approaches for present and future generations.

Shared traditions and rituals, activities within social and religious institutions, and cooperative community projects represent occasions for interaction that encourage recognition of affinity and in turn greater commitment to each other. Case studies also reveal that programs that facilitate host language acquisition, vocational preparedness, and good health are among the most promising practices for immigrant integration, in the United States (Godziak and Martin 2005) and elsewhere (Reed-Danahay and Brettell 2008; Segal, Elliott, and Mayadas 2010). Demography and histories certainly affect formulation and efficacy of policies. Concentrations of immigrants and uneven geography can have major implications for services and programs that enhance integration. In the end, though, broad commitment encourages overall success, as does the extent to which inclusive norms are favorably perceived and cosmopolitan identities created or reinvented, whether through trial and error or with insight.

Immigration thus takes on deeper significance than accorded by most contemporary discourse. The dream of a vibrant society, of multiple hues and views coming together to build a better future, has never been more critical—and more threatened. Today little is more tragic than unfulfilled prospects of integration. Anger in the face of a diminishing sense of security and ability to make a difference can easily be magnified and misdirected into concern about threats posed by outsiders. Environmental decline and alarmist headlines about terrorism generate still further fragmentation and pessimism, deepening divisions rather than unity. Retrenchment into idealized homogeneity is likely to continue until deglobalization and inclusion efforts become more visible and acceptable. A healthier future, moreover, will be grounded in freedom to move, between places and across new understandings and viewpoints.

Next Generations: Our Greatest Resource

It is said that children are the future, and that the true measure of a society is how it treats its most vulnerable members. Contrary to common wisdom, however, the realities faced by many children are often sobering. In the United States, as in most of the world, children tend to be among the poorest sectors of a community, and also the most likely to experience various disruptions in their lives. These frequently mean moving. So, it not surprising that children comprise a large proportion of people on the move—whether refugees, homeless families, or communities rent apart by loss of viable livelihoods. Sometimes youth comprise the majority or even entirety of disrupted populations, such as the "lost boys of Sudan" (Deng, Alephonsion, and Ajak 2005), or young people riding the rails north through Mexico to find their parents (Cammisa 2009), and others forced to leave communities devastated by global economic demands. They are also affected greatly when parents and close family members migrate, particularly as they experience abandonment or loss of moral guidance (Nazario 2006; Dreby 2010).

Children of immigrants are also the fastest-growing sector in many countries. This includes the United States, where 20% of children live in households in which at least one parent migrated from another country (Suárez-Orozco and Suárez-Orozco 2001). Among Latinos, 36% are under the age of 18. Educational attainment and other measures of "success" vary widely depending on ethnic and social class origins and other characteristics, including funding and language use in schools. Youth adjustment, identity formation, and family communication patterns are shaped by the stresses of migration, changes in family composition, and shifts in gender and generation roles (Orellana 2009; Rumbaut and Portes 2001; Estrada and Loucky 2006).

The effects of persistent poverty, which many immigrants—and therefore also many children, experience—include significant risks for health, graduation rates, and stable employment. A study following 380 infants from infancy into their third year reveals that undocumented parents avoid valuable resources, including programs and agencies that provide food subsidies and child care, out of fears relating to their legal status. Some 4 million preschool-age children of immigrants are US citizens, and delays in cognitive development, and potential school and job prospects, are ominous (Yoshikawa 2011). Isolation and poor working conditions further compound the problem. Clearly, the price of ignoring this reality is serious decline in the future contributions of maturing children.

Ultimately the future of youth and potential contributions they may make to society are strongly determined by the degree to which community resources and national policies include them. Such understanding is reflected in court decisions granting access to public education to children, regardless of immigration status. This includes a decision by the California Supreme Court, in November 2010, that all students are eligible for in-state tuition rates at public colleges and universities in a state where Latinos now make up more than half of all students in public schools. These are critical issues, however much they may be avoided amid the alarm that circulates about borders and security.

Further crisis looms in the form of worldwide demographic trends. Ninety percent of population growth is occurring in developing countries, while industrialized and postindustrialized regions are experiencing some of the lowest reproductive levels ever known. The aging population of countries such as Italy, with a fertility rate below 1%, would be even more calamitous were it not for immigrants, whose younger age and higher fertility represent crucial productivity and progeny for the future. Production and reproduction are both matters of common concern. Investing in good education, health, and experiences to plan and work together are as essential for long-term prognoses in the United States as they are for humanity as a whole.

Borders of Mind and Body Politic

In contrast to social boundaries, whose universality gives them a transcendental quality, state borders are complex creations of equivocal, even perverse character. Neither inevitable nor often very logical, they require assertion to have meaning. Existing through enforcement as well as image management, they are the most visible arena against which are counterposed people on the move. Their function goes beyond physical movement alone; they also have the capacity to limit or delimit possibility, aspirations, even intellect. This makes it even more important to think beyond territoriality as immutable.

An alternative conceptualization of borders is essential, particularly in light of contemporary global trends in which a world of "flows" is overlaying, if not replacing, one of fixed places (Agnew 2008). Witness how globalized forms of economic organization have expanded, including the near-detachment of capital from allegiance to nationality. At the same time, the ability of states to regulate groups is diminishing. Identification and loyalty associated with social group, including shared cultural values and religious beliefs, have persisted long before nation-states, and will persist beyond as well.

If territories and flows must coexist, the challenge ahead is monumental. It is both practical and ethical. As the world changes, configurations or borders and the ethos of institutions that determine them also change. So, too, does the fate of human dignity and posterity. Borders, like movement, can enhance and not just restrict life and liberty. A borderless world may not be practical, and is certainly not inevitable, but the sense of bordering as an edging together points a way forward. Blurring of borders, far more than hardening them, offers the best chance for mobilizing the full potential of a collective human intellect, built on shared well-being rather than a privileging of occupancy, territoriality, and competition.

The case for (more) open borders should not be too readily dismissed. Ethical and humanitarian contentions for open borders are solidly rooted in recognition that all human beings are equally free and moral persons. While this may sound idealistic in the real world, power to admit or exclude rests on equally debatable notions of sovereignty and utilitarian worth of different people (Carens 1987). Current political realities are hardly a basis for continuing or intensifying closed borders. What is practiced or believed today is likely to look quite different some years hence. Faulty assertions and fears about immigrants are especially likely to recede, in the face of overwhelming evidence of the capacities of newcomers and of common cumulative experiences to transform them and established residents alike.

Given the alacrity and uncertainties associated with global interdependence, a long-term perspective is constructive. This includes acknowledging that needs for safety and belonging are a human commonality and that people everywhere are modified by unexpected experiences and, in turn, modify plans as they also create new spaces. More democratic ideals and practice with respect to movement will be needed if resource competition compounds structural violence or provokes greater conflict and subsequent movement of more people seeking life-giving resources or refuge. Equally important are greater efforts to shift opportunities to people in the homes, families, and familiar cultural worlds where most prefer to stay.

The dilemmas are serious, the solutions unclear. Societies and institutions can easily lose sight of the long term, especially during periods, like today, of dramatic shifts in social relations, populations, and economic accumulation. Writers from Durkheim to Achebe (1958) have recognized how anomie or normlessness builds in times of rapid change. These are the times we must recall the tremendous benefits associated with migration, known through extensive empirical research as well as in personal accounts of immigrant America (Portes and Rumbaut 2006). The vibrancy of new populations, emerging in interconnections and intermarriage, as well as through numerical growth, is an essential feature of a shared future. There may still be a lag in full recognition of that promise. Public deliberation can be clouded by alarmism, or lost amid other worries about busy lives, jobs, or climate. Thoughtful consideration of evidence and voices from within as well as beyond the United States can clarify shared commitments and goals and, in turn, guide decisive action toward a better world shared by all.

Affirming Humanity, Incubating Our Future

> It is in the shelter of each other that people live.
> —Irish proverb

No culture, much less country or civilization, survives long without being grounded in commitment to social good. Commitment to the common good, or what in contemporary phrasing is increasingly referred to as the commons (Ostrom 1990), is basic to community formation and continuity. Commons sense is common sense. As societies grow in size and spread, affirmation of the common good may be extenuated, but it rarely disappears altogether. In fact, ethical commitment to others is fundamental to most cultural codes of conduct and religious principles across history and worldwide, as well as more recent international conventions. A moral imperative to affirm, through material as well as social support, is required in times of need and for those who are more vulnerable in society.

Disruptions and conflicts associated with migration understandably receive a great deal of attention by the media and researchers alike. Yet, while mobility can complicate kin-based or face-to-face bases for cooperating or maintaining mutually beneficial arrangements for working and dwelling, social networks nonetheless remain central to how people plan and pursue migration (Menjívar 2000). Furthermore, we can identify numerous arrangements to extend safety to people on the move, such as refugee camps, disarmament zones, and structures like churches and immigrant service centers (Mitchell and Hancock 2007). These places and the people who serve them also provide much beyond protection alone, most notably related to education, health, and other kinds of anchoring and adaptation when dislocation is prolonged and even permanent.

Whether humanity can sustain a collective social ethic when crises loom on a global scale is the question at hand—or perhaps more accurately, whether humanity can risk not sustaining that ethic. As evidence of planetary environmental stress becomes ever more incontrovertible, the imperative for a more universal ethic becomes even greater. References to tipping points, environmental refugees, and climate responsibility were nearly nonexistent only a few years ago. Today, they are becoming the defining issues of our time. Borders, national sovereignty, and notions of citizenships are very much in contention. So, too, are rights associated with movement, whether involuntary or relatively more by choice.

An ecocultural ethic, one that encompasses human communities within a "commons" perspective, has never been more vital than in the face of multiple mobilities and mounting insecurity, with more and more people on the move. There are no guarantees that we can easily supersede long-standing maldistribution of resources. People in transition or uprooted from physical and social supports rarely have the same rights and privileges as more stationary and "propertied" people (Rossomanno 2009; Widdows 2007). The contemporary situation is even more alarming in light of scenarios for greater food insecurity and migration, and the potential for more intensive lockdowns and lockouts rather than more humanitarian response.

The challenges facing humanity as a result of misdirected priorities and policies, or through climate change, are profound. But, ultimately, so too is the creative power of the human spirit and the collective capacity that transpires when people come together for a higher purpose (Dalai Lama 1999; Hawken 2007; Korten 2010; Stiglitz 2010; Suzuki 2002). As people everywhere come to realize that actions anywhere have consequences everywhere, they face a fundamental moral challenge of creating or re-creating a new global ethic (Parekh 2005; Booth, Cox, and Dunne 2001). Increasingly vibrant dialogue within and between societies suggests exponential growth in awareness that common problems require common solutions. Discerning what is entailed in asserting the most basic human right—to life—will (and must) emerge organically, as a kind of species response to adapt by promoting the common good, grounded in optimism associated with action and orientation to a future world of ordinary people recommitted to life-sustaining principles.

"One team, one country" was the vision of Nelson Mandela and the slogan of the Springboks, a rugby team closely associated with the whites of South Africa, during the very difficult early postapartheid days. Just as that lesson didn't come easily, neither will progress toward reasonable migration policy.

All too often, human-imposed borders—whether straight lines through deserts and forests, or convoluted gerrymandering of US congressional districts—have little to do with human cultural communities or common sense, much less environmental integrity or "commons sense." The Pacific Northwest provides ample evidence of fallacies and folly that prevail often and widely, but also of how rational minds sometimes prevail. Decades of significant cross-border pollutants from a smelter in Trail, British Columbia, for example, finally led to advances in international law with respect to environmental responsibility. Years of bickering over salmon runs at last yielded binational agreements. Colonial nomenclature of the Strait of Georgia and Puget Sound, north and south of the 49th parallel, was at last acknowledged to be parts of a single watershed, through official affirmation of the "Salish Sea" in 2010. During two centuries of political "geo-mangling," of course, the Salish peoples (whose homelands extend from contemporary Oregon to southern Alaska) had continued to maintain, through lore as well as legal battles, that the border between the United States and Canada was as unjust as it was recent. Of course, no one polled the salmon or whales, whose migratory routes cross international boundaries, in support of partisan claims they "belong" to one nation or another.

In the space of a decade, efforts to meet shared challenges through cooperative and transparent approaches have been severely truncated. Growing emphasis on security and hardening of borders across the globe is echoed in a politics of retrenchment, in the United States and elsewhere, yet long-range multilateral efforts to promote broad environmental health and socioeconomic parity are needed more than ever. They can, and must, include reasonable approaches based on the realities as well as positive potentialities of human movement.

Looking beyond immediate events and quick fixes, we can approach human migration as part of an essential endeavor for common ground. Movement on at least some levels is a right shared by all; it also entails shared responsibility. Migration ultimately turns our focus to what it means to be human. Our species is not just 7 billion featherless bipeds. We have

become climate itself, while also exhibiting astonishing hubris to rational-
ize our inordinate impact. Yet we are also astoundingly resilient, in spite of
ourselves. We can affirm the shelter of each other, in part by acknowledging our interdependence on other people far beyond immediate relatives
or compatriots alone.

By affirming a species perspective we find the greatest hope. Humans
can, and often do, encourage living that is respectful of the fullness of culture, gender, generations, and kith and kin. Those human characteristics, at
least as much as nationality, are essential to reaffirm as we consider new
mixes and movement, here and everywhere.

References

Achebe, Chinua. 1958. *Things Fall Apart*. London: Heinemann.

Adler, Rachel H. 2007. *Yucatecans in Dallas, Texas: Breaching the border, bridging the distance*. Second Edition. Boston: Pearson.

Agnew, John. 2008. "Borders on the mind: Re-framing border thinking." *Ethics and Global Politics*. DOI, 10: 3402/egp.v1i4.1892.

Alba, Francisco. 2010. "Mexico: A crucial crossroads." *Migration Information Source*, February.

Alden, Edward. 2008. *The closing of the American border: Terrorism, immigration, and security since 9/11*. New York: HarperCollins.

Al-Hibri, Azizah Y. 1999. "Is Western patriarchal feminism good for Third World/Minority women?" In *Is multiculturalism bad for women?* edited by Susan Moller Okin, 41–46. Princeton, NJ: Princeton University Press.

Al Jazeera English. 2009. "Thousands flee Taliban-held town." May 15, http://english.aljazeera.net/news/asia/2009/05/200951512551688563.html.

Allen, Lila. 2009. "The dark side of the Dubai dream." *BBC News*, April 6, http://news.bbc.co.uk/2/hi/uk_news/magazine/7985361.stm.

Alper, Donald K., and James Loucky. 2006. "U.S.-Canada border." In *Immigration in America today*, edited by James Loucky, Jeanne Armstrong, and Larry J. Estrada, 337–40. Westport, CT: Greenwood Press.

———. 2009. "Canada-U.S. border securitization: Implications for bi-national cooperation." *Canadian-American Public Policy*, No. 72. Canadian-American Center, University of Maine, Orono, ME.

Amnesty International. 2009. *Jailed without justice: Immigration detention in the USA*.

Anderson, Benedict. 1983. *Imagined Communities*. London: Verso Press.

Andreas, Peter. 2000. *Border games: Policing the U.S.-Mexico divide.* Ithaca, NY: Cornell University Press.

Ansley, Fran. 2005. "Constructing citizenship without a license: The struggle of undocumented immigrants in the USA for livelihoods and recognition." In *Inclusive citizenship: Meanings and expressions,* edited by Naila Kabeer, 199–215. London: Zed Books.

Archibold, Randal C. 2010a. "Arizona endorses immigration curbs." *New York Times,* April 15, http://www.nytimes.com/2010/04/15/us/15immig.html?emc=tnt&tntemail1=y.

———. 2010b. "Grief across Latin America for migrant killings." *New York Times,* September 1, http://www.nytimes.com/2010/09/02/world/americas/02migrants.html.

Arendt, Hannah. 1986. *The origins of totalitarianism.* New York: Andre Deutsch.

Argueta, Luis (dir.). 2011. "abUSed." Documentary. www.abusedthepostvilleraid.com.

Bacevich, Andrew. 2010. *Washington rules: America's path to permanent war.* New York: Metropolitan/Henry Holt.

Bacon, David. 2008. *Illegal people: How globalization creates migration and criminalizes immigrants.* Boston: Beacon Press.

Barry, Tom. 2009. "The new political economy of immigration." *Americas Program Report,* February 16, 1–6. Center for International Policy, Americas Program.

Basok, Tanya. 2002. *Tortillas and tomatoes: Transnational Mexican harvesters in Canada.* Montreal: McGill–Queen's University Press.

Batalova, Jeanne, and Michael Fix. 2008. *Uneven progress: The employment pathways of skilled immigrants in the United States.* Washington, DC: Migration Policy Institute.

Battisti, David S., and Rosamond L. Naylor. 2009. "Historical warnings of future food insecurity with unprecedented seasonal heat. *Science* 323 (January 9): 240–44.

Bawer, Bruce. 2006. *While Europe slept: How radical Islam is destroying the West from within.* New York: Doubleday.

Behdad, Ali. 2005. *A forgetful nation: On immigration and cultural identity in the United States.* Durham, NC: Duke University Press.

Benhabib, Seyla. 2004. *The rights of others: Aliens, residents and citizens.* Cambridge: Cambridge University Press.

Berkeley, Bill. 2009. "Stateless people, violent states." *World Policy Journal* 26(1): 3–15.

Bhabha, Homi. 1992. "Double Visions." *Artforum,* January, 82–90.

Bhattacharyya, Gargi. 2005. *Traffick: The illicit movement of people and things.* London: Pluto.

Bigo, Didier. 2002. "Security and immigration: Toward a critique of the governmentality of unease." *Alternatives* 27 (January–March): 63–92.

Binford, L. 2003. "Migrant remittances and (under)development in Mexico." *Critique of Anthropology* 23(3): 305–36.

————. 2009. "From fields of power to fields of sweat: The dual process of constructing temporary migrant labour in Mexico and Canada." *Third World Quarterly* 30(3): 503–17.

Blake, Michael, and Mathias Risse. 2006. "Is there a human right to free movement? Immigration and original ownership of the earth." Kennedy School of Government Faculty Research Working Paper Series RWP06-012. Cambridge, MA.

Bodley, John H. 2008. *Victims of progress.* Fifth Edition. Lanham, MD: AltaMira Press.

Booth, Ken and Michael Cox and Timothy Dunne, eds. 2001. *How might we live? Global ethics in the new century.* Cambridge: Cambridge University Press.

Borjas, George J. 2006. "The new economics of immigration: Affluent Americans gain, poor Americans lose." In *The migration reader: Exploring politics and policies,* edited by Anthony M. Messina and Gallya Lahav, 318–28. Boulder, CO: Lynne Rienner.

Bosniak, Linda. 2001. "Denationalizing citizenship." In *Citizenship today: Global perspectives and practices,* edited by T. Alexander Aleinikoff and Douglas Klusmeyer, 237–52. Washington, DC: Carnegie Endowment for International Peace.

Brahic, Catherine. 2009. "Billions could go hungry from global warming by 2100." *New Scientist,* January 8, http://www.newscientist.com/article/dn16384-billions-could-go-hungry-from-global-warming-by-2100.html.

Brysk, Alison, and Gerson Shafir, eds. 2004. *People out of place: Globalization, human rights and the citizenship gap.* New York: Routledge.

Bryson, Donna. 2009. "Zimbabwean girls seek opportunity in South Africa." *Miami Herald,* May 16, http://www.miamiherald.com/news/world/AP/story/1051718.html.

Cammisa, Rebecca (dir./prod.). 2009. *Which way home?* BullfrogFilms.

Carens, Joseph H. 1987. "Aliens and citizens: The case for open borders." *Review of Politics* 49(2): 251–73.

Castañeda, Jorge G. 2007. *Ex Mex: From migrants to immigrants.* New York: The New Press.

Castle, Stephen. 2010. "Anti-immigrant party rises in Sweden." *New York Times,* September 14, http://www.nytimes.com/2010/09/14/world/europe/14ihtsweden.html?emc=tnt&tntemail1=y.

Castles, Stephen. 2007. "The factors that make and unmake migration policies." In *Rethinking Migration: New Theoretical and Empirical Perspectives,"* edited by Alejandro Portes and Josh DeWind, 29–61. New York: Berghahn Books.

————. 2010. "Neo-liberal's global workforce: The end of a dream?" University of Chicago, School of Social Service Administration, November 1.

Castles, Stephen, and Alistair Davidson. 2000. *Citizenship and migration: Globalization and the politics of belonging.* New York: Routledge.

Castles, Stephen, and Mark J. Miller. 2003. *The age of migration.* Third Edition. New York: Guilford Press.

————. 2009. *The age of migration.* Fourth Edition. New York: Guilford Press.

Cavanagh, John, and Jerry Mander, eds. 2004. *Alternatives to economic globalization: A better world is possible.* Second Edition. San Francisco: Berrett-Koehler Publishers.

Cernea, Michael, ed. 1999. *The economics of involuntary resettlement: Questions and challenges.* Washington, DC: World Bank.

Chavez, Leo R. 1998. *Shadowed lives: Undocumented immigrants in American society.* Second Edition. Fort Worth, TX: Harcourt Brace College Publishers.

———. 2001. *Covering immigration: Popular images and the politics of the nation.* Berkeley: University of California Press.

———. 2008. *The Latino threat: Constructing immigrants, citizens, and the nation.* Stanford, CA: Stanford University Press.

Chen, Michelle. 2010. "Slavery in our time." *In These Times,* July 21, http://www.inthesetimes.com/main/6192.

Chio, Jenny. 2010. "China's campaign for civilized tourism." *Anthropology News,* November, 14–15.

Chisti, Muzaffar, and Claire Bergeron. 2010. "Increasing evidence that the recession has caused the number of unauthorized immigrants in the U.S. to drop." *Migration Information Source,* March 15.

Chomsky, Aviva. 2007. *"They take our jobs!" And 20 other myths about immigration.* Boston: Beacon Press.

Coenders, Marcel, Merove Gijsberts, and Peer Scheepers. 2004a. "Resistance to the presence of immigrants and refugees in 22 countries." In *Nationalism and exclusion of migrants: Cross-national comparisons,* edited by Merove Gijsberts, Louk Hagendoorn, and Peer Scheepers, 97–120. Hants, England: Ashgate.

Coenders, Marcel, Merove Gijsberts, Louk Hagendoorn, and Peer Scheepers. 2004b. "Introduction." In *Nationalism and exclusion of migrants: Cross-national comparisons,* edited by Merove Gijsberts, Louk Hagendoorn, and Peer Scheepers, 1–25. Hants, England: Ashgate.

Cohen, J. 2001. "Transnational migration in rural Oaxaca, Mexico: Dependency, development and the household." *American Anthropologist* 103(4): 954–67.

———, and L. Rodriguez. 2005. "Remittance outcomes in rural Oaxaca, Mexico: Challenges, options, opportunities for migrant households." *Population, Space and Place* 11(1): 49–63.

Congressional Budget Office. 2005. "The role of immigrants in the U.S. labor market." *Congressional Budget Office,* Washington, DC, November, http://www.cbo.gov/doc.cfm?index=6853&type=1.

Cornelius, Wayne, Thomas Espenshade, and Idean Salehyan, eds. 2001. *The international migration of the highly skilled.* Boulder, CO: Lynne Rienner.

Cornelius, Wayne A., David Fitzgerald, and Pedro Lewin Fischer. 2007. *Mayan journeys: The new migration from Yucatán to the United States.* La Jolla: Center for Comparative Immigration Studies, University of California.

Cresswell, Tim. 2006. *On the move: Mobility in the modern Western world.* New York: Routledge.

Croucher, Sheila. 2009. *The other side of the fence: American migrants in Mexico.* Austin: University of Texas Press.

Dalai Lama. 1999. *Ethics for the New Millenium.* New York: Riverhead.

Daley, Suzanne. 2010. "Roma, on move, test Europe's 'open borders.'" *New York Times,* September 17.

Daniels, Roger. 1981. *Concentration camps: North America. Japanese in the United States and Canada during World War II.* Malabar, FL: Robert Krieger.

Danticat, Edwidge. 2008. *Brother, I'm dying.* New York: Vintage Books.

Davison, John. 2007. *Human tide: The real migration crisis.* London: Christian Aid.

De Certeau, Michel. 1984. *The practice of everyday life.* Berkeley: University of California Press.

Deng, Alephonsion, Benson Deng, Benjamin Ajak, and Judy Bernstein. 2005. *They poured fire on us from the sky.* New York: Public Affairs Publishers.

DeParle, Jason. 2007. "Border crossings: Rising breed of migrant worker—skilled, salaried and welcome." *New York Times,* August 20.

———. 2010. "Defying trend, Canada lures more migrants." *New York Times,* November 12.

Doty, Roxanne. 2003. *Anti-immigrantism in western democracies.* New York: Routledge.

Dowie, Mark. 2010. "Conservation refugees." *Cultural Survival Quarterly* 34(1): 28–35.

Dreby, Joanna. 2010. *Divided by borders: Mexican migrants and their children.* Berkeley: University of California Press.

Durand, Jorge, and Douglas S. Massey, eds. 2004. *Crossing the border: Research from the Mexican migration project.* New York: Russell Sage Foundation.

Dyer, Gwynne. 2010. *Climate wars.* Oxford: Oneworld.

Editorial. 2010a. "Arizona goes over the edge." *New York Times,* April 18, http://www.nytimes.com/2010/04/18/opinion/18sun3.html?emc=tnt&tntemail1=y.

———. 2010b. "Jobs for the picking." *New York Times,* July 18, http://www.nytimes.com/2010/07/18/opinion/18sun3.html?_r=1&scp=1&sq=jobs%20for%20the%20picking&st=Search.

———. 2010c. "Xenophobia: Casting out the un-French." *New York Times,* August 6, http://www.nytimes.com/2010/08/06/opinion/06fri2.html?emc=tnt&tntemail1=y.

Egan, Timothy. 2006. *The worst hard time: The untold story of those who survived the great American dust bowl.* New York: Houghton Mifflin.

———. "Building a nation of Know-Nothings." 2010. *New York Times,* August 25, http://opinionator.blogs.nytimes.com/2010/08/25/building-a-nation-of-know-nothings/.

Escobar, Arturo. 1995. *Encountering development: The making and unmaking of the Third World.* Princeton, NJ: Princeton University Press.

Estrada, Larry J., and James Loucky. 2006. "Families." In *Immigration in America today,* edited by James Loucky, Jeanne Armstrong, and Larry J. Estrada, 108–14. Westport, CT: Greenwood Press.

Falk, Richard. 1999. *Predatory globalization: A critique.* Cambridge: Polity Press.

Farmer, Paul. 2003. *Pathologies of power: Health, human rights and the new war on the poor.* Berkeley: University of California Press.

Farrer, James, and Devin T. Stewart. 2010. "Defining a right to move?" *Reflections on "ethics of migration" conference.* Carnegie Council for Ethics in International Affairs, www.policyinnovations.org/ideas/briefings/data/000156.

Fernandez, Manny. 2010. "Guilty verdict in killing of Long Island man." *New York Times,* April 20, http://www.nytimes.com/2010/04/20/nyregion/20patchogue .html?ref=jeffrey_conroy.

Fitzgerald, David. 2009. *A nation of emigrants: How Mexico manages its migration.* Berkeley: University of California Press.

Fix, Michael. 2007. *Securing the future: U.S. immigrant integration policy, a reader.* Washington, DC: Migration Policy Institute.

———, Demetrios G. Papademetriou, Jeanne Batalova, Aaron Terrazas, Serena Yi-Ying Lin, and Michelle Mittelstadt. 2009. *Migration and the Global Recession: A Report Commissioned by the BBC World Service.* Washington, DC: Migration Policy Institute, http://www.migrationpolicy.org/pubs/MPI-BBCreport-Sept09.pdf.

Foner, Nancy. 2005. *In a new land: A comparative view of immigration.* New York: New York University Press.

Foucault, Michel. 1991. "Governmentality." In *The Foucault effect: Studies in governmentality,* edited by Graham Burchell, Colin Gordon, and Peter Miller, 87–104. Chicago: University of Chicago Press.

Fox, Jonathan, and Gaspar Rivera-Salgado, eds. 2004. *Indigenous Mexican migrants in the United States.* La Jolla: Center for Comparative Immigration Studies, University of California.

Foxen, Patricia. 2007. *In search of providence: Transnational Mayan identities.* Nashville: Vanderbilt University Press.

Frontline. 2011. "Lost in Detention." Rick Young, Producer. WGBH Boston: Corporation for Public Broadcasting. October 18.

Gabriel, I. 2008. "The political economy of remittances: What do we know? What do we need to know?" Working Paper Series No. 184, University of Massachusetts, Political Economy Research Institute.

Galeano, Eduardo. 1997. *Open veins of Latin America: Five centuries of the pillage of a continent.* New York: Monthly Review Press.

———. 2000. *Upside Down: A Primer for the Looking-Glass World.* 2000. NY: Picador.

Ganster, Paul, and David E. Lorey. 2008. *The U.S.-Mexican border into the twenty-first century.* Second Edition. Lanham, MD: Rowman and Littlefield.

Gardner, Andrew M. 2010. *City of strangers: Gulf migration and the Indian community in Bahrain.* Ithaca, NY: Cornell University Press.

Giddens, Anthony. 1990. *The consequences of modernity.* Stanford, CA: Stanford University Press.

Gijsberts, Merove, Louk Hagendoorn, and Peer Scheepers, eds. 2004. *Nationalism and exclusion of migrants: Cross-national comparisons.* Hants, UK: Ashgate Publishing.

Gillis, Justin. 2010. "As glaciers melt, science seeks data on rising seas." *New York Times,* November 14.

Godziak, Elzbieta M., and Micah N. Bump. 2008. *New immigrants, changing communities: Best practices for a better America.* Lanham, MD: Lexington Press.

Godziak, Elzbieta M., and Susan F. Martin, eds. 2005. *Beyond the gateway: Immigrants in a changing America.* Lanham, MD: Lexington Books.

Gray, Mel, and Kylie Agllias. 2010. "Australia: The world in one place." In *Immigration worldwide: Policies, practices, and trends,* edited by Uma A. Segal, Doreen Elliott, and Nazneen S. Mayadas, 53–170. Oxford: Oxford University Press.

Guibernau, Montserrat. 2007. *The identity of nations.* Cambridge: Polity Press.

Guskin, Jane, and David L. Wilson. 2007. *The politics of immigration: Questions and answers.* New York: Monthly Review Press.

Hagan, Jacqueline M. 2008. *Migration miracle: Faith, hope and meaning on the undocumented journey.* Cambridge, MA: Harvard University Press.

Hardin, Garrett. 1968. "The Tragedy of the Commons." *Science* 162 (3859): 1243–48.

Harris, Collin. 2010. "NAFTA and the political economy of immigration." *Z Magazine,* July 13, http://www.zcommunications.org/contents/170676.

Harris, Nigel. 1995. *The new untouchables: Immigration and the new world worker.* London: I.B. Tauris.

———. 2002. *Thinking the unthinkable: The immigration myth exposed.* London: I.B. Tauris.

Harvey, David. 1990. *The condition of postmodernity.* Cambridge: Blackwell Publishers.

———. 2003. *The new imperialism.* Oxford: Oxford University Press.

Hatton, Timothy J., and Jeffrey G. Williamson. 2005. *Global migration and the world economy: Two centuries of policy and performance.* Cambridge, MA: MIT Press.

Hawken, Paul. 2007. *Blessed unrest: How the largest movement in the world came into being and why no one saw it coming.* New York: Viking Press.

Held, David, and Anthony McGrew. 2007. *Globalization/anti-globalization: Beyond the great divide.* Cambridge: Polity Press.

Hill, Steven. 2010a. *Europe's promise: Why the European way is the best hope in an insecure age.* Berkeley: University of California Press.

———. 2010b. "The plight of the Roma minority: Signs of hope amidst this challenge to Rainbow Europe." http://www.washingtonmonthly.com/hows_europe_doing/archives/individual/2010_10/026116.php.

Hirschman, Charles, and Douglas S. Massey. 2008. "Places and peoples: The new American mosaic." In *New faces in new places,* edited by Douglas S. Massey, 1–21. New York: Russell Sage Foundation.

Ho, Christine G.T. 1993. "The internationalization of kinship and the feminization of Caribbean migration: The case of Afro-Trinidadians in Los Angeles." *Human Organization* 52(1): 32–40.

———. 2010. "Who will do the work?" *Miami Herald*, August 15, http://www.miamiherald.com/2010/08/15/1776251/who-will-do-the-work.html?story_link=email_msg.

———, and Keith Nurse, eds. 2005. *Globalization, diaspora and Caribbean popular culture.* Kingston, Jamaica: Ian Randle Publishers.

Hoefer, Michael, Nancy Rytina, and Bryan C. Baker. 2010. "Estimates of the unauthorized population residing in the United States: January 2009." Washington, DC: U.S. Department of Homeland Security, Office of Immigrant Statistics.

Holo, Selma. 2004. *Oaxaca at the crossroads: Managing memory, negotiating change.* Washington, DC: Smithsonian.

Hossain, Farhana, and Shan Carter. 2007. "Snapshot: Global migration." *New York Times,* June 22, http://www.nytimes.com/ref/world/20070622_CAPE VERDE_GRAPHIC.html.

Hugo, G. 1996. "Environmental concerns and international migration." *International Migration Review* 30(1): 105–31.

Huntington, Samuel. 2004. "The Hispanic challenge." *Foreign Policy* 141 (March/April): 30–45.

Immigration Justice Clinic. 2009. "Constitution on ice: A report on immigration home raid operations." New York: Cardozo School of Law.

Inda, Jonathan Xavier. 2006. *Targeting immigrants: Government, technology, and ethics.* Malden, MA: Blackwell Publishing.

International Organization for Migration. 2008. "Migration and climate change." *IOM Migration Research Series* no. 31. Geneva: IOM International Organization for Migration.

Jiménez, Tomás R. 2011. *Immigrants in the United States: How well are they integrating into society?* Washington, DC: Migration Policy Institute.

Johnson, Chalmers. 2010. "It's the beginning of the end for the American empire." *Alternet,* August 17, http://www.alternet.org/story/147880.

Johnson, Tim. 2009. "China's newest export: Laborers." *Miami Herald,* February 2, http://www.miamiherald.com/business/story/882588.html.

Jonas, Susanne. 2010. "Increasing visibility of Guatemalan immigrants: The great raid of Postville, Iowa." *ReVista—Harvard Review of Latin America* (Fall 2010–Winter 2011), http://www.drclas.harvard.edu/publications/revistaonline/fall-2010-winter-2011/increasing-visibility-guatemalan-immigrants.

Kabeer, Naila, ed. 2005. *Inclusive citizenship: Meanings and expressions.* London: Zed Press.

Kandel, William, and Douglas Massey. 2002. "The culture of migration: A theoretical and empirical analysis." *Social Forces* 80(3): 981–1004.

Kaye, Jeffrey. 2010. *Moving millions: How coyote capitalism fuels global immigration.* Hoboken, NJ: John Wiley and Sons.

Kivisto, Peter, and Thomas Faist. 2007. *Citizenship: Discourse, theory, and transnational prospects.* Malden, MA: Blackwell.

Klare, Michael T. 2001. *Resource wars: The new landscape of global conflict.* New York: Metropolitan/Holt.

Knight Foundation. 2010. *Soul of the community: Why people love where they live and why it matters.* http://soulofthecommunity.org.

Kobelinsky, Carolina, and Chowra Makaremi, eds. 2008. "Alien exclusion: Between circulation and confinement." *Cultures et Conflits, Special Issue Number 21.* Autumn.

Korte, Tim, and Manuel Valdes. 2010. "AP enterprise: More immigrants getting licenses." *Miami Herald,* August 13, http://www.miamiherald.com/2010/08/13/1774979/ap-enterprise.html.

Korten, David C. 2001. *When corporations rule the world.* San Francisco: Berrett-Koehler Publishers and Kumarian Press.

———. 2010. "Essential priorities." In Korten, *Agenda for a new economy,* 102–16. San Francisco: Berrett-Koehler.

Kunichoff, Yana. 2010. "A long stay." *Truthout,* August 1, http://www.truth-out.org/a-longstay61888.

Kurzban, Ira J. 2008. "Democracy and immigration." In *Keeping out the other: A critical introduction to immigration enforcement today,* edited by David C. Brotherton and Philip Kretsedemas, 63–78. New York: Columbia University Press.

Lendman, Stephen. 2009. "Big brother U.S.A.: Police state raids against immigrants." *Global Research, Centre for Research on Globalization,* September 25.

LeVine, Robert A., and Donald T. Campbell. 1972. *Ethnocentrism: Theories of conflict, ethnic attitudes, and group behavior.* New York: John Wiley and Sons.

Levitt, Peggy. 2001. *The transnational villagers.* Berkeley: University of California Press.

Long, Lynellyn D., and Ellen Oxfeld. 2004. *Coming home? Refugees, migrants, and those who stayed behind.* Philadelphia: University of Pennsylvania Press.

Lopez, Ann Aurelia. 2007. *The farmworkers' journey.* Berkeley: University of California Press.

Loucky, James, and Donald K. Alper. 2008. "Pacific borders, discordant borders: Where North America edges together." In *Transboundary policy challenges in the Pacific border regions of North America,* edited by James Loucky, Donald K. Alper, and J.C. Day, 11–37. Calgary: University of Calgary Press.

Loucky, James, Jeanne Armstrong, and Larry J. Estrada, eds. 2006. *Immigration in America today.* Westport, CT: Greenwood Press.

Loucky, James, and Marilyn Moors. 2000. *The Maya diaspora: Guatemalan roots, new American lives.* Philadelphia: Temple University Press.

Lovato, Roberto. 2008. "Building the homeland security state. In terror incognita: immigrants and the homeland security states." *NACLA Report on the Americas* 41(6): 15–20.

Lucassen, Leo. 2005. *The immigrant threat: The integration of old and new migrants in Western Europe since 1850.* Urbana: University of Illinois Press.

Marfleet, Philip. 2006. *Refugees in a global era.* New York: Palgrave Macmillan.

Martinez, Samuel. 2009a. "Introduction." In *International migration and human rights: The global repercussions of U.S. policy,* edited by Samuel Martinez, 1–22. Berkeley: University of California Press.

———, ed. 2009b. *International migration and human rights: The global repercussions of U.S. policy.* Berkeley: University of California Press.

Massey, Douglas S. 2009. "The political economy of migration in an era of globalization." In *International migration and human rights: The global repercussion of U.S. policy,* edited by Samuel Martinez, 25–43. Berkeley: University of California Press.

———, Jorge Durand, and Nolan J. Malone. 2002. *Beyond smoke and mirrors: Mexican immigration in an era of economic integration.* New York: Russell Sage Foundation.

Menjívar, Cecilia. 2000. *Fragmented ties: Salvadoran immigrant networks in America.* Berkeley: University of California Press.

Messina, Anthony M., and Gallya Lahav, eds. 2006. *The migration reader: Exploring politics and policies.* Boulder, CO: Lynne Rienner.

Migrants Rights International. 1990. "Basic rights provided by the migrant workers convention," http://www.migrantwatch.org/1990Convention.html.

Mitchell, Christopher, and Landon E. Hancock. 2007. "Local zones of peace and a theory of sanctuary." In *Zones of peace,* edited by Landon E. Hancock and Christopher Mitchell, 189–215. Bloomfield, CT: Kumarian Press.

Mize, Ronald L., and Alicia C.S. Swords. 2011. *Consuming Mexican labor: From the bracero program to NAFTA.* Toronto: University of Toronto Press.

Moran-Taylor, M.J. 2008. "Guatemala's Ladino and Maya Migra landscapes: The tangible and intangible outcomes of migration." *Human Organization* 67(2): 111–24.

Moreno Gonzales, John. 2009. "Immigrant detainees hunger strike over conditions." August 6, http://www.miamiherald.com/news/nation/AP/story/1164934.html?story_link=email_msg.

Muller, Benjamin J. 2008. "Governing through risk at the Canadian/U.S. border: Liberty, security, technology." Border Policy Research Institute, Working Paper no. 2, Western Washington University.

———. 2010. "Securing the political imagination: Popular culture, the security dispositif and the biometric state." *Security Dialogue* 41(6): 199–220.

Muzaffar, Chishti, and Claire Bergeron. 2010. "New Arizona law engulfs immigration debate." Washington, DC: Migration Policy Institute, May 17, http://www.migrationinformation.org/USFocus/display.cfm?ID=782.

Myers, Dowell. 2007. *Immigrants and boomers: Forging a new social contract for the future of America.* New York: Russell Sage Foundation.

Myers, Norman. 2005. "Environmental refugees: An emergent security issue." *13th Economic Forum,* May, Prague.

NACLA. 2008. "Terror incognita: Immigrants and the homeland security state." *Report on the Americas* 41(6). Special edition.

Nagengast, Carole. 2009. "Afterword: Migration, human rights and development." In *International migration and human rights: The global repercussion of U.S. policy,* edited by Samuel Martinez, 253–69. Berkeley: University of California Press.

National Immigration Law Center. 2009. *A Broken System.* Los Angeles.

National Network for Immigrant and Refugee Rights. 2010. *Injustice for all: The rise of the immigration policing regime.* December, Oakland, CA, http://www.nnirr.org/resources/docs/InjusticeforAllNNIRRHURRICANEReportDec182010.pdf.

Navarro, Armando. 2009. *The immigration crisis: Nativism, armed vigilantism, and the rise of a countervailing movement.* Lanham, MD: Altamira Press.

Nazario, Sonia. 2006. *Enrique's journey: The story of a boy's dangerous odyssey to reunite with his mother.* New York: Random House.

Ngai, Mae M. 2004. *Impossible subjects: Illegal aliens and the making of modern America.* Princeton, NJ: Princeton University Press.

Nyamu-Musembi, Celestine. 2005. "Towards an actor-oriented perspective on human rights." In *Inclusive citizenship: Meanings and expressions,* edited by Naila Kabeer, 31–49. London: Zed Press.

Okin, Susan Moller. 1999. *Is multiculturalism bad for women?* Princeton, NJ: Princeton University Press.

Ong, Aihwa. 1999. *Flexible citizenship: The cultural logics of transnationality.* Durham, NC: Duke University Press.

Oppel, Richard A., Jr. 2011. "Arizona, bowing to business, softens stand on immigration." *New York Times,* March 19, http://www.nytimes.com/2011/03/19/us/19immigration.html?_r=1&emc=tnt&tntemail1=y.

Oppenheimer, Andres. 2006. "Border fence bill a grand political deception." *Miami Herald,* September 24.

———. 2007. "Inside the real costs of immigration crackdown." *Miami Herald,* April 29.

———. 2010a. "Why don't they come legally? They can't." *Miami Herald,* April 29, http://www.miamiherald.com/2010/04/29/1603473/why-dont-they-come-legally-they.html.

———. 2010b. "Spanish classes thriving in U.S. colleges." *Miami Herald,* December 18, http://www.miamiherald.com/2010/12/18/1980331/spanish-classes-thriving-in-us.html.

Orellana, Marjorie. 2009. *Translating childhoods: Immigrant youth, language, and culture.* New Brunswick, NJ: Rutgers University Press.

Ostrom, Elinor, ed. 1990. *Governing the commons: The evolution of institutions for collective action.* Cambridge: Cambridge University Press.

Page, Scott E. 2007. *The difference: How the power of diversity creates better groups, firms, schools, and societies.* Princeton, NJ: Princeton University Press.

Papademetriou, Demetrios G., and Madeleine Sumption. 2011. *The role of immigration in fostering competitiveness in the United States.* Washington, DC: Migration Policy Institute, http://www.migrationpolicy.org/pubs/competitiveness-US.pdf.

Parekh, Bhikhu. 2005. "Principles of a global ethic." In *Global ethics and civil society,* edited by John Eade and Darren O'Byrne, 15–33. Aldershot, UK: Ashgate Publishing.

Payan, Tony. 2006. *The three U.S.-Mexico border wars: Drugs, immigration and homeland security.* Westport, CT: Praeger Security International.

Pecoud, Antoine, and Paul de Guchteneire, eds. 2007. *Migration without borders: Essays on the free movement of people.* New York: Berghahn Books.

Pfaelzer, Jean. 2007. *Driven out: The forgotten war against Chinese Americans.* New York: Random House.

Physicians for Human Rights and the Bellevue/NYU Program for Survivors of Torture. 2003. *From persecution to prison: The health consequences of detention for asylum seekers.* June, http://physiciansforhumanrights.org/library/documents/reports/report-perstoprison-2003.pdf, 5.

Pickford-Gordon, Lara. 2009. "Hanging with the Chinese." *Trinidad and Tobago's Newsday,* October 19, http://www.newsday.co.tt/commentary/0,109439.html.

Portes, Alejandro, and Rubén G. Rumbaut. 2001. *Legacies: The story of the immigrant second generation.* Berkeley: University of California Press.

———. 2006. *Immigrant America: A portrait.* Third Edition. Berkeley: University of California Press.

Portes, Alejandro, and Alex Stepick. 1993. *City on the edge: The transformation of Miami.* Berkeley: University of California Press.

Povoledo, Elisabetta. 2010. "Immigrants rally for a nationwide strike in Italy." *New York Times,* March 1, http://www.nytimes.com/2010/03/02/world/europe/02iht-italy.html?emc=tnt&tntemail1=y.

Preibisch, Kerry. 2010. "Pick-your-own-labor: Migrant workers and flexibility in Canadian agriculture." *International Migration Review* 44(2): 404–41.

Preston, Julia. 2010. "Work force fueled by highly skilled immigrants." *New York Times,* April 15, http://www.nytimes.com/2010/04/16/us/16skilled.html?_r=1&emc=tnt&tntemail1=y.

———. 2011. "Immigration program is rejected by third state." *New York Times,* June 6, http://www.nytimes.com/2011/06/07/us/politics/07immig.html?_r=1&emc=eta1.

Putnam, Robert D. 2007. "'*E pluribus unum*': Diversity and community in the twenty-first century." *Scandinavian Political Studies* 30(2): 137–74, http://www.blackwell-synergy.com/doi/full/10.1111/j.1467-9477.2007.00176.x.

Rampersad, Indira. 2009. "Turbulence within the Cuban diaspora in South Florida." *Practicing Anthropology* 31(2): 29–34.

Reed-Danahay, Deborah, and Caroline B. Brettell, eds. 2008. *Citizenship, political engagement, and belonging: Immigrants in Europe and the United States.* New Brunswick, NJ: Rutgers University Press.

Riley, Jason L. 2008. *Let them in: The case for open borders.* New York: Gotham Books.

Risse, Mathias. 2008. "On the morality of immigration." *Ethics & International Affairs* 22(1), http://www.carnegiecouncil.org/resources/journal/22_1/essays/001.html.

Robbins, Richard H. 2011. *Global problems and the culture of capitalism.* Fifth Edition. Boston: Pearson.

Rodriguez, Cristina. 2010. "14th amendment is key to the American experiment." *CNN.com,* August 17, http://www.cnn.com/2010/OPINION/08/17/rodriguez.14th.amendment/index.html?hpt=Mid.

Rogers, Tim, and Carlos Dada. 2007. "Perspectives in the Americas and the Caribbean: Proposed reforms in the U.S. spark policy changes and worries." *Miami Herald,* June 10.

Rossomanno, Anthony. 2009. "The ethics of heat: Fundamentals and challenges in allocating the global commons." *University of Illinois Law Review* 2009(2): 551–82.

Roy, Arundhati. 2001. *Power Politics.* Second Edition. Cambridge, MA: South End Press.

Ruiz, Ramón Eduardo. 2000. *On the rim of Mexico: Encounters of the rich and poor.* Boulder, CO: Westview Press.

Rumbaut, Rubén G., and Alejandro Portes, eds. 2001. *Children of immigrants in America.* Berkeley: University of California Press.

Rushdie, Salman. 1991. "In good faith." In *Imaginary Homelands,* 393–414. London: Granta Books.

Sabar, Ariel. 2008. *My father's paradise: A son's search for his Jewish past in Kurdish Iraq.* Chapel Hill, NC: Algonquin Press.

Samuels, Robert, and Jacqueline Charles. 2009. "Interdiction of Haitian migrant boat touches off drama at sea." *Miami Herald,* May 29, http://www.miami-herald.com/news/southflorida/story/1070991.html.

Sassen, Saskia. 2007. *A sociology of globalization.* New York: W.W. Norton and Company.

Segal, Uma A., Doreen Elliott, and Nazneen S. Mayadas, eds. 2010. *Immigration worldwide: policies, practices, and trends.* New York: Oxford University Press.

Semple, Kirk. 2010a. "Attacks on Mexicans leave neighborhood in turmoil." *New York Times,* July 31, http://www.nytimes.com/2010/07/31/nyregion/31staten.html?scp=48&sq=semple,%20kirk&st=cse.

———. 2010b. "Mexican New Yorkers are steady force in workplace." *New York Times,* September 23, http://www.nytimes.com/2010/09/23/nyregion/23mexicans.html?scp=9&sq=semple,%20kirk&st=cse.

Sheller, Mimi, and John Urry, eds. 2006. *Mobile technologies of the city.* New York: Routledge Publishers.

Shiva, Vandana. 2002. *Water wars: Privatization, pollution and profit.* Cambridge, MA: South End Press.

Shoer-Roth, Daniel. 2007. "Remittances refine town's way of life." *Miami Herald,* February 14.

Singer, Audrey. 2011. "The rise of new immigrant gateways." Washington, DC: Brookings Institution Center on Urban and Metropolitan Policy, http://www .brookings.edu/~/media/Files/rc/reports/2004/02demographics_singer/ 20040301_gateways.pdf.

Slackman, Michael. 2010. "Book sets off immigration debate in Germany." *New York Times,* September 3, http://www.nytimes.com/2010/09/03/world/europe/ 03germany.html?emc=tnt&tntemail1=y.

Smart, Josephine. 2011. "Labour mobility in the 21st century: The temporary foreign workers program in Canada." Paper presented at *Society for Applied Anthropology,* 71st Annual Meeting, Seattle, WA, March 31.

Smith, Robert Courtney. 2005. *Mexican New York: The transnational lives of new immigrants.* Berkeley: University of California Press.

Southern Poverty Law Center. 2007a. *Close to slavery: Guestworker programs in the United States.* Montgomery, AL: Southern Poverty Law Center.

———. 2007b. "Neo-Nazi attacker sentenced in vicious teen assault." *Intelligence Report,* Spring 2007 (issue 125): 6.

Stanford, Lois. 2008. "Globalized food systems: The view from below." *Anthropology News* 49(7): 7, 10.

Staudt, Kathleen, and Irasema Coronado. 2002. *Fronteras no mas: Toward social justice at the U.S.-Mexico border.* New York: Palgrave Macmillan.

Stephen, Lynn. 2007. *Transborder lives: Indigenous Oaxacans in Mexico, California, and Oregon.* Durham, NC: Duke University Press.

Stepick, Alex. 1998. *Pride against prejudice: Haitians in the United States.* Boston: Allyn and Bacon.

———, Guillermo Grenier, Max Castro, and Marvin Dunn. 2003. *This land is our land: Immigrants and power in Miami.* Berkeley: University of California Press.

Stiglitz, Joseph E. 2010. "Moral bankruptcy." *Mother Jones,* January/February, http://motherjones.com/politics/2010/01/joseph-stiglitz-wall-street-morals.

Stuteville, Sarah. 2009. "Caught in Pakistan's crossfire." *Globalpost,* April 24, http:// www.globalpost.com/print/1204961.

Suárez-Orozco, Carola, and Marcelo Suárez-Orozco. 2001. *Children of immigration.* Cambridge, MA: Harvard University Press.

Suárez-Orozco, Carola, Marcelo M. Suárez-Orozco, and Irina Todorova. 2008. *Learning a new land: Immigrant students in American society.* Cambridge, MA: Harvard University Press.

Sumner, Jennifer. 2007. *Sustainability and the civil commons: Rural communities in the age of globalization.* Toronto: University of Toronto Press.

Suzuki, David. 2002. *Good news for a change: How everyday people are helping the planet.* Vancouver: Greystone.

Tancredo, Tom. 2006. *In mortal danger: The battle for America's border and security.* Nashville: Cumberland House.

Tirman, John, ed. 2004. *The maze of fear: Security and migration after 9/11.* New York: The New Press.

Tobar, Héctor. 2005. *Translation nation: Defining identity in the Spanish-speaking United States.* New York: Riverhead Press.

Todd, Douglas. 2010. "Metro is ethnically much different than experts predicted in the 1980s." *Vancouver Sun,* November 12.

United Nations Global Compact. 2011. "Human Rights Working Group meets under new terms of reference," Geneva, http://www.unglobalcompact.org/news/149-09-29-2011.

Valtonen, Kathleen. 1996. "Bread and tea: A study of the integration of low-income immigrants from other Caribbean territories into Trinidad." *International Migration Review* 30(4): 995–1019.

———. 2008. *Social work and migration: Immigrant and refugee settlement and integration.* Surrey, UK: Ashgate Publishing.

Wadhwa, Vivek. 2009. "Why skilled immigrants are leaving the U.S." *Yahoo News,* March 3, http://news.yahoo.com/s/bw/20090303/bs_bw/feb2009tc20090228990934.

Walia, Harsha. 2010. "Why we should welcome boatful of refugees into Canada." *Vancouver Sun,* August 14, http://www.vancouversun.com/news/should%20welcome%20boatful%20Tamil%20refugees%20into%20Canada/3398770/story.html.

Webb, Jim. 2009. "Why we must fix our prisons." *Parade Magazine,* March 29, 4–5.

Wessler, Seth Freed. 2010. "How the Dems' attempt at immigration reform led to major expansion of deportations." *AlterNet,* October 8, http://www.alternet.org/immigration/148453.

Widdows, Heather. 2007. "Is global ethics moral neo-colonialism? An investigation of the issue in the context of bioethics." *Bioethics* 21(6): 305–15.

Wilcove, David S. 2008. *No way home: The decline of the world's great animal migrations.* Washington, DC: Island Press.

Wilson, Edward O. 1978. *On human nature.* Cambridge, MA: Harvard University Press.

Witte, Griff. 2009. "Taliban is foiling Pakistani military." *Washington Post,* May 24, http://www.washingtonpost.com/wp-dyn/content/article/2009/05/23/AR2009052300725_pf.html.

Wolf, Eric. 1982. *Europe and the people without history.* Berkeley: University of California Press.

Wolfert, Jacqueline. 2008. "Reality vs. rhetoric: *Lozano v. Hazleton* and the state and local tax contributions made by undocumented immigrants." *Pittsburgh Tax Review* 6(1): 83.

Yoshikawa, Kirokazu. 2011. *Immigrants raising citizens: Undocumented parents and their young children.* New York: Russell Sage Foundation.

Zimmerman, Wendy, and Michael Fix. 2002. "Immigration and welfare reforms in the United States through the lens of mixed-status families." In *From immigration controls to welfare controls,* edited by Steve Cohen, Beth Humphries, and Ed Mynott, 59–80. New York: Routledge.

Zinn, Howard. 1980. *A people's history of the United States.* New York: Harper-Collins.

Index

in immigration policy, 87
civil rights, 94, 163
climate fluctuations, 168
  climate refugees from, 156–57, 159
  drought, 156
  flooding from, 157–58
  in history, 156, 157
  migration from, 156–59
  sea levels and, 157
Clinton, Bill, 49, 103–4
Close to Slavery (SPLC), 27
Colbert, Stephen, 45
colonization, 32–33, 150
"the commons," 18–19, 182–83
"communities of practice," 164
Commonwealth Immigrants Act
  (1962), 32
Conroy, Jeffrey, 60
Contract Detention Facilities
  (CDFs), 89
cooperation
  groups and, 155–56, 182–85
  for undocumented migration,
    164–65
  violence from, 61
corporations, 172–74
  multinational, 150
Corrections Corporation of America
  (CCA), 95–96
costs
  of detention, 96
  of developing countries' debt,
    24–25
  for guest-worker programs, 27
  of ICE, 87
  of immigration bonds, 90–91
  of US-Mexico border enforcement,
    64, 71–72
  of water business, 23
coyotes, 40, 58
creative survival, 38–40
crime
  aggravated felons, 98–99

deportation and, 91–92
governing through, 96–98
hate, 60–61
immigration conflated with, 98–99
Mexico-US migration compared to,
  50–51
undocumented migration compared
  to, 94–96, 133–34, 163
Criminal Justice System, US, 64
Cubans
  Adjustment Act, 103
  African Americans against, 104
  Haitians compared to, 102–4
  wet foot, dry foot policy for, 104
culture, xi, 12, 67, 183, 185
  American identity and, 50–52
  ethnocentrism and, 79–80
  of migration, 35, 134–35
  multiculturalism, 115, 141, 176
  sense of place in, 169

Daniels, Roger, 62
Danticat, Edwidge, 102, 191
Danticat, Joseph, 102
The Dark Side of the Dubai Dream,
  28–29
debts
  foreign aid related to, 25
  from guest worker program, 27
  from World Bank and IMF, 24–25
democracy, 156, 166, 181–82
democratic citizenship, 129, 164
Department of Homeland Security,
  87–88, 94, 137, 145
  reclassifications from, 94–95
deportations, 107, 144
  crime and, 91–92
  in guest-worker programs, 27
  of Haitians, 101
  in Mexico-US migration, 38
  politics of, 88
  unemployment related to, 75
detention, 14